Sniper on the Ypres Salient

Sniper on the Ypres Salient

An Infantryman's War In The Royal Welsh Fusiliers

Based on the War Diaries of William McCrae

Sue Boase

Pen & Sword
MILITARY

First published in Great Britain in 2022 by
Pen & Sword Military
An imprint of
Pen & Sword Books Ltd
Yorkshire – Philadelphia

Copyright © Sue Boase 2022

ISBN 978 1 39909 557 0

The right of Sue Boase to be identified as Author of this work has been asserted by her in accordance with the Copyright, Designs and Patents Act 1988.

A CIP catalogue record for this book is
available from the British Library.

All rights reserved. No part of this book may be reproduced or transmitted in any form or by any means, electronic or mechanical including photocopying, recording or by any information storage and retrieval system, without permission from the Publisher in writing.

Typeset by Mac Style
Printed in the UK by CPI Group (UK) Ltd, Croydon, CR0 4YY.

Pen & Sword Books Limited incorporates the imprints of Atlas, Archaeology, Aviation, Discovery, Family History, Fiction, History, Maritime, Military, Military Classics, Politics, Select, Transport, True Crime, Air World, Frontline Publishing, Leo Cooper, Remember When, Seaforth Publishing, The Praetorian Press, Wharncliffe Local History, Wharncliffe Transport, Wharncliffe True Crime and White Owl.

For a complete list of Pen & Sword titles please contact

PEN & SWORD BOOKS LIMITED
47 Church Street, Barnsley, South Yorkshire, S70 2AS, England
E-mail: enquiries@pen-and-sword.co.uk
Website: www.pen-and-sword.co.uk

Or

PEN AND SWORD BOOKS
1950 Lawrence Rd, Havertown, PA 19083, USA
E-mail: Uspen-and-sword@casematepublishers.com
Website: www.penandswordbooks.com

For all those families whose loved ones did not return from the Great War.

There are two voices in this book, mine and my grandfather's, William McCrae. William's writing is at the heart of this account, and all his words are therefore in a contrasting font, in order that the reader can easily differentiate his narrative from my own. SB

Contents

Foreword   viii
Introduction   x
Prologue   xii

Chapter 1   The Journey to War   1

Chapter 2   Rouge Croix and Christmas   18

Chapter 3   Trench and Billet   32

Chapter 4   A Sanctuary and Holding a Line   52

Chapter 5   The Raid   70

Chapter 6   Craters and the Colour Blue   86

Chapter 7   The Somme and Mametz Wood   95

Chapter 8   A Respite of Sorts   114

Chapter 9   The Yser Canal   125

Chapter 10   Sniping School and Observation   143

Chapter 11   1917–1918   165

Epilogue   183
Notes   185
Abbreviations   198
Glossary   199
Bibliography   202
Acknowledgements   206
Index   208

Foreword

It is a huge honour to be asked to write this foreword. I first became aware of this fascinating diary when Sue Boase made contact with the Royal Welch Fusiliers Museum in September 2018. Sue's grandfather, William McCrae, had enlisted in the 15th (1st London Welsh) Battalion, the Royal Welch Fusiliers shortly after the outbreak of the First World War. He went on to serve with that battalion, part of the 38th (Welsh) Division, including a year and a half on the Western Front, before being commissioned into the Duke of Wellington's Regiment.

As a serving officer of both the Royal Welch Fusiliers and its antecedent regiment, the Royal Welsh, I have had a long-standing interest in the history of our regiment. We have an unrivalled literary tradition in the regiment, particularly in our poets and writers of the First World War. The 15th (1st London Welsh) Battalion was a prime example of the literary and artistic talent that emerged from the conflict. Hedd Wyn, David Jones and Llewelyn Wyn Griffith all served with the battalion. Llewelyn Wyn Griffith prided himself on the fact that, whilst not as well known as Sassoon and Graves, he was actually a Welsh-speaking poet. David Jones penned an extraordinary semi-autobiographical account of his character Private Ball. Ball volunteered in London to join 15 RWF, trained in North Wales and served with the battalion in France much as William McCrae did. Finally, Ellis Humphrey Evans, is better known by his Bardic name *Hedd Wyn*. Evans was a farmer from the village of Trawsfynydd, in southern Snowdonia.

As a Scotsman, it is surprising that McCrae chose 15 RWF, the majority of those joining the 15th Battalion being Londoners of Welsh origin. As time went on, however, the supply of London Welshmen started to dry up and once the battalion moved to Llandudno in North Wales, their ranks were bolstered by new recruits from the area.

Reading this diary, I am struck by William's eloquence and perceptiveness. It is perhaps a true indication that this was a citizens' army, made up of men from all walks of Edwardian life. They had been thrown together by circumstances rather than the very different demographics of the pre-war Regular Army. It is also therefore not a surprise that William would go on to be awarded a commission in the Duke of Wellington's Regiment.

His employment, first as a company runner and then as a sniper also marks him out as having been identified as far from an average soldier. The skills he would learn and employ required a soldier with the right temperament and aptitude for this demanding role. Patience, self-discipline and excellent observational ability were all prerequisites that were not present in most of the rank and file of the army. Reading William's account of his experiences as a sniper, I am struck that he was part of the cohort who developed the original tactics and doctrine of British military sniping. I am also struck that the basic concepts and employment of snipers has changed very little in the last hundred years. Technology has significantly improved the sniper's ability to observe and acquire targets, particularly at night. The tactics, the need to deploy snipers in pairs, the observational abilities required and the highest possible standards of soldiering skills remains unchanged. William's granddaughter's research into the inception and evolution of British Army sniping brings context and a greater understanding to William's account.

This is a remarkable book, the very fact that accounts such as William's are still emerging from the conflict over a hundred years later is a testament to the profound impact the Great War had on a generation of young men. The fact that many such accounts were never finished or published by their original authors suggests that this may have been a cathartic process. Perhaps these men were driven to record their experiences for their own personal restitution rather than to be published. We are indeed fortunate that Sue has done both William and the historical record a great service by publishing this diary for new generations to understand the experiences of a generation that was irrevocably changed by their experiences of war. I am sure you will enjoy reading it as much as I did.

Colonel Nick Lock OBE (Retd.)
Trustee, The Royal Welch Fusiliers Museum
December 2021

Introduction

The aim of this book is to bring to light the previously unpublished words of William McCrae, my grandfather, whom I knew as a child. These words describe his experience as a private infantryman in the 15th (1st London) Royal Welsh Fusiliers when, at the age of 19, he went to fight on the Western Front in the First World War.

Long after his death, I was to discover his handwritten account, composed and copied into two exercise books, and on the back of old, loose, insurance ledger sheets.

He describes a world of Very lights, rain, mess tins and mud, of tortuous days and nights spent in the trenches, in cold, damp billets and near starvation. His account of the day-to-day activities which he endured reveals a great deal of interesting detail, such as when the men were first issued with 'tin hats', as they marched towards the Somme in June 1916. He does allude to the many horrors around him, though none of it can be thought of as gratuitous, and his story is told with compassion and an eye for humour.

The account includes his first exposure to the front line near La Rouge Croix, Neuve-Chappelle, volunteering for a raid on enemy trenches, acting as a runner in the attack on Mametz Wood during the Battle of the Somme, being a patient in an army field hospital, and training and becoming a sniper in the 38th Divisional Sniping Company when he was posted along the Yser Canal, on the northern edge of the Ypres Salient.

I can be almost certain that William had written much of his account by the end of 1926. The amount of detail points to the use of carefully logged notes and diaries taken at the time of events, although sadly none of these has survived. Several of the first pages were copied into the back of his officer's training notebook from 1918. It then moved into another exercise book, and then all the rest has been composed in pencil on the back of printed, loose, discarded sheets, blank 'tester reports' for the Royal London Mutual Insurance Society where he worked, both before and after the war. On the other side of one of the sheets is a half-finished draft of a letter inquiring about the sale of a house advertised in *The Times*. This is dated 18 September 1926.

His writing stops abruptly, seemingly while in mid-flow. Perhaps his need to write further may have been curtailed by the arrival, two months early, of my mother, in January 1927. The focus of his life, as a result, changed forever.

Beyond that, on a separate sheet of paper, in different ink, there is a brief description of the day the Armistice was declared, noting the retreat of the Germans and his incredulity that the war had ended.

William also left some photos, and sketches he made of the view across to the enemy trenches when he was standing in a sniper's observation post. There are several maps, that I believe he may have used when he went behind enemy lines, later in the war. From this material and with further research, I have been able to create a picture of his time training in North Wales before travelling to the Western Front; of the time beyond his account when he went on to train as a temporary officer in the 18th Officer Cadet Battalion, in Prior Park, Bath; becoming a second lieutenant in the Duke of Wellington's Regiment (West Riding Division); and, as such, serving with the 1/5 Lancashire Fusiliers until the end of the war.

Over one hundred years after these events, the words of this infantryman are added to those of so many others. Unique to him but so much in common with millions of men who served in the First World War.

I believe this was the only occasion William travelled overseas. Afterwards, understandably, never driven to explore too far, but forever grateful to be alive, I know he considered every day beyond his return to be a gift.

Prologue

Mametz Wood, Northern France, 2019

One cool sunny day in June 2019, I make my way through the village of Mametz, heading north and turning right down a narrow single-track lane. A few hundred metres later I unknowingly pass Queen's Nullah to my right, now just a slight indent in the land; a little further, a shady tree-tunnel, marked on my map as Death Valley. Back into the sun again and looking northwards, Mametz Wood stands, large and dense, seemingly without malice, surrounded by agricultural fields.

Facing it, on a small hill set above the road, strong and defiant, its front claws entwined in barbed wire, is the Red Welsh Dragon, the memorial of the 38th (Welsh) Division of the British Army. Alone now, keeping watch over the place where so many Welsh soldiers lost their lives in one of the bloodiest battles of the First World War.

Following its gaze, I look again at the wood, rising gently towards a ridge.

There is no obvious path across between maize and wheat field, just a margin where one stops and another begins. No signs. I pick my way along this line, a few red poppies flowering amongst the cereal, spanning time with their presence.

All I can see is sun, a few clouds, lush green growth and beauty. I step into the gentle shade of the wood. Mixed deciduous, lime and hornbeam. Some of the trees have been felled and stacked to dry. Edible snails, strikingly huge, and birdsong.

I walk along an ill-defined track with dense undergrowth on either side. In some places it looks as though the ground has caved in, down a hole. A sinister disruption in the lie of the land.

Small stacks of rusting, unexploded artillery shells, stand beside the track, collected by previous visitors, softened now by the blades of grass and greenery growing in amongst them. Here and there a tree trunk and branch, festooned with strings of knitted red poppy flowers. Welsh flags, rugby scarves and memorabilia of the Swansea Pals. Red against the green.

Gentle rain falling now, and incredibly a nightingale singing.

I try hard to imagine the overpowering cacophony of the artillery bombardment, blocking out the barked commands, the cries and screams of the men, the horror and despair. So many words have been used attempting to capture the depth of destruction. There are no words here now. Silence, enhanced by gentle rainfall and birdsong. I look around. A green blanket of nature wrapped over the horror so many men experienced. For some, the agonizing few minutes or perhaps hours that marked the end of their lives, for others a deep scar that would haunt their remaining days.

The compass

I remember it feeling heavy in the palm of my hand. It was made of brass, with a hinged lid, and was slightly dented in places. Overall it had a somewhat battered, perhaps military appearance. Once opened, on the back of the compass face, there was a smooth flat disc. I think this was made of ivory. Nestled and held in the side in some way, was a minute pencil, used for making notes on this shiny, now forbidden, off-white surface. I can remember being fascinated, opening and closing it, and trying the pencil out myself, but not being quite sure what to write.

I was about 14 years old when I lost this compass. We were moving to another house. I had what was known as a 'toy cupboard', into which anything that didn't seem to fit anywhere else was tossed. It was not something you could organize, but a heap of jumbled objects haphazardly thrown in there. I thought the compass was in the cupboard, but I was never to see it again after that move.

My grandfather William had given it to me when I was around 10 years old. He died just before my twelfth birthday. He used to take me walking on Dartmoor. A quiet, gentle, softly spoken man with a hint of a Scot's accent. I knew that he had fought in the First World War, and I remember trying to ask him questions, naïvely and innocently. 'What was it like fighting… did you shoot anyone?' He gave me placid answers which satisfied my curiosity, but carefully gave me no idea of what he had really experienced.

Years later, when my grandmother died, my mother found some of his writing, describing a year of his time in the war. Also pencil sketches of views from trenches, and maps of the terrain behind enemy lines, marks in pencil, and red and blue crayon. An exercise book full of photographs, faded and worn, of people he knew at that time, some labelled, so many others leaving questions. A training manual from when he trained as an officer later in the war.

As a child, I am sure I could not have understood what a precious gift this compass had been. I try to remember in vain how he gave it to me, what he said. The symbolism is something I now find hard to ignore. I cannot now think why else it was so well worn, other than it had been close to him, while he navigated his way through the Great War.

Chapter 1

The Journey to War

Winnall Down Camp, Winchester 1st December 1915
It was our last night in camp before leaving for France. Everyone had just had embarkation leave, and, with the possible exception of one or two deserters, had returned to camp. All was bustle and preparation in Hut 30, for orders had been issued for an early start in the morning, … The wailing, heart-piercing notes of the "Last Post" had just sounded. The regimental drum and fife band was playing outside the Officers' Mess a hundred yards away.

Jones, Sayer and Dean had spent the evening in the Canteen and were in a merry mood, and by their horseplay and repartee were keeping the rest of the occupants of the hut amused. Jones with some difficulty had made his bed. Laying the usual three six-foot planks on two low trestles, placing thereon his straw palliasse and with many grunts [he] wrapped himself in his two blankets and laid down. "Well boys … This is our last night in Blighty, … The Lord only knows where I shall rest my old bones next. Tomorrow we fare east, some of us shortly afterwards will go west, our bones being left to whiten on some foreign soil."

I lay there for some time listening to the band and thinking of the future. I remember also wondering why all the other ranks were sent to bed early, and why the officers could have a band and stay up enjoying themselves so much longer. Of course, on the long march on the morrow those who had no horses would only have to carry a stick whereas we would be borne down by almost our own weight in equipment.

Thus did our last evening in camp end. Rather like, outwardly anyway, to any other of the many evenings we had already spent there. Similar jokes, the same horseplay, the same songs and laughter. Who could tell however now that all was quiet how many of the 30 odd men and boys, mostly between 19 and 21 in Hut 30 were lying awake, thinking of the recent farewells, the kiss of the wife or sweetheart or mother, the tears of the kiddies, or possibly the unuttered feeling in the last firm handshake of father or brother. How many were striving to pierce the future. Lucky for all that it was veiled.

The next morning it was one big rush from reveille until parade time. The hut and contents had to be left tidy and clean ready for the next batch of recruits.

When we lined up at 9 o'clock the weather was fine, but rain threatened. The 15th RWF [Royal Welsh Fusiliers] were to be the rear guard of the brigade and so were last on the road. We marched down the hill nearly into Winchester, and then, turning to the left soon came into the road to Southampton.

For the first few miles we were fresh and enlivened the way with songs. We were at last launched on the Great Adventure, going to take our places in that then khaki line which was fighting our countries foes and preventing them from invading this fair land which we were marching thro', many of us for the last time.

My grandfather William was the fourth child of seven, four boys and three girls who were born to Robert and Isabella McCrae, a couple from Glasgow in Scotland, who had moved away during the last years of the nineteenth century, from the overcrowded, cramped conditions of the southern bank of the Clyde to settle in London, just after the birth of their first child.

Isabella died at the age of 52, at the end of 1913, a few months before the war broke out. The wording on the death certificate captures a shadowy glimpse of the day she died, of 'exhaustion', having struggled with tuberculosis for the last ten years of her life. Her husband Robert was by her side, her children, deep in sorrow, waiting quietly, during the long dark nights of that winter. Her youngest child Agnes was only 9 years old. With such tragedy, Nettie, as the oldest girl, would have had to work hard to keep the family together, her older brothers still living at home, but employed in London as clerks. Their bereft father would continue to work as a manager for a cork merchant. The two older brothers, Robert and Andrew, would also travel to the Western Front with William following soon after.

There were no thrills down our spines on that march on the Southampton road, yet we were marching to war. However, there was a very real persistent ache in that quarter where our packs bore heaviest. We had in addition to our usual pack a blanket to carry. Turner weighed the whole of his equipment later and it was about 80lbs.The rain which soon came down in torrents must have added considerably to this weight. The march soon became a question of mere endurance, for the most of us would have sooner suffered, in fact often did suffer agonies, rather than disgrace ourselves and our company by falling out. By the time we had reached the vicinity of Southampton, where the road skirted the common, a good many men, having reached the limit of their endurance did fall out, and from this spot until we reached the end of our 14 miles march at the quayside, men continued to fall out in ever increasing numbers.

On entering Southampton, the rain ceased and the band, who had had less to carry than the rest of us, found enough wind to give us a short tune. We all brightened up and even managed a song or two thinking that we must be near the end of the march, not knowing that we had nearly 2 miles further to go thro' the town to the quay.

From those inhabitants of Southampton who were out and about, in spite of the rain, we got nothing but encouragement, even a little cheer now and again, above all we felt their sympathy. How different were to be our feelings on the other side of the Channel.

Reflections on war

Woven into his description of the last few hours on his home soil, are William's reflections on war which I understand were written, as was all his account, in the 1920s.

His reflections display a strong criticism of the war, which I believe was intended to be on behalf of all the ordinary people caught up in it. He moves from the notion of a Great Adventure to, as with so many others, his feelings of being duped, led into battle, believing what they had been told, and even predicting what was to come, as in this first paragraph:

At the time we firmly believed, owing to the patriotism engendered by propaganda in the press and elsewhere, that all Germans were scum, and the more that were killed the better for the world. How many, now that the war is over and facts purposefully withheld then have now seen the light of day, have now come to look upon their one-time enemies and themselves as common dupes fooled by politicians, financiers and petty kings for their own ends and ultimate aggrandisement. These same vampires, or those of them on the so-called winning side, have since made of the peace, which fell like a benediction on warring men, nothing but a farce, sowing the seeds of further wars which will be more terrible than the last.

Strange it is that these very foes, if approached individually on the matter would for the most part have forsworn any desire to see this country or any other country but their own, and would have been delighted to have returned to their own home in peace.

There is nothing finer or more stirring to the imagination than descriptions in poetry and in prose of young men in their full health and vigour going forth to War in defence of their country, in defence of the weak and in support of their ideals. Poets and other writers must have well-nigh exhausted their stores of well-sounding words and beautiful spine thrilling phrases on this very theme. How different is the actual experience to most men, and how disillusioning it must be to poets. Such descriptions are only of use to instil in the hearts of the susceptible a false patriotism, and spur them on in time of need to greater sacrifice, or greater folly, or on the other hand to comfort a grief-stricken mother or wife, making them forget the poignancy of their bereavement in the thought that their son or husband died in Glory, whereas his last moments must have been just the opposite, filled with noise, explosions, smoke, shrieks of pain, yells and curses of passion, a very world gone mad.

There is no glory in War, none whatever, only suffering, despair, and death.

One hundred or so years later, we understand so much more, and see from the writings of the well-known First World War writers and poets such as Wilfred Owen, the misery and pain resulting from experiencing the wholesale slaughter of so many human beings. Some of these, such as Siegfried Sassoon and Robert Graves, were also in the Royal Welsh Fusiliers, and indeed Llewelyn Wyn Griffith and David Jones were in the same battalion as William, the 15th (1st London) Royal Welsh Fusiliers, or 15 RWF.

However, many still believed that the war, no matter how horrific, needed to be fought to contain German aggression. Both Frank Richards, in his book *Old Soldiers Never Die*, and Captain James Dunn in *The War the Infantry Knew*, both in the 2 RWF, demonstrate this.

Reflections and opinions of the war at that time were in no way unusual amongst those who had been able to return and were attempting to come to terms with what they had experienced. Many of the classic war memoirs and novels that are available to us now were written in the late 1920s and the 1930s. Edmund Blunden's *Undertones of War* was published in 1928, Robert Graves's *Goodbye to All That* in 1929, Siegfried Sassoon's *Memoirs of an Infantry Officer* in 1930, David Jones's *In Parenthesis* in 1937 and Llewelyn Wyn Griffith's *Up to Mametz* in 1931.

William's thoughts on the impact of propaganda on both sides of the war, what they were made to believe, and his reference to the signing of the Armistice opening up the possibility of further war, all resonate very much in the present day, even though it is so far away in time. The strong feeling of sympathy they felt from the crowds in Southampton as they were leaving, despite the encouragement and the odd cheer, portrays those bleak and heavy doom-laden days, over a year since the war began. The 15 RWF, to the rear of brigade, were the last to leave. There was little feeling of glory.

Confined

```
When we reached the end of the quay we were marched into
a large store-shed and having dressed by the right and
dressed by the left, been shouted at and told to wake up:
etc. etc. [we] were allowed to place our packs in neat
lines and recline on them. Oh! The delight of stretching
our unencumbered bodies on even this rough couch and
feeling free from that dead weight, which not only seemed
to pull the shoulders right off the body, but also seemed
to keep our hearts in our boots. We did not embark until
the next night, and in the meantime were kept confined
to the shed and adjoining quay. No men were allowed to go
into the town. No doubt there was sufficient reason for
this, but at the time it seemed hard to us that we should
be denied the last few hours of freedom in our native
country, just because one or two men, who would be useless
anyway in the face of the enemy, might desert.
```

Recruitment and training

William was a private soldier in an infantry battalion, and the march to Southampton on that rain-drenched day to embark for France, marked over a year since he had signed up to join the army at Gray's Inn in Holborn, London, towards the end of 1914.

Lloyd George, who was to become the prime minister later in the war, but was at this time Chancellor of the Exchequer, had been very keen to have a specific Welsh Army Corps when he first gave his full support to the war in a speech in September 1914. (A corps is made up of a minimum of two divisions and is allocated the appropriate number of divisions for a specified mission or role.) Initially this did not meet the agreement of the then Secretary of State for War, Lord Kitchener, who was not in favour of national regiments. However, Kitchener eventually conceded, and the formation of the Welsh Army Corps was approved on the 23 September 1914.[1] It should be noted that by the time recruiting was fully under way for the Welsh Army Corps, many men from Wales had already volunteered for the army and been allocated to new (Service) battalions. The 8th, 9th, 10th, 11th and 12th RWF were raised in North Wales before the Welsh Army Corps started recruiting.

Following the initial rush to volunteer to fight, when Great Britain declared war on Germany on 4 August 1914, recruitment had declined, and much was being done to encourage the Welsh to join up. As well as across Wales, recruitment for the Welsh battalions was also taking place in London, Liverpool and Manchester.

My grandfather was working just outside the City of London, in Finsbury Square when the 15th (1st London) Battalion Royal Welsh Fusiliers was raised in the Inns of Court as part of the New Army. It was first inaugurated at a meeting of Welshmen in London on 16 September 1914, presided over by Sir Vincent Evans, and was officially recognized on 29 October 1914.[2] This became one of the new battalions in the long-established Royal Welch Fusilier Regiment, with a distinguished history of campaigns dating back from 1689.[3]

The Inns of Court Hotel was made their headquarters, and the Benchers of Gray's Inn lent the adjoining garden and square to be used as an initial drill ground for the volunteers before they left London for further training.[4] Marking the place where they first enlisted, there is now a memorial to those of this battalion who were lost in the Great War.[5, 6]

Gray's Inn was a mile away from where my grandfather worked as a clerk in the policy department, at the Royal London Mutual Insurance Society. It would have taken him about half an hour to walk there but was not in the direction of his daily journey home, which would have been more towards London Bridge. I wonder what made my grandfather volunteer with this Welsh regiment. To my knowledge the family did not have any direct connection with Wales.

Was he alone when he made his journey to the recruitment office after work, on that ninth day of November 1914? Or would he have been with other work colleagues, some of whom may have been from Wales or had connections with the people and that land of mountains and valleys? Did the receipt of some particular news from his brothers who were already fighting in the war, drive him to make the decision that particular day? What spurred him on?

Perhaps it was to do with his religious beliefs. He was, I discovered, a non-conformist, the branch of the Christian church with which Wales, at the time, had a strong national identity. The need for the Welsh to have non-conformist chaplains alongside them in the front lines was successfully negotiated by Lloyd George. Although Kitchener was initially against it, Lloyd George realized this was going to be an important consideration for effective recruitment. He successfully argued that Indian troops – both Sikhs and Gurkhas – already had chaplains of their own faith with their regiments.[7]

It was clear that by then, the euphoria and excitement, particularly in London, when the British first declared war on Germany on 4 August 1914,[8] was now giving way to a more sober and sombre mood.

After enlisting, William would have returned home and continued with his job until he received further instruction and orders by post.

The officers of the newly formed 15 RWF were given a banquet in the capital, which Lloyd George attended, to wish them 'Godspeed'. In his speech, the prime minister referred to his two sons, one of whom, Gwilyn, joined the battalion as an aide-de-camp in the office of the commanding officer, Ivor Philipps.[9] Major General Ivor Philipps was a retired Indian Army officer, a Liberal MP, and friend of Lloyd George. He was brought out of retirement and appointed to command the 38th (Welsh) Division. Such political patronage was to be an unusual factor in the formation of this division.[10]

Just over a month later, on 15 December 1914, the whole battalion left for Llandudno under the command of Lieutenant Colonel W. A. L. Fox-Pitt of the Grenadier Guards. The 15 RWF thus joined what was initially referred to as the North Wales Brigade and later designated the 113th Infantry Brigade, one of the three brigades that made up the 38th Welsh Division. Although the total fighting strength of this division was 18,500 men, hardly any of them had military experience, apart from a few officers and some non-commissioned officers (NCOs) brought back from retirement, who were often referred to as 'dugouts'.[11]

The commander of the 113th Brigade was Brigadier General Owen Thomas, another Liberal politician, Anglesey landowner and another Lloyd-George-influenced appointee. Thomas was a long-term volunteer soldier having raised his own unit, the Prince of Wales' Light Horse, to serve in the Boer War. His three eldest sons all joined the RWF and all three were killed during the war.[12] The 113th Infantry Brigade was made up entirely of North Wales recruited 'Pals' battalions: 13 RWF (1st North Wales), 14 RWF (Caernarfon and Anglesey), 15 RWF (1st London Welsh) and 16 RWF (2nd North Wales). The 15 RWF with its eclectic mix of Cockney Welshmen and more recent émigrés to London would certainly have stood out amongst the Welsh-speaking North Wales soldiers of the other battalions in their brigade.[13]

It was to be a whole year before they were to leave for France. Most of them were aged between 18 and 20 as was William. They were to spend the first eight months of this time training in Llandudno, billeted in hotels and boarding houses. The first two months were taken up with marching and drilling, mainly on the seafront in front of many local interested spectators.[14]

There was a shortage of suitable training equipment, and the men had to either use something like a broomstick or a walking stick instead of a rifle. At best they would have had a dummy rifle. There was also initially a shortage of uniforms, with some men still wearing their own civilian clothes. Eventually most of the Welsh regiments would have been dressed in uniform made of a Welsh black and white sheep's wool known as *Brethyn llwyd*. The shade of this fabric was varied, some describing it having a blue-grey tone, some more khaki, and gave the Welsh their own identity apart from the rest of the British Army, while also helping with the local economy. The division was issued with a mix of Brethyn llwyd, standard khaki and Kitchener blue uniforms. However, the man who was instrumental in raising the 15 RWF, Lieutenant Colonel Ivor Bowen, refused to allow them to wear the Welsh homespun, so this battalion would have been dressed in the regular khaki[15] (see plate 1). Once in France, on their shoulder they would wear a cloth badge with the words 'London Welsh' embroidered in orange thread, and on their sleeve a yellow triangle of cloth, a tactical recognition flash, in order that they could be recognized as a member of the 15 RWF when at the front.

Lloyd George came to Llandudno to inspect the men on 1 March, St David's Day in 1915. Liverpool's *Daily Post* provided a rousing description of the crowds gathering to see the men dressed in blue and khaki and specifically mentions the 'stalwart London Welsh', the 15 RWF.[16]

Although there is some indication that boredom and drunkenness were rife,[17] the photos and postcards William collected during that time (which he eventually carefully displayed in an old exercise book), give the impression that he lived comfortably. There are small, sepia photos of the Great Orme with a group posing at the summit. A number of images show William with a group of around seven others, the four men in uniform, three younger women and one older, perhaps a chaperone. The images suggest that this group had had a day out perhaps, walking, and taking tea outside in the garden of a farmhouse near Trefriw. All the group smiling for the camera, William looks particularly happy (see plate 2). Another picture is of a group of five or six men and women out walking, the men in uniform, standing on a bridge leading to Llyn Geirionydd, deep in the heart of the Welsh mountains.

A particular postcard, written by William which he must have had returned to him, perhaps when he came back to the office after the war, was addressed to a Mr W. C. Woodroffe, Policy Dept., Royal London House, Finsbury Square, London EC (see plate 3).

The stamp has been torn off. The sepia picture on the front is of sixteen uniformed men, arranged formally for the camera, in front of quite a grand-looking house. Some are standing, including William; some seated. In the centre are three women, the central one dressed in perhaps a housekeeper's or nurse's uniform. It is likely this is Redcliffe House, Church Walks, Llandudno (see plate 4). The message is short:

> Just to show you what kind of company I am in. They are
> a very mixed lot, but we get on fairly well together.
> Kind regards to all the Policy Dept
> W. McCrae

All the while the next step in their march to war was looming, and on 19 August 1915, the battalion and the rest of the division moved to Winnall Down Camp in Winchester, for their final three months of training.[18] The move had been delayed until these camps had been vacated by the first and second new armies. This purpose-built camp was comprised of a series of huts for accommodation, and several specifically for training, such as lecture halls and gas rooms, a canteen and space for recreation such as a YMCA building.

William, along with twenty-two other men in the 7 Platoon, resided in Hut A30. A photo in his collection shows the men posing in front of their accommodation in quite a relaxed manner, with one smoking a cigarette, another a pipe, some with their army jackets on and some in shirt sleeves; one holds a mop, another a broom and perhaps a cook sits in amongst them with a carving knife and fork in his hands. They seem strong and healthy. Some are squinting in the bright sun. Perhaps they have only recently arrived and have a day free from exercises and training (see plate 8).

Despite the more suitable accommodation, there was still a shortage of equipment. Even though they had been in training for a year in Wales and Hampshire, this factor had overall greatly reduced their ability to reach an effective level of training. Also, in this early period of the war there was very little instruction in trench warfare back in Britain. (Later when subsequent drafts were taken into training at the new very large Kinmel Park Camp, practice trenches were built in the parkland around Bodelwyddan Castle. These can still be seen from the air today.) As rifles continued to be lacking up to this point, the division was forced to use the rifle ranges on Salisbury Plain, to put each man through a hurried course to familiarize themselves with their new SM (short magazine) Lee–Enfield rifles just before leaving for the Western Front [19].

Winnall Down, Magdalen Hill and Avington Park were collectively known as Morn Hill and could accommodate 50,000 soldiers. In 1917, Morn Hall became the US training camp when America joined the war, accommodating their soldiers before they moved across to the Western Front.[20]

In late November 1915, the entire 38th Division was ordered to move to France.

The journey to France

We embarked on board the transport just as light was fading on the evening of 2nd Dec 1915, and by the time we had explored the ship and donned our life belts it was quite dark.
 Ward and I decided that it would be best to remain on deck if possible as we were less likely to be seasick. As the sailors cast off, we took our last look at the land. The quay was now deserted except for a stray sailor or two, the lights of Southampton glowed drearily through a kind of damp, grey mist which had followed the recent heavy rains. Soon we were out of the shelter of the harbour and could feel the ocean swell. The lights of Southampton faded out of sight and we seemed alone on the ocean. The ship was in darkness as a precaution against submarines, and all that could be heard was the thud of machinery and the wash of the paddles, for it was a paddle steamer used before the war for river traffic.
 Ward and I laid ourselves down amid-ships, where we thought the rocking of the boat would be least, in the shelter of a deckhouse of some kind, but the rain and the wind soon drove us to shelter in the gangway close to one of the paddles where we watched the gleaming, boiling surge from the paddle and occasionally got drenched with spray. We remained here huddled up close together, until we were stiff with cold and then went below. As we entered the hatchway the pungent smell of seasickness greeted our nostrils, mingled with the warm oily smell of machinery. The interior of the ship was dimly lit with oil lamps, and everywhere were sprawling heaps of humanity in various stages of seasickness. The few who still seemed well were mostly grouped round the engines, watching the huge pistons revolve and the engineers as they oiled and tended their charges. The noise was so great, the atmosphere so thick, that we soon went on deck again and took refuge in our corner by the paddle. The cold wind and rain were better than that pandemonium below.

William's description of travelling across the sea to war, in just one of the many vessels carrying their load of unknowing and apprehensive men, moving inexorably towards their fate, introduces the idea of liminality which is explored in Erich Maria Remarque's book *All Quiet on the Western Front* where he describes the novel existence that the fighting men of the Great War had, in these terms.[21] This concept helps to explain the way in which the soldiers are removed, to another world, separate and liminal, where they become detached, and exist outside their normal environment. As with William's journey across the English Channel, they travel over a threshold, to the trenches on the front line. They stay, and continue to fight, until they die or are wounded, or until the end of the war – a seismic shift that can never be undone.

The title of David Jones's poem *In Parenthesis* also alludes to the other life, the interruption or interval, the different place in time and space and memory, that was the war.

For those that are left behind – the children, the women and the older people – outside this position of liminality, all they can do is wait. They may reach across, attempting to touch, in thought and strength of feeling, as they cling on, teeth gritted, waiting for an end to the horror. As was so tragically realized, once the war was over, nothing was ever to be the same again. Siegfried Sassoon also refers to this separation and the lasting impact it had: 'And the man who had really endured the War at its worst was everlastingly differentiated from everyone except his fellow soldiers.'[22]

The other side of the Channel

The lights of France were now in sight and before long we were moored to the quay at Le Havre. Everything seemed strange. There directly in front of us, that dark shadowy mass was a foreign country and not only that, but a country in which not many miles away there were two opposing armies, perhaps at that very moment at death grips with one another. The shuddering machinery of the ship was now strangely silent after five hours of incessant thudding and clamour. Le Havre seemed a city of the dead. It wanted of course several hours to daylight and the occasional foreign sing-song cries of the French waterman or watchman only seemed to add to the weirdness of it all.

We were not to disembark until daylight and my friend and I, going below, found perching space and that is all it could be called, as there were already a number of men asleep there on a heap of equipment, and [we] actually slept for a couple of hours.

At 7 o'clock, just as dawn was breaking, we fell-in on shore and marched through the town of Le Havre to the railway sidings. What a scrubby crew we must have looked, unwashed, unshaved, worn out by our experiences the night before, and I am afraid, hungry. There was perhaps little wonder that the few natives of the town about the streets at that early hour took but little notice of us. Here were we, a battalion of men 1000 strong, a small part of an enormous army which had been raised in order to help this very people to drive an invader from their soil, and they took less notice of us than if we had been a gang of prisoners being marched to prison. We did not notice this attitude very much at the time, we were too busy drinking in all the strange impressions of a foreign town, but later, on closer acquaintance-ship with the French, and to a lesser extent of the Belgians, this first impression of indifference, if not actual ingratitude, was never altered. ... They never expressed or seemed to feel any gratitude to us whatsoever. For the most part (of course there were many and notable exceptions) they never were even kindly to us. They would charge us exorbitantly for what little extras in the way of food we could afford out of our meagre pay. Our papers often gave accounts of the brave population of the immediate war area who remained for years in the danger zone rather than leave the homes to which they were so much attached, although those homes were usually shell-torn. Brave they may have been, but they made good money out of Tommy and were well recompensed for the danger.

In our own country during the war, householders often had to give up rooms in their houses as billets for the troops. Not so in France. We were housed in what were for the most part vile venomous barns, sometimes stables and even piggeries and our Government paid the owners for this privilege.

It is interesting to reflect on how William thought they may have been received once they stepped ashore in this foreign land, his expectations perhaps being directed towards thanks and gratitude. He captures with poignancy his first impressions. He was aware of the extent of the commitment and effort in creating the force that he was part of, to arrive at this point. Marching through this port city, in this foreign land, in the chill December dark and rain, already tired, hungry and disoriented, the experience cannot have been uplifting.

He saw the British troops as coming to save the French and Belgians from an enemy. He maybe had not anticipated, as he had not known, how it was to come upon another people with a different culture, and different attitudes and beliefs. Had his thinking been influenced by the propaganda meted out back on the shores of 'Blighty'? The French population was suffering greatly with the entire Western Front war machine encroaching upon their existence, finding themselves immersed in the company of those who had come to fight, who were also seeking out their bars, cafés and women, not necessarily always sensitive to the culture of another country. At the same time their towns, villages and farmland were being destroyed. By then, wave upon wave of troops would have already arrived from across the world, completely overturning any sense of normality they may have had, and replacing it with uncertainty, horror and dread. His perspective is that of the private infantryman, never before having travelled to another country, for whom the living conditions in their billets were basic to the extreme. The British officers were billeted in comparative comfort, occupying rooms in houses and chateaux across France and Belgium.

For France and Belgium, the war is still there now, in their fields and their woods, still littered with metal fragments of munitions, spent bullets and buckles. Human remains are regularly disturbed and unearthed by the farmers, to this day. The immaculate memorials and graves still trace the footsteps of the men that once trooped across their land.

```
We had to march two or three miles to the rail head, and
it shows how worn out we were that men had to fall out
even on this small march. It may have been caused partly,
however, by our first experience of the rough cobble
streets so common in France. When we reached the railway,
we were sheltered in some cattle-sheds, which however
were thoroughly clean. They were open on one side and had
a stone floor with a gutter in the middle.
    We were here able to have breakfast, which consisted of
bully beef and army biscuits. Bully beef was issued to
```

the troops in tins holding nearly a pound [weight] and there was usually a key attached to facilitate the opening thereof. The manipulation of this key and the extraction of the meat whole was quite an art. More-often-than-not the key failed to act, and then recourse had to be made to the tin opener in our jack-knives, a very inefficient weapon. The bottom of the tin, and often pieces of flesh from our hands, were wrenched off with this instrument and the meat extracted in a more-or-less mauled condition. It did not taste exactly like meat, or quite like string, but something in between the two. The nearest approach to the army biscuit, is the larger variety of dog biscuit, only it was usually harder. They tasted just like one would expect a dog biscuit to taste and were in fact made in some cases by the big dog biscuit firms.

What we were even more thankful for that morning was a mess-tin of tea from our Company Cookers. It not only warmed us up but put new life into us.

The journey towards the front line – cattle trucks and oily tea

We waited all day in these sheds, and at nightfall our platoon was detailed to go as guard or fatigue party on a supply train running, if one may use this verb to describe our 2 mile an hour progress, in the direction of the war area. We did not travel 1st class or even 3rd but made our first acquaintance with those afterwards so familiar carriages de-luxe, labelled '40 hommes 8 chevaux'. There were two of these cattle trucks to this train and so our platoon of sixty odd men ought to have been quite comfortably disposed thirty in each. We all bagged our places and were so crowded that there was scarcely room to remove our equipment. Where we could have put another ten men to make up forty, without putting one on top of another was a matter for deep conjecture. By the light of a candle end or two we disposed ourselves as comfortably as we could, claiming each man 15" of wall space and placing the pack against it. When we lay down, we had to wedge ourselves with our legs interlacing with those men on the other side of the truck.

The train started off with a jerk and was soon travelling slowly forward with much puffing and creaking. Our speed scarcely ever exceeding two or three miles an hour, and frequently there were long stops, when if we looked through the crack of the sliding door, we saw a deserted, dreary station with an unfamiliar name. Not many of us got the sleep we needed so much, we were too uncomfortable and cold, and there was, all through the night the clank-clank, rumble-rumble of our slow progress.

When dawn broke, we opened the doors on each side of the truck so that we could view the country we were passing through. It was mostly flat and uninteresting. As we passed through the villages the children came out and greeted us with shrill cries for "Bully Biff" and "Biscuits". We were plentifully supplied with these commodities and moreover had not yet overcome our reluctance to eat such unsavoury food. The consequence was that we amused ourselves, as we crawled slowly on, in throwing biscuits to them, as long as supplies lasted, watching their greedy scrambles. Now and again the train stopped for a considerable time, and we were able to get out and stretch our legs. We had been thoughtfully furnished with tea and sugar, mixed together in a biscuit tin, but we had little water in our bottles, and anyway no means of heating it. During one of these long stops one of us had a brainwave and seeing that the engine was discharging hot water put some tea and sugar in his mess tin and filled it with this water. There was soon a string of men waiting their turn at the pipe. The resultant beverage was not tea in the usual sense, the water was oily and certainly not boiling but we were glad of even this warm drink. When the train restarted after these stops there was always a big scramble to get aboard amid much shouting.

All that day we rumbled on and all the next night, but early the second morning we detrained at a small station near Aire, Pas de Calais. Our officer[s] had not been told exactly where to find our battalion and we wandered about all the morning looking for them and were very thankful when we at last did find them in a small village.

So, William finds himself, a private soldier, across the sea, in an alien world. The almost mystical, other-worldly existence during the journey, travelling often at night, waiting, pushing on and waiting again for the next step that brought him to the shores of France and eventually to the Western Front.

The rhythm and the beat of time that started with his first walk to the recruiting station in Gray's Inn from Finsbury Square, to the journey home that night thinking of what was to come. Leaving the comfortable routine of work, to travel to Wales and what was likely to have been in some ways, a wonderful experience, spending time surrounded by the beauty of the mountains and the sea of North Wales – no longer tied to an office job in the heart of a city but gathering stamina and strength. Then the move to Winchester and Winnall Down, and the comradery of platoon No. 7 in Hut A30.

They are sucked in, just another group of men being fed as cannon fodder across the Channel. The inglorious march to Southampton docks, the pumping of the packet steamers laden with men packed together. Ashore, their feet marching, painfully across the pavé, weighed down by the size of their packs. The long, painfully slow journey by train, lurching and graunching, wheels clanking, as it inched its way towards danger, ready to expel its load of already hungry and exhausted soldiers, nearer the front. Marching until they were within earshot of the deafening clamour and deadly exchange between the two armies, to then move deeper into the world of rain, mud, Very lights and trenches.

Chapter 2

Rouge Croix and Christmas

The overnight train journey had taken William and his fellow Royal Welshmen to Blendecques near Aire-sur-la-Lys. They disembarked on that chill winter's day, and then marched for another ten kilometres to a small village called Warnes. Once they finally met their officers, billets were found, and headquarters was established.[1] They were to stay for two weeks from 5 December until 19 December for further training. Compared to the hills of North Wales, even to the landscape around Winnal Down Camp, this flat land must have seemed exceedingly featureless. Everything at this point in William's description appears as new, as with a fresh pair of eyes. Each step was carrying them further away from that with which they were familiar.

Closer to the front line

The platoon was billeted in a barn and as it was typical of many of our billets merits a short description. It was a big barn which took up one side of a square, opposite was the farmhouse, and the other sides were composed of various outbuildings such as stables and storehouses. Entrance to this square was gained by an opening by the side of the farmhouse. Taking up most of the space inside this square was the cesspool surrounded by a pathway of rough cobble-stones. All the waste products in connection with the farm were … cast into this receptacle and left to rot, forming a semi-solid, pestilent mass. The smell from this was always present in our nostrils and tended to become worse after rain, or when it had been disturbed in one way or another. Up against the farmhouse, and within a few feet of this cesspool was the pump [which was] the sole water supply of the inmates. We used this water for washing in, but only drunk it when it had been chlorinated by the Water Section attached to the Battalion, or boiled by the cooks to make tea. (I used to wonder if the natives drunk it in its raw state, but supposed that they only used to make coffee, no doubt the impurities added strength and body to that beverage.) The Entrance to the barn [was] a small door cut out of the larger double door which was large enough to admit a loaded cart. Within, the barn was divided by beams of rough wood, into sections. In the first section was fixed the threshing machine, and other rather primitive farming implements. The walls were made of a very inferior kind of plaster interspersed with thick beams at uneven intervals. The floor was earth well hardened and covered with one or two feet thickness of broken dusty straw, evidently accumulated during the passage of years. The only means of lighting this palace was by leaving the door open and even that only sufficed to lessen the gloom inside. Ventilation was excellent, too excellent in fact, the cold wind blowing in through many cracks.

As the short December day [began] drawing to an end, my friend and I sallied forth to view the village. It consisted only of some score or so of farms and small houses straggling along a single road. There were two Estaminets or inns. We entered one and found it crowded with men, drinking beer or coffee and talking in the light of a single dim oil lamp. We here sampled for the first time a café and did not [think] much of this national beverage. For economy sake the French put too much chicory in the drink and render it insipid. Soon tiring of the noise in here we made our way back to our barn and reaching our own particular corner lit a candle.

Douglas Ward, a good friend

Here perhaps it is expedient to give some kind of a description of my friend and comrade Douglas Ward as for the next 12 months or so we were to pass through many new experiences and untold dangers together.

He was verging on 30 years of age, ten years older than myself and was a tall burly looking man … A year or so before the war he had left his native town of Bromyard and come to London, where he was employed up to the time of joining the army, as a draper's assistant in the firm of Wallis Holborn, at the princely salary of 8 shillings per week and his keep, such as it was. … In character he was a good staunch friend, unselfish, narrowminded, gentle, uncouth, painstaking, inefficient. He was a strong Anglican, even bigoted at times. Despite ridicule and even blasphemy he quietly and unobtrusively stuck to his [ways], read his bible and said his prayers where and when he thought fit. To his comrades credit it must be said that they soon ceased to annoy him when thus engaged, and even at times ceased their noise and horseplay.

A connection with home

Before long the remainder of the platoon began to drift back into the barn, more candles were lit, and there was quite a hum of conversation. Jones was reviling the quality and effects of French beer. Sayers had been luckier and found an Estaminet where they dispensed "Café au rhom" (Rum and coffee), and being filled with delight at this resounding name, and with that warming beverage [inside him], persisted in repeating it over and over again with relish.

  The arrival of a man with the first post that we had had since leaving Winchester increased the hub-bub. The letters were mostly those forwarded from there. It seemed strange to be brought suddenly in touch with Blighty in this way. Even the envelopes upon which was the well known "Hut 30, Winnal Down, Winchester" seemed weird. It appeared as if our life previous to crossing the water was a separate existence. So it always appears if there has been a great upheaval in life, or when a complete change in environment has taken place. Our address was now, in so far as locality was concerned, merely B.E.F. [British Expeditionary Force] France. We were of no fixed abode, our different billets and resting places would only know us for a few days and then on [we] wafted here and there with no control over our own volition, just so it seemed, sports of chance and circumstance. Yet marvellously kept in touch with home and kin by these few letters.

As the men move further towards the Western Front, they begin to realize the implications of being an itinerant force, marching, resting and temporarily settling, and then marching again as directed.

  For those in the armed forces and their families, keeping in touch was crucial to morale, and communication by letter, or perhaps telegram, was the only way this could happen at that time. To cope with the vast numbers of letters and packages being sent out to the Western Front, a huge wooden sorting office was erected in London, covering five acres of Regent's Park. This London depot employed 2,500 mostly female staff and handled two billion letters and 114 million parcels during the war. The static nature of trench warfare enabled a reliable network of lorries and carts to deliver their loads to those at the front and to return correspondence back to their loved ones.

It is hard to imagine the extent of the service provided by the Post Office at the beginning of the twentieth century. In 1914 it was the largest single employer of labour in the world. Prior to the First World War, even in a rural town you could expect twelve deliveries of post a day. As a result of the conflict, this had to be scaled back enormously. Also responsible for the telegraph and telephone systems, the role of the Post Office was crucial to communications during the war effort.

In addition to this, as many as 75,000 staff were released to fight mostly in their own battalion, the Post Office Rifles. They were to fight on the Western Front, both at Ypres and the Somme.[2]

Rations

Soon after this the platoon's rations were brought to the barn and the sergeant dispensed them to us. "Here you four in this loaf", (Cries of "But sergeant, this one has been sat on") "You five in this tin of jam" ("Ticklers again") "Corporal divide this piece of cheese between the men of your section. I'll leave this tin of biscuits here for you to help yourselves" Needless to [say] the generosity of this last offer was fully appreciated as we seldom ate biscuits unless very hungry. It was received with a cheer and Jones remarked "Perhaps Sergeant dear you would be so kind as to bring me a couple with my early morning tea".

The tea, condensed milk, sugar, bacon and meat was taken to the company cooker or field kitchen (a cooker on wheels).

We were soon all asleep, as we had had no sleep or at best only an hour or so since leaving Southampton 4 nights before.

The next day

The next morning reveille was at 7am. Our toilet had to be made under the pump. Three men washing at the same time while a fourth worked the handle. We rejoiced in the fact however that we had not to clean our buttons or polish buckles for we were now on active service. Anything bright or shining about our uniforms at this period of the War was deemed dangerous as it would make us an easier mark for the enemy. Strange to say however before many months were passed we had to buy cleaning implements and paste out of our meagre pay, and were expected to be as clean and bright behind the line, or even at times in the trenches, as we had been while on home service. Evidently the higher command came to the conclusion that the salutary effect of bright buckles and buttons on discipline and morale, was great enough to cancel out the question of danger.

At eight o'clock the mess orderlies (we were detailed daily for this onerous job) were dispatched to the Company Cooker which stood in an adjacent farm-yard and soon reappeared with breakfast. There was a large dixie of tea with very little milk and sugar in it and a dixie lid full of bacon. We lined up in a queue with our mess tins, and in turn received about a pint of tea and a piece of fat bacon 4"x2", from the sergeant and corporal respectively who were doing the honours. When the bacon was all served out there was a rush of nearly the whole platoon with slices of bread to bag the "dip" or fat left in the dixie-lid. In the melee Sayers upset his tea in Hoar's boot which happened to be near, and Jones highly delighted at the discomfort of his friend, let his bacon fall in the straw dust and had to scrape it with his knife the while Sayers laid claim to Hoare's tea as said he "You've got the benefit of my tea in your boots. I should have your tea to quench my bloomin' thirst".

For dinner that day we had so-called stew. The Company's meat ration was cut up into cubes and boiled in the dixie. Each man received about four of these swimming in half a mess tin full of this muddy fluid. We tried soaking army biscuits in it but they were so hard that invariably the soup got cold before the biscuits softened. Tea served just before dusk consisted of tea, made evidently in the same dixie that had contained the stew, and as most of us had already consumed our bread, biscuits spread with jam.

The meagreness of our rations, especially at this time was always a cause of grousing. We could not understand why we did not get the full ration of 1lb of meat per diem and so many oz of bacon etc to which we were entitled. The rations, especially perhaps these two items, were phenomenally short. Our conjecture was that the rations passed through so many hands A.S.C. [Army Service Corps], Batt Q.M.S. [Battalion Quarter Master Stores], B/C [Battalion Cook] M.S. [Mess Sergeant] etc on the way down to Tommy, that by the time these people, and the officers and sergeant messes had each the pick of the best cuts, the bone and grisle only were left for the ordinary private. Undoubtedly however the inexperience of the cooks had a great deal to do with it. They had not the knack of making use of everything.

The first trenches

The next stage of their journey took them to La Gorgue, and Lavantie.[3]

One morning when we had been in this locality [for] two or three weeks we had orders to proceed up to the firing line. To our delight we found that we had not to march the whole way as a fleet of General Omnibuses had been placed at our disposal. These buses were painted a uniform grey and alas the direction boards with familiar names such as Charing Cross, Victoria Station etc. had been removed, but yet they were real buses and a link with home. We travelled some 30 kilometres or so in these buses and when we de-bussed were within 4 miles or so of the trenches. We marched about a mile further on, and then halted in a farm yard to await dusk before going into the trenches. While here we saw our first enemy shell-burst. Fritz was shelling a gun position some ½ mile away and quite a group of us gathered to watch.

For the purpose of instruction into the details of trench warfare the Battalion was split up and attached to various units of a Brigade of Grenadier Guards. A section of RWF to a platoon of Guards.

No 2 Section 7th Platoon was detailed to a platoon of No 2 Company GG who were already in the trenches.

Soon after dark the platoon fell in and marched away to the spot where they were to meet the guides. We marched along a main road leading towards Neuve Chapelle. It seemed absolutely straight. There was the usual line of poplar trees on each side. The position of the line was plainly defined by the numerous Verey lights, which seemed to rise slowly from the horizon, hover for a few seconds and then, as slowly, subside again. Small parties of Guards passed us at intervals, going in the opposite direction, and I remember well admiring their carriage and steady swinging stride. If we halted for a few minutes limbers and lorries passed us taking up ammunition and food to the forward areas.

We pressed on and soon could hear the occasional rattle of machine guns and the report of single shots from rifles. The Verey lights began to furnish us with a flickering ghostly light in which we could see the ruined walls of farmhouses, the jagged, splintered trunks of trees, and the dark shapes of our fellows marching on in silence to their first ordeal. Then we reached the area where spent bullets whined their way passed to their final resting places. It gave one an eerie feeling to hear this menacing, mournful whine and to know that was possible injury or even death in it. I do not think, however that any of us were really frightened. We had not yet seen or felt the effects of these same deadly missiles. Shortly afterwards we came to a spot where a road left the main road to the left. On the corner was a scarred, red coloured crucifix towering up above us, although the houses and trees in the vicinity seemed to be mostly blown to pieces. This was the well-known Rouge-Croix of Neuve-Chappelle. Here our guards met us. A tall Guardsman took charge of our section, and with a curt "Come along" led us along this side turning for two hundred yards or so, and then turned into a communication trench leading to the right. Wending our way along this trench for some fifteen minutes we reached our destination which was a so-called fort some 500yds from the front line trenches. This fort, which was only a circular formation of trench and fire-bay was manned by a platoon of Guards, and we were again split up, a few men being attached to each section.

The Guards treated us with some disdain, evidently thinking how green we were compared with their noble selves, and rather patronised us. I know the feeling as later we ourselves took some of the Bantams into the trenches for instruction. We spent most of the night sitting on the fire-step, but of course took our turn on sentry with a Guardsman, standing on the fire step gazing at mostly nothing, the occasional Verey light only serving to show a little barbed-wire and a sandbag or two. There was the usual pop of bullets overhead, followed later by the report of the rifle showing that the bullet had travelled considerably faster than the sound. Strange that the bullet at close quarters, although much more deadly than the spent variety mentioned before, should have a less menacing sound. The pop or rather crack, caused by the impact of the bullet on the air as it passed was formidable enough but not so bad as the sound of the spent one. We soon learnt to disregard these as there was little chance of stopping one, they were only fired at random by the enemy. It was a different matter however when a machine gun also firing at random, was swung round in our direction. That rapid crack-crack, swish-swish caused even a Guardsman to duck his lordly head.

Just as the first glimmer of dawn appeared the word came along the trench from mouth to mouth "Stand to". Those of us who were dozing were awakened and we all stood on the fire-step. "Stand to" (literally "Stand to your posts") was the order from ½ an hour before daybreak until ½ hr after, and again in the evening for the same period before and after dark. It was recognised that these times were the most likely ones for an attack.

As the light grew, so did the desultory rifle and machine gun fire, which had been going on all night, die away. Both armies we knew were manning their trenches within a few hundred yards of each other in an attitude of expectancy. An army of hundreds of thousands stretching, from the English Channel well down into Alsace and Lorraine, in a long irregular line, and only separated by a few yards from similar hundreds of thousands of enemy troops. There was scarcely a sound.

As the light grew stronger we could distinguish the ruins of Neuve-Chapelle on our right. The ground in front of our post was very much broken up by shell-fire and scarred with disused trenches. Barbed wire[,] old tins etc. were littered about and many of the shell holes were filled with water. The ground had been well fought over during the first big attack carried out by the British Army. Somewhere in this broken ground was our front line trench and that of the enemy. To the left was a row of tall trees, for the most part still standing, but with here and there a gap, where in place of a tree there was a splintered stump. At the foot of these trees we could see the sandbag communication trench by way of which we had arrived the night before. Most of the trenches in this part of the line were built above the ground. Sandbags were filled with earth and placed to form a parapet and parado, the space between forming the trench. The ground was so flat and boggy that it would have been impossible to have dug trenches in the ground itself.

As soon as it was broad daylight there came the order along the trench "Stand down" and with the exception of a sentry left on the fire step, we all got down into the trench and made preparations for breakfast. Our friends the Guards soon had little wood fires going, and the smell of bacon cooking was very appetising. We enjoyed our breakfast, although the tea was made from water out of a shell hole and most of us burnt our bacon.

All day long we lounged in the trench, feeling cold miserable and hungry. The Guards did not treat us badly, but we could see they despised us for undersized tenderfoots. They seemed happy in comparison with us. Towards evening one would persist in singing at the top of his voice seated on the top of the parapet. His friend remonstrated with him for taking this risk, but he would not come down and sat for quite a time with his back to the enemy. It would have been a good shot however that could have winged him in the uncertain light as we must have been 800yds or so from the Germans.

After dark we were relieved by another platoon of Guards with whom were a few of our own battalion, and marched back to billets in some huts three miles behind, and glad we were to get away from the trenches.

Back from the front line

We were billeted in a camp consisting of wooden huts built amongst the trees of an orchard. No.7 Platoon were allotted one of these huts to themselves and although it was very crowded we were glad to have a roof over our heads and dry boards as our bed. During the next two days we paraded with the Guards and were rather put through our facings, the NCO's not thinking much of our drill. It was always the Fusiliers that were getting shouted at.

Back to the trenches

The end of the second day however, once more found us in the trenches, as luck would have it, in the same place as before. We had been attached to the wrong platoon of Guards in the first instance.[4]

Unfortunately the weather turned colder and decidedly wet and we spent two uncomfortable days and nights. The only shelter we had was a couple of sheets of corrugated iron across the top of the trench. The Guards of course chose the driest spots under this shelter, and the poor Fusiliers had to take outside places. There was six inches or so of wet mud in the bottom of the trench, and everything, ourselves included, was wet and muddy.

A Christmas fire

One of the Guards was an Irishman, and he kept us lively with his banter and songs. Towards the end of the second day, as it was getting dark, he came singing, back from a working party loaded with wood he had salv[ag]ed from some ruined farmhouse. "It's Christmas Eve, lads and I have brought the wherewithal for a Christmas fire" he said and forthwith lit a proper blaze which must have been seen for miles round. It was impossible to pass along the trench owing to the heat. Later on in the war a foolhardy act like this would have brought over several salvoes of shells from Fritz.

When one of his comrades remonstrated with him he laughed and threw on more wood. He insisted that it was his Christmas fire, and anyway he was not going to leave any wood behind for those damned Jocks who would not leave a bully beef tin behind them if they could possibly carry it away. (The Scots Guards were relieving us that night.) We were content to bask in the warmth and dry our sodden garments.

A sign

William emerged from his first experience of trench life on Christmas Eve, 1915, an experience that caused him to reflect and search for some kind of solace:

We were relieved at 6'o'clock and made our way down the communication trench on to the road, where we halted for a few minutes. Wet, weary and hungry we stood there in a dejected group. A stranger more wretched Christmas Eve we had never spent. There were the usual sounds of desultory firing from the front line, and occasionally a spent bullet winged its way by us or fell with a "phut" in the wet ground around us.

Suddenly a "Verey" light from the nearest portion of front line sprung into the air and in its flickering, ghostly light we could see the road glistening with inches thick of semi-liquid mud, standing out like a strip of silver ribbon from the dark shadows of the surrounding fields. Silhouetted against this light background we could see the motionless shapes of our comrades in front, and overshadowing all, standing out clear and glowing against the deep black of the night, the Croix Rouge. The Prince of Peace nailed thereon with head bent down in sorrow and pity, looking on the very antithesis of all he lived and died for in this world. The scene only lasted a few moments and, as the Verey light dropped, faded out leaving the darkness, the mud and our miserable selves. It left also however, a message of comfort. That this image, serene and alone, should be standing, when so much else around had been shot to the ground, seemed to show us that in spite of the terrors, the chaos, the blood, the utter bestiality of a world gone mad, there was still hope for humanity, and that sooner or later the Prince of Peace would again come into his own.

Away from the trenches for Christmas Day

As we marched back to our billets our spirits began to revive a little. We had been cramped up so long in a trench that it was a pleasure to be on the move. At least we had been spared the hardship of Christmas Day in the trenches and were marching back to a camp where we would get a hot drink, be able to remove some of our sodden garments and roll ourselves in blankets, above all be able to sleep. On arrival at the camp we re-joined the other portions of the platoon, who had returned earlier and were already installed in two huts. We were too tired to talk much that night and were soon in a dreamless sleep.

Christmas Day 1915

The next morning we were aroused at 7 a.m. We looked a scrubby lot. Three days without wash or shave had wrought a wonderous change in us all. Dean, a dapper neat little man usually, was in a parlous state as were we all. That portion of his face not covered by the thick black growth of his beard was smeared with dried mud. His cap, stuck on at a rakish angle was crumpled and dirty. Thick, half-dried mud was coated on his legs up to and above the knees. Sayers was in like condition, with the addition that he had fallen sideway into a shell hole and taking roughly a line of demarcation down his middle was one half mud and one half khaki. These two scarecrows spent precious minutes, when they should have been getting on with their breakfast, telling each other what they looked like. Said Sayers, gradually raising his voice, "Just look at you, you black, dirty ruffian. What a mess you are in. Your own mother wouldn't own you. Look at you hat" (the last was nearing a squawk). Dean retorted "You red-faced piebald baboon. I should like to know I should, how you came to fall into that there shell-hole. The rum ration must have been too much for your silly head and you couldn't walk straight." This altercation ended in a wrestling match during which several pieces of dried mud becoming detached, fell to the floor. One piece fell into Jones' tea. He philosophically went on stirring it however, with a lead pencil remarking "My barman, having forgotten to bring the sugar perhaps a little mud will do as well. Thank you very much boys."

Much is spoken of the Christmas Truce in 1914, which occurred only five months from the start of the war. Germans and the Allied troops sang Christmas carols and exchanged gifts, and the artillery temporarily ceased their fire, in an act of goodwill and recognition of their mutual humanity.[5]

In recent years evidence has come to light that there was an attempt to do the same during Christmas Day in 1915, along part of the front line being held by some members of William's battalion. As he describes, during their first few days of trench life different companies of the 15 RWF were allocated to different companies of the Guards. In William's case, being in B Company, he was with the 3rd Battalion of the Grenadier Guards.[6] Thus, his group came out of the trenches on Christmas Eve.

Bertie Felstead, another private in the 15 RWF, this time D Company, who died in 2001 aged 106, related hearing the Germans singing 'Silent Night' that Christmas Day in 1915, and how the Royal Welsh Fusiliers sang 'Good King Wenceslas' in reply. He remembered how the two sides met in no man's land and played football together.[7]

Another recently discovered account regarding this 1915 Christmas 'truce' is from the diary of Robert Keating, another private in the same battalion, who recounts how the two sides shouted Christmas greetings to each other, with carols and Welsh songs being sung, amidst much cheering and encouragement from the other side. Robert also describes how one of the Germans told him that he was born in Northampton and was looking forward to the day he could return, hoping that the war would end soon.[8, 9]

Reference to the singing and friendly interaction between the Allies and the enemy on this Christmas Day has also been made by David Jones,[10] and Llewelyn Wyn Griffiths. The latter describes seeing 'a rush of men from both sides, carrying tins of meat, biscuits and other commodities. How no man's land almost became everyman's land with 'a suggestion for peace for the day and a football match in the afternoon …[which] came to naught', discouraged by an 'irate Brigadier … breathing fury everywhere'. Back in England however, it was reported in the newspapers that there had been no friendly interaction with the enemy during Christmas Day in 1915.[11]

```
We washed and shaved as best we could, some of us using
the remains of our tea for that purpose, others finding
puddles of water, washed in them. The mud was a worse
problem. Scraping it off with our knives and rubbing the
clothing in our hands. We had of course no brushes. It
was all we could do to get even the worst of it off as it
was scarcely dry. After a busy hour or so spent thus, we
paraded for Church Service. The inspection by the Guards
Sergeant Major was something to be remembered. He had a
word to say to each of us. Said to me "Dig yourself out of
some of that mud m'lad" To Douglas "Who the hell taught
you to carry your chest down there?" giving the offending
spot a prod with his stick. "Pull your shoulders back man!"
The Non-comformists were then separated from the rest and
marched away to Service in a large barn. We thought how
much better off we were in this shelter compared with the
others standing in the cold taking part in the C of E
```

[Church of England] Service. After this Service, we took leave of the Guards and marched to billet in a barn a mile or so away, where we joined the rest of the Company. Here we had dinner. Our Christmas Dinner. The cooks had surpassed themselves. There was a slice of roast beef, a great change from the usual stew, no vegetables of course, but followed by real Christmas pudding, piping hot, served in the tins in which they were received. We then had tea in which the rum ration had been mixed. Various delicacies were then given out, gifts of figs, dates, sweets etc. to the battalion by friends at home. There were also gifts of woollens, socks, gloves etc. To our delight we heard that the Post had arrived, then that there were several bags of parcels or "convoys" for No.7 Platoon alone. The bustle, expectation and excitement reached its highest pitch when they were actually brought into the barn. Names were called, parcels and letters claimed and we each took our share of the spoil to our own particular corner of the barn, read and re-read the letters from home and gloated over and sampled the contents of the parcels. The letters were full of news, full of kindly thought, full of Christmas, and of love, linking us with the folks at home. Who can ever describe the feelings aroused in the breasts of us men, or rather boys, by these letters written in the full knowledge that the recipients were far from home and in need of comfort.

Thus, finally arriving at his first destination on the front line near Laventie, William's description impresses on us how it must have felt to the men as they adapted to their new and changing environment. The cold, dark, cavernous barn next to a stinking cesspool as their first sleeping place. The paucity of food rations and resulting hunger was a theme that was to continue throughout his writing. Plate 9 illustrates the mess tins the infantry used for every meal while in the trenches. The pleasure in being excused from polishing their buckles and buttons was tempered by having to wash in tea or puddles of water, in a futile attempt to cleanse themselves of the ubiquitous claggy, clinging mud. Their new way of life was beginning to take shape.

Once escorted to the front line, they admired the confident stride of those who knew how it was. Full of trepidation, they realized that despite their training, they were naïve to this way of life.[12] Christmas arrived to serve as a temporary balm to soothe their nerves.

Chapter 3

Trench and Billet

'In time of danger the greatest burden of them all is enforced inactivity.'[1]

Christmas marked the end of the 15 RWF's initiation into trench warfare, and January 1916 sees their first experience of manning trenches on their own, taking complete charge of a sector for the first time. They were to spend five months in this region, from Givenchy-lès-la-Bassée and Cuinchy in the south, to Laventie and La Gorgue in the north.[2]

Taking over a section of the firing line

A fortnight or so after Christmas, the Division (38th) having passed out as it were, took over a sector of the firing line. Our Brigade, being Divisional Reserve did not immediately go into the trenches but were billeted in villages some five miles back in the neighbourhood of Merville.

It soon, however, came to our turn for a spell in the trenches and one day starting at 10am we marched to Richebourg St Vaast each company being followed by its field kitchen in full blast, cooking the midday meal.

Richeberg St Vaast had been a small village of half a hundred houses clustered round an old church. A small portion of the church tower remained standing and the rest of it littered the small churchyard, which was in a terrible condition. Huge pieces of masonry lay propped up against broken tombstones. Close to the road there was a huge hole at which we gazed in awe as we heard it had been made by a Jack Johnson shell. At the bottom of this hole, amongst other debris was the whitened bones of a one-time inhabitant of the village disrupted from his last resting place.

Of the houses little was left except broken walls and fallen roofs. The peaceful inhabitants had long since fled. The battalion halted just past the church and we fell out to partake of dinner. It was here that the battalion suffered its first casualty. A stray shell burst close to A Company's cooker, killing a cook and wounding several others.[3, 4]

Ruins

When it was dark our platoon moved forward up the road, a section at a time, into the village of Richebourg L'Avoué. This village was in a worse condition than the one we had just left. It was within 700 or 800 yds of the front line, a mere double line of ruins one each side of the Rue de Bois, a road which a little further on, led across no mans' land into enemy country. As we waited for the guides, I looked up this road. I could not see far, but could visualise it passing our front line, manned by our khaki comrades, and then across the confusion of no mans' land a few hundred yards only, to similar trenches manned by the grey clad enemy. From thence leading back far into that unknown land and used by the Germans in the same way as we used it on our side of the front line. The guide soon appeared and led us in single file along the road. We were greeted by a burst of machine gun fire which however was aimed too high to hurt us. The bullets were knocking pieces of brick from the walls above our heads.

No. 8 Post, across the boggy mud and water

Trenches were an impossibility at this part of the line as the ground was too flat and boggy. The front line, so called was a series of posts formed by raising sandbagged barricades on the top of the ground or mud. These posts were reached by tortuous, precarious paths of duckboards laid across the intervening mud and water.[5]

We soon reached one of these paths and turning off from the road were soon carefully wending our way along it, our pace slow usually, but quickening at times as a Verey light occasionally lit the way.

Trenchboards or duckboards are made by nailing short pieces of boards crossways on to two parallel supports, something in the form of a rough ladder. They were treacherous things to walk on, as upon one end being stepped upon, the other end evinced a strong desire to rear itself up to see who has trod on its tail. A very disconcerting movement when one was loaded with equipment etc., it was pitch dark, and the surrounding terrain was anything but firm.

After 20 minutes of such progress, we came at the end of the track to No.8 post, which was to be held by the platoon. The post first appeared to us as a low dark barricade stretching 30yds or so on each side of us. We filed along the trench board laid behind this, and proceeded to take over from a platoon of the Welch regiment who had been there four days. From the outgoing garrison of the post we learned the various particulars concerning it [such as] how the enemy were entrenched only 300yds away, the risk we ran from enemy snipers if we showed ourselves during daylight, where the stores of bombs and other ammunition were, and many other things inseparable from trench-relief.

They then filed out of the post and we could hear the faint jingle of their accoutrements gradually fading away as they made their way back over the trench board track in the direction of the rest billets.

We were soon set to work filling sandbags and building a parados so as to make our position more comfortable. The barricade or parapet before mentioned was an adequate protection from bullets and from shells bursting in No Mans' Land, but until we finished this parados, we stood in great danger from shells bursting in our rear.

We worked in pairs, one holding the sandbag open while the other shovelled in the wet clayey earth. Ward and I worked together, and when we had filled several carried them to Corp[ora]l Meadows, who in an exposed position on top of the parodos, was laying them into position.

Jones and Sayers were having their usual words with each other, "Sayers you great fat fungus, what is the good of you trying to shove a yards square into that small bag?" Sayers retorted "If you would only shut your mug and open the bag properly I should get on quicker, or better still, if you would only stow yourself in a sandbag I will have much pleasure in tying you up and placing you on the fortifications. You might be some good there." A shell coming over at this moment and bursting on the Rue de Bois behind us, Jones remarked "Sayers, what do you mean bringing your infernal air-pillow up here and then letting it go off in that fashion. You quite made me jump."

The night passed on quietly enough however. There was the usual desultory fire. Now and again, as an officer and orderly approached on visiting rounds the sentry would challenge "Halt, who are you?" On receiving the answer "15 R.W.F." he would say "Righto" and allow them to approach.

Dawn and isolation

The last visitors appeared just before daylight and had to hurry back as they had to make the shelter of the village before the fast-gaining daylight caught them napping on the duckboard track. We were of course isolated during the day. The only communication being in the hands of the signallers, who had a telephone line laid out.

When quite light we could take stock of our position. The post was merely some 50yds or so of barricade and was quite isolated from its neighbours, the next post on the left lying in our rear and quite 400yds away. We could see little movement in these posts but could plainly see their regular outline standing out in contrast to the surrounding confusion of shell-holes, water and mud. About 600yds to our right we could see the ruins of Neuve Chappelle. The only link with the outside world was the duckboard track winding back, sometimes in sight, sometimes disappearing in a hollow, until, where it joined the Rue du Bois, it looked like a mere ribbon. The village seemed but a line of curiously shaped ruins mingled with which were a few crippled trees. Further back still in the misty distance, we could see trees in a more natural state, and over these hung the sausage-shaped observation balloon kept captive by a rope which disappeared down behind the trees. Other balloons, gradually decreasing in size as the distance increased, hung motionless, like so many solemn-eyed gods watching over us, at regular intervals as far as we could see on either side. Further away, behind the German lines were a similar line of balloons.

Our position, now we could view it in daylight, did not seem a very happy one. It seemed to my mind a very easy matter for an enemy raiding party to pass through the gap in between our post and the next during the hours of darkness, and to attack us in our defenceless rear. Behind the parapet we were able to move about fairly freely, which was an advantage when compared with the narrow confines of an ordinary trench.

We had been warned about looking over the top but most of us had quick glances at the enemy terrain, not that we could see anything much, only more mud and broken ground.

Bacon, tea and letters from home

From the direction of the enemy lines, out of No Man's Land, a small stream, it was really only a ditch draining the waterlogged ground, came under the barricade and flowed on towards the village. The water looked fairly pure, but we were rather doubtful about using it as Jerry might have poisoned it. However the outgoing garrison had recommended it and it came in very useful for tea and for washing in.

We soon had several little fires going, and round each fire were grouped 3 or 4 men. Necessity had soon made us adept at fire lighting. Even the most sodden piece of wood by judicious chipping, could be made to yield fire enough to cook by. We started with very small chips indeed, kindling them with one match, matches were scarce, and gently blowing with the mouth, afterwards increasing the size of the chips, until quite large pieces of damp wood would burn.

We fried our bacon in our mess-tin lids, with the cheese ration. Our appetites, after a night spent fasting, were whetted by the savoury smell. Our tea we made in our mess tins, waiting, until the water boiled freely and then casting therein tea and sugar, and immediately removing it from the fire. How eagerly we blew on the tea, the quicker to feel its warming comforting passage down our throats into our chilled innards. The day passed very quietly. There were one or two rifle shots, snipers at work, and we afterwards learned that [the] O.C. no.6 platoon, a tall officer over six feet high, had been killed outright with a bullet through his head.

During the afternoon the regimental postman paid us a visit bringing up our letters. It was a foolhardy journey but he did not realise his danger. Luckily the enemy snipers must have been looking elsewhere. When within a few yards of the post a shot rang out, and I saw the postman thinking it was meant for him, duck rapidly and turn colour first white and then red. We watched his stooping figure as he rapidly made his way back, expecting every moment to see him crumple up with a bullet in him. Shortly after this, Fritz began to shell the village, sending up clouds of smoke, red brick-dust and debris. As the light of the short January afternoon faded so did the usual noises of the night increase. We stood to and then stood down. The most active noisiest period of the 24hrs had commenced.

A party of men were told off to go back for the next day's rations, the rest of us, when not on sentry, continued our work of the night before. Hard, unpleasant work it was. The wet, clayey soil would only break up into big lumps, and the shovels got very sticky. I was glad when it was my turn to go on sentry, and I could stand on the fire step with my fellow sentry, and gaze with unseeing eyes across at the German trenches for an hour.

We stopped in this post for 4 days and 4 nights. The only sleep we got was an hour or two during the day time, stretched out on the ground, or on the fire step. Our only shelter was a few pieces of corrugated iron, propped up to form a roof. The only two small dugouts were occupied by the officer in charge and the signallers respectively. The weather was raw and damp.

Handing over

At the end of the 4th day we were relieved by the 13th R.W.F. With what eagerness we waited for an hour or so after dark, our eyes strained along the duckboard as far as we could see, our ears listening for the first sign of the approaching relief.

These same ears gave us the first indication, a vague indefinable sound of movement, increasing until we could hear the click-click of the slung rifles knocking against the entrenching tool handle, then we could hear footsteps, and at last faintly discern dark, shadowy shapes loaded with equipment, rations and stores, emerging out of the gloom and advancing towards us in single file. Following the hoarse challenge of the sentry, and the quieter reply, the relief were soon amongst us, muttering and swearing in their quick Welsh way, about the unevenness of the track, their too heavy loads, and the God-forsaken hole they had come to.

The handing over of the post was soon complete, and we joyfully left it behind us, rejoicing in the freedom of moving once more, stretching our legs over the track and making light of the bullets that popped past us. Reaching the road we joined the rest of the company. We learned that our Captain (Allison) was no longer in command. Suffering from fright he had re-coursed to his whiskey flask and being found drunk by the C.O. was removed from his command [and] afterwards cashiered. He was a man disliked by all, a veritable bully. At the first sign of danger he had shown up in his true colours, and would now worry us no more.

Back from the front

We marched back to Richebourg St Vaast and were billeted in rooms on the ground floor of houses of which the 1st floor and roof had been demolished by shell fire. Blankets were served out to us by the Q.M.S. [Quarter Master Sergeant] and we soon made ourselves comfortable on the brick or tiled floor. The floor was undoubtedly hard, but we had soon learnt to appreciate a dry level floor, where there was shelter over our heads and room to be at full length.

We spent four days in this billet. Actually we were in the support line to the front line, but as far as I can remember there were no trenches to man.

Movement, during the day in the village street was restricted, very much owing to the fact that we could easily be seen from the enemy country, but behind our ruinous billets we were screened from observation and could move about more freely. However, every now and then we heard three shrill whistles and had to take cover as an enemy aeroplane was approaching, emerging when we heard the 'All clear' one single blast from the same whistle. We paraded several hours a day for drill.

Night work

During the night we were mostly on RE [Royal Engineer] working parties. One night we were working erecting a trench amidst the ruins of Richebourg L'Avoué. There were 40 or so of us working in a small space of open ground between the unfinished trench and the ruins. The ghostly flicker of a distant Verey light or the livid flare of a nearer one, were continually showing us the grotesque shape of the ruins and the black figures of our comrades; sweating, toiling, cursing and grousing, some filling sandbags, others staggering across the boggy ground loaded with the filled ones to the point where the parapet was being continued. One or two on the top of this parapet, placing them in position, and banging them into shape with their shovels. Frequently a burst of enemy machine gun fire would pass us and crack-crack on the walls behind, causing pieces of brick to fall about us.

After four days we came out of the line for eight days rest. We next went into the trenches directly on the right of the village of Givenchy. This village stood on a small hill. Our front line curved round the eastern boundaries of it.

The trenches here were actually dug out of the ground as there was plenty of fall for drainage.

Llewlyn Wyn Griffith refers several times to the feeling there was something bad about Givenchy, 'a focus of evil', something that gave it a bad reputation. He felt there was an ugliness about the area, completely destroyed at the time, with no hint of softness, 'a feeling of malignant fate hovering above this hillock'. He particularly refers to the sadness of seeing new buildings destroyed that had recently been built with so much hope for the future.[6]

A sort of dugout

With five other men, I occupied a so called dugout in a communication trench ten yards or so from the front line. We were not exactly the front line garrison but were there to protect the C.T. [communications trench] in the event of an attack. The dugout, was very dilapidated.

A space six foot square had been dug out of the side of the CT, roofed with a double thickness of sandbags, about enough to make it rifle-grenade proof, [when] placed on a few beams. There was a narrow entrance from the trench, flanked on each side by a column of sandbags 4ft high, which was also the height of the inside. We had a piece of sacking hung over this opening to make it cosier. In this damp, dark, dirty hole four or five of us would stow ourselves, there always being one or more on sentry in a kind of sap, which led off and overlooked the C.T.

Miners and listening duty

At this time, [in] February 1916 the miners of both sides were very active around Givenchy. Within a few yards of our dugout was the shaft of one of our mines. A small hole in the trench, half covered in with boards, a small windlass for bringing up sandbags full of earth, just the ends of the ladder which reached down into the depths, and a hand-pump with pipe attached for pumping out the water from the mine. There was nearly always one of the miners lounging about outside this shaft, smoking and evidently taking his turn for a breather. The windlass shaft top, spare pit props, surrounding ground, even the miner himself from head to foot, were covered with a pale grey sediment of clay, and there was the smell peculiar to earth which has never seen the light of day. Below ground there were various saps and tunnels, some actually under the enemy trenches, and other[s] merely for protection, running parallel to above and at the side of the main tunnel in which men were placed to listen for sounds of enemy miners at work. This listening was very important as the opposing forces were continually endeavouring to countermine (that is, digging a mine under that of the enemy and blowing his works sky-high). I never was on this listening duty, which was done of course when our miners were not working, but can well imagine the horror of it. Nothing to do but crouch in a narrow, wet tunnel, lighted by one flicking candle, many feet below the surface, listening in the awe inspiring silence of such places, where surface sounds could not penetrate, for the thud of the enemy miners at work. Possibly within a few yards of an enemy listener, or worse still a huge charge of cordite, which might be exploded under him at any minute. What terrors this duty must have had for [the] oftentimes, mere boys who had to undertake it. (Their ears were sharper than those of the older men, or possibly they were not so good at the hard work.)

The thought of a sudden deep concussion, the narrow sap in which they were closing on them, utter darkness and death, or being pushed by the force of the explosion through yards of intervening clay to the surface, and then up into the air and, at last falling, killed and broken, God knows where[, was terrifying].

Even on the surface the dread of this hidden menace added a new terror to a life already full of anxieties and fears. Dugouts at other parts of the line looked upon as a godsend, were here counted a very mixed blessing, for, even when situated outside the immediate area of an exploding mine, the concussion might easily cause the dugout to fall in, burying the inmates alive.

One night there were five of us dozing in our dugout. Sleep very seldom came to my relief when in the trenches however tired I was, or however long I had been without, but its place was taken by a kind of doze which was not nearly so refreshing as genuine sleep. I suppose the ever-present fear of some sudden danger, an attack, a raid, a near shell explosion, a gas attack, to name a few of them, prevented me sleeping in any other manner than with all my senses at the alert. Many hours both during the day and the night have I spent lying in dugouts, or sitting on fire-steps, dozing, trying to get an hour or so of refreshing real sleep. Sometimes I would just be dropping off when I was disturbed by a shattering explosion, or some other noise, and would have to start all over again.

Lack of sleep was one of our greatest trials.

A close shave

In my doze on this occasion I suddenly realised that the ground under me was shaking and heaving. Immediately I instinctively made for the opening of the dugout, groping with my hands in the dark, and arousing my comrades. I realized almost without thinking that the dugout was a decidedly unhealthy place, that it might fall in at any moment. My precipitancy was nearly the cause of my undoing as just as I was drawing back the screen a huge

```
lump of earth, a cubic yard or so, fell with a thud just
in the entrance, half blocking it. If I had been half
a second quicker in getting out of the dugout I should
have received the benefit of this cartload of earth right
on the top of me, giving me a nasty jar if not seriously
injuring me. We were soon all out of the dugout standing
to arms in case Fritz meant business, but we soon learnt
that he evidently had only blown up a countermine under
some of our own saps, two of our miners having very
narrow escapes. The next day we could see our side of
the crater, within 2 yards or so of our front line at its
nearest spot. It looked like a circular mound of freshly
turned up earth 50yds or so in circumference.
   If the Germans had meant it for our front line they
were far out.
```

Within the first six months of the war, both sides realised that something needed to be done to break the stalemate of trench warfare, and both turned to the idea of mining and explosives as a possible solution.

In February 1915, the Allies decided to form eight tunnelling companies, although more were to come later. The decision to do this has been described as the quickest intentional act in the war, with men who had been working underground in the UK being underground at Givenchy only four days later, such was the urgency.[7]

These companies were made up of drafts of civilian miners and sewer workers, and also 'clay-kickers' who had worked on the construction of the London Underground network. Men who had worked on the Manchester sewer system were key to the construction of the mines in the Givenchy region, supported by miners from various regiments from Wales and Staffordshire.[8] Although their mining skills were not initially used, many miners had already signed up to fight in the war seeing an opportunity to be released, at least temporarily, from their subterranean existence. However, when mining along the front line, there was a marked differential in the rate of pay, with civilian tunnellers being paid six shillings per week, against the ordinary infantryman's wage of one shilling per week.[9]

Where it was possible, due to the underlying geology of the region, mines were constructed, going deeper and deeper, mining and countermining, as quietly as possible, listening for the enemy, perhaps only a few metres away. If enemy mining activity was detected, explosives would be planted, destroying not only the targeted enemy tunnels but also inevitably their own system of mines. The main target was enemy trenches, and explosions of underground munitions, very often ammonal, a dangerous unstable substance,[10] produced enormous craters some of which are still visible today, such as the Lochnagar Crater in the Somme. The lesser-known Duck's Bill and nearby Red Dragon Crater are situated in the Givenchy-lès-la-Bassée area. A few weeks later William found himself defending a trench close to the top edge or lip of Duck's Bill Crater as he describes in Chapter 6.

Rifle grenade alerts

The opposing trenches were so close together at this part that rifle-grenades could be used. A sentry was specially posted to listen for the discharge of the Germans grenades, quite a different sound from the report of an ordinary shot, watch for the rise of it and blowing a whistle, shout "Rifle Grenade Right" or "Rifle Grenade Left" as the case might be, to warn the rest of the garrison. On hearing the plop of the discharge however, most of us were already on the 'qui vive' and saw the peculiar stick with a blob on one end go hurtling up turning over and over until it reached a good height, when it appeared to steady, and then drop like a stone with its business end downwards. The ensuing explosion was a sharp angry one, but as the grenade was mostly shrapnel and high explosive it exploded upwards and unless it actually fell into the trench did little damage. One grenade fell clean on top of a shrapnel helmet, killing the wearer immediately. I remember examining the helmet afterwards. The dome-like top was opened out like a tulip.

Brigade support

After this spell in the trenches we were relieved, and becoming brigade support, took up our quarters in a small village called Nouix.[11] This village although within 3 or 4 kilometres of the front line was scarcely touched by shellfire. It owed this immunity to the fact that it was well screened from enemy observation by trees. Compared with most others in the vicinity it was rather a pretty little village. It had two estaminets and even one small shop.

It was rumoured that the girl in this shop had a baby by a German officer, the Germans having been in occupation at the very beginning of the war. Whatever truth there was in this rumour there was certainly a baby in the house.

We were billeted in a loft over a huge barn, which took up one side of an unusually large farmyard. It was reached by climbing a ladder and entering through a small door. It was rather dark inside but the floor was of wood and quite level and clean. Altogether it was an admirable billet and almost roomy enough for the whole company. We spent a very comfortable four days in this village and then went into one of the posts in front of Richebourg l'Avoué. This post was on the left of the previous one, and in a more advanced state of completion. Four of us had quite a nice new little dugout. We also had the foresight each to take a loaf of French bread in with us. We spent a rather more comfortable time than before.

Back to Givenchy shadowed by Bantams

Following this spell in the trenches we had eight days rest in billets. At the end of this period we assembled one night to again take over trenches in Givenchy. It was bitterly cold. We had been joined by some of the Bantams for instruction purposes in the same manner as we ourselves had joined the Guards. There was at this time I believe a Division of Bantams, mainly recruited from men a few inches too short to enlist in the usual battalions.[12] A good number of boys, however, between the ages of fourteen and seventeen had seized the opportunity of becoming soldiers, and moreover had succeeded in passing out of the training and getting out to the front. One of the Bantams was getting on for 6ft in height. When he joined up at the age of 15 he had been only 5' 4".

When about half way to Givenchy we came to La Bassée Canal and turned to the left along the tow path. At this spot there was a half demolished house which had been converted into a pumping station, for the purpose, we believed, of keeping the level of the water in the canal so low as to render it useless to the Germans further on. The steady pulsation of the engine through a kind of exhaust pipe, which like an inverted L protruded through the top of the building, went on day and night and could be heard on quiet days for miles around. It was strange to hear this sound sometimes when in the front line. We marched along by the side of the canal for 1km or so, passing a lock where a branch canal joined the main one on the far bank. The front line lay directly in front of us as we could see by the frequent Verey lights. I thought it would be rather interesting to see where it was bisected by the canal. There was supposed to be a German Master Sniper active in this spot. I do not remember his exact exploits, but my impression [was] that he was a mysterious, bearded, wild-man-of-the-woods kind of person. We left the canal taking a road to the left, which was well screened from observation during the day by a high hedge. This road led us to the renowned "Windy Corner" owing to the fact that it was liable to sudden bombardments by whizz-bangs and was at times swept by machine-gun fire. We turned to the right here and entered the northern end of Givenchy-en-...[Bassée]. Guides met us at this spot and we entered a CT leading off by the Inn of the Red Hart. This CT zig zagged up the hill, past the demolished church of Givenchy, through the ruined houses to the front line on the further slope.

We took over a post in the front line just to the left of the village, where the line sloped down to Festubert.

Blizzard conditions

Thus began one of the worst spells we ever had in the trenches. There were 6 men in our section to which were attached 4 of the Bantams. We had to place ammunition boxes on the fire-steps to enable them to gain a firing position over the parapet.

The next morning we were able to take better stock of our position. The view over the parapet was rather restricted directly in front. We could see little further than the German front line. Mixed up in their barbed wire entanglements some 200yds distant we could plainly see the body of a British officer lying on his side facing us. To our left we could see the little that was left of the village of Festubert. A few broken walls and tree stumps. Surrounding these ruins, grey and cold looking in the early morning light was a desolate, trench scarred, shell-pitted expanse, plentifully sprinkled with barbed wire. It looked absolutely devoid of life, but hidden in its muddy wastes were many soldiers of both armies undergoing unbelievable hardships and miseries. Before long huge, swirling clouds of snow swept across the valley alternately hiding and revealing the landscape. It beat upon us, half blinding us, and getting into all the crevices of our clothing. I glanced over the top at the dead officer. He was already coated into a white pall. I half envied him. However agonising his last moments had been, he was now where German bomb or bitter weather could not touch him. He was at peace, while we were very conscious of the bitter cold and the abject misery of our position. The weary day drew on. The landscape looked even more desolate in its thick mantle of snow. The little shelter we had under a few pieces of corrugated iron was insufficient to hold us all. Only the men in the very inside were protected at all from the penetrating blizzard.

The six inches of snow in the trench rendered movement in order to keep ourselves warm, difficult. It melted on our boots making our feet wet. All that day and all the next night the snow continued falling. The night was worse than the day. Those of us not on sentry sat on the fire step under, or half under our shelter, huddled up close to one another, trying to keep what warmth we could in our frozen bodies. One little fellow, a Bantam who was still under 16 years of age was next to me at one time. I could hear him quietly weeping, from sheer misery and cold.

I awakened once or twice from a doze to find myself groaning, and had to get up and stamp to get any feeling at all into my legs. Our rations were very poor. Five persons shared a 2lb loaf [of bread]. The quantity of fresh meat and bacon were almost negligible, the ration being made up with bully beef. We could scarcely get two good drinks a day out of our tea and sugar ration. There was no milk. The snow came in very handy to make the tea however, as we had only to melt sufficient in our mess tins over tiny fires we lit for the purpose.

Douglas and I found a small half collapsed dugout on the second day situated just behind the trench. We could only just gain entrance to it by lying down on the ground and wriggling our bodies through the narrow opening. When inside we could not sit up but had to assume a reclining attitude. We retired here when able and I can well remember making café au lait (I had bought a tin before coming into the line), boiling the water by means of a few pocket fires received in a parcel. It did not snow on the second day, but it was bitterly cold and lasted so for the whole of our spell in the trenches. Some of us found a German rifle grenade and beguiled some time examining it, a very dangerous practice with a weapon of this nature which might go off if shaken or jerked about. An Irishman O'Hara seemed to enjoy playing with it, he used it as a dumb-bell and swung it round his head, finally hurling it over into no man's land where it promptly exploded. Why it did not do so before I cannot say. None of us would have minded very much, we were in such desperate straits. The time dragged on, each hour seemed a day, each day a month. We were wretchedly cold, hungry and suffering from lack of sleep. We gazed at the drab confines of our narrow prison, hating the very sandbags and boxes of ammunition [and] longing for the time which never seemed to grow nearer for our relief. The ennui[,] discomfort and lack of sleep attendant on a stay in the trenches were harder to bear than the fear of sudden dangers. To remain for days together pent up in a muddy ditch, little to do, nowhere to rest, wet, hungry and miserable was little short of torture. There was not a single man amongst us who would not have welcomed a wound, as long as it was not too serious, that would take him out of it all. To many, death itself if it came suddenly would have been a welcome release. The feeling almost akin to revolt against everything, which came over us at times, and not natural bravery, was the cause of many a deed of daring. Often, heartily sick of a struggle along a congested trench, (loaded as we often were with heavy trench stores), through mud, round awkward corners and past many obstacles, we would, cursing and blaspheming, get out of the trench and walk along the top, not caring a damn for the bullets which popped past us every second.

There never is, and moreover there never has been any glory in actual warfare. All the glory comes afterwards and is indulged in by people who never experienced war. Take for instance the historic Charge at Balaclava rendered glorious in verse. What was the actual feelings of the men engaged? Judging by what I know of attacks over the top even more terrible than the one in question, every man was cursing his hard fate, a very real fear of sudden death, tearing at his victuals.

The Inn of the Red Hart, Cuinchy

Our relief was never more welcome than when it arrived at the end of the 4th day. We were absolutely worn out. Luckily we had not far to go as we were billeted in the Inn of the Red Hart, Cuinchy. We were asleep within a few minutes of our entry into the one habitable room in the inn.

This inn stood at the crossroads, on the east side of the main street, at the northern end of Cuinchy. Opposite was a road leading back out of the trench area along which, at all times of the day and night, supplies of ammunition, rations etc were continually arriving in limbers, carts and lorries. The road should have continued up by the side of our billet to Givenchy, but shell fire and debris from the fallen houses had completely obliterated it. The only clue to show that it had existed was a direction label on the wall of the inn which read "Givenchy 1km". Looking in the direction of the front line, we could see two communication trenches zig-zagging up the slope and losing themselves in the heap of bricks and fallen masonry which marked the village of Givenchy. The front line was not visible to us although only some 1200 yards away. It was situated just over the brow of the rise. To our left was the road leading along to "Windy Corner", and to our right the long straggling village street with its ruined houses on each side, leading along to the area known as the Brickfields. The village although sadly battered was not under direct observation from the enemy's territory and while we were there we were not troubled with much shell-fire, and could move about freely even in daylight although so near the front line. It was a different matter 200 yds away at "Windy Corner". This spot could be seen by the enemy and suffered accordingly.

Our billet appeared as if it had had the 1st storey knocked clean out of it, the roof collapsing and resting in a slanting position over the ceiling of the ground floor. We could still see the name of the estaminet on the wall although the letters were much torn with shrapnel.

Suspended on an iron bar and creaking on its rusty hinge, was a shot riddled signboard which bore an image which could still be recognised as an animal of some kind.

Next door, or rather in the next ruin, there was no door left, its place being taken by a curtain of sacking, was the Divisional Soup Kitchen. Savoury odours were emitted from the kitchen at intervals but we never discovered who received the soup. We received none ourselves.

Porridge

The next day Douglas and I on a tour of discovery amid the adjacent ruins, found a canteen. The only things in stock were writing pads, oatmeal and condensed milk. We purchased some of the last two items and returning to our billet made ourselves some porridge. Fuel was very plentiful here, the woodwork of the fallen houses furnishing an almost limitless supply.

We had a couple of braziers formed out of oil drums in the room and we made our porridge on one of these. It was awkward balancing our mess tins on this kind of fire.

Douglas was already guzzling his porridge with much gusto and smacking of his thick lips. Upon attempting to remove my mess tin from the fire I grasped the handle, which was almost red hot and dropped the lot. When I retrieved it from the depths of the fire with the end of my bayonet half the porridge was lost and the remainder was mixed with charred wood. I ate it however.

An underground attack

That night we were ordered out onto trenches just behind our billet. Our engineers were blowing up three mines simultaneously under the works of the enemy. We stood gazing in the direction of the expected explosion, glad that we were out of its immediate neighbourhood. At ten o'clock, to the second, we felt the ground under our feet tremble and could see what looked like a cloud suddenly appear, poised over the crown of the hill. A second or so later we heard the rushing, rumbling sound of the explosion. The desultory firing of rifles suddenly ceased. It was as if everyone was holding their breath, startled at the suddenness of the catastrophe. Following swiftly on this short silence came the renewed, accentuated noise of rifle fire, to which was added the rat-tat-tat of machine guns. Red lights, green lights and white lights all appeared above the horizon, and showed us plainly the cloud of smoke and descending debris over the scene of the explosion. Some of these lights were signals to the enemy's artillery who added considerably to the din, putting down a barrage on our front line. The noise seemed to wax and wane, one minute comparative quiet, the next a very tornado. One or two shells seemed to emerge from this stormy area, hum over our heads, and explode with a crash behind us. Bullets whined and ricocheted about us. Evidently the Bosch expected some kind of a raid.

The din gradually subsided until, in ten minutes time all was as quiet as before the explosion. We returned to our billets to sleep. How many poor devils had entered their last sleep, killed and buried in the same minute?

Thus, the men of the 15 RWF learnt the routine of trench warfare: the four-day-on, four-day-off rhythm of trench and billet. During the long periods they spent in the front line, all they would often see beyond the confines of their immediate surroundings, would be the sky. Throughout the war in fact, they would rarely, if ever, see the enemy. They were hungry, cold and wet, constantly exhausted and constantly in terrible danger. They became disoriented and 'lost'. The men, relatively untrained, were not fighting. Theirs was a passive, disconnected role shoring up defences and waiting in a bubble of mud, barbed wire and sandbags, with little opportunity or ability to respond in any way to an attack.

When in the marshlands they were aware of being watched by the enemy situated above them on the ridges, by planes flying overhead and by snipers waiting for any chance to claim another victim. 'Dug in' to the mud and water that surrounded them, they waited for the next opportunity to be relieved by another group of men, so they may make their way back along the duckboards which created the tenuous link with the outside world.

When posted around the ruins of Givenchy, elevated from the mud, they were placed in even more danger, not only from enemy artillery but also from the work of miners, both ally and enemy, placing munitions underneath the opposing trenches. Each man was constantly 'waiting to be blown up'. There was never a time when a mind could be at rest.[13]

No wonder that William describes how many came to not care what might happen. Rather, there was a wooden acceptance of their lot, which he describes as 'nothing short of torture' causing a deadening of the mind and almost a preference for death.

Chapter 4

A Sanctuary and Holding a Line

Alongside the tedious and dangerous way of life that William and his fellow soldiers endured in the trenches, there were times when it was possible to relax a little. Such moments were cherished as the men continued their journey through the war.

Two half minutes

When we had spent four days in Cuinchy the battalion was relieved and entered billets in a very small village 4 kilometres from Béthune. Our platoon had a large barn to themselves. The next day we spent cleaning ourselves and our equipment. Our platoon fell in for baths after breakfast, the order being clean fatigue with towels, and we marched off to the Divisional Baths. We enlivened the way with song being accompanied by Sayers on a mouth organ he had just received from home. He had great difficulty in pitching on the right key. We passed other parties of the Battalion returning from their baths, everyone seemed light hearted and gay. We were out of the trenches, were not carrying our usual deadening weight of equipment and moreover we were on our way to get rid of by drowning, the many insects which infested our bodies and clothing.

Arriving at the Baths which were in a barn, we were allowed in 20 at a time. This barn was divided into three portions, the two side ones for dressing and undressing and the central portion for washing. We undressed, placing our clothing on a bench which ran around the wall and lining up, clad only in our identity discs, at a small aperture like that of a booking office, we received a clean set of underclothing in exchange for our venomous old ones from the hands of a RAMC [Royal Army Medical Corps] man. Taking our clean change back to our places we took up our positions under the sprays which were a foot or so above our heads. The RAMC corporal in charge called out

"The water will run for one half minute only" and promptly turned it on. There was much splashing and shouting. The water was too hot. Jones called out to the man in charge. "Too hot you b--- fool, too hot, are you trying to boil us." At this and many other noisy complaints he turned on more cold water and had just as many epithets flung at him as the water was too cold. At the end of the half minute the water was turned off, and grasping the soap provided we hurriedly lathered ourselves and each other, pushing, shoving, cursing and laughing. Two minutes were allowed for this operation and then the tap was turned on for another half minute. We then returned to our places and dried ourselves.

The fitting on of our clean underclothing caused a great deal of fun. It had been indiscriminately served out to us. In consequence Hoare a very small man, who was some months later killed, had a large shirt reaching down to his ankles. He was chaffed about his nightgown until he espied Ward who with nothing on his nether regions, arms waving above his head, which was hidden in the folds of his shirt was frantically endeavouring to don a shirt which when he did succeed in getting it on, barely reached his waist. Jones meantime had been quietly examining the seams of his pants, muttering to himself. He suddenly burst out into a vituperative outburst against the whole army and that section of it which compromises the RAMC in particular. "Give me back my old dirty pants will you you b……. representative of the Rob All My Comrades. I at least knew the insects on that garment. They had stuck to me through thick and thin and many an hour have I beguiled chasing the b…….s. This lot crawling along the seams of these pants are a bastard lot". He was given a cleaner pair of pants. When we were dressed we assembled outside, and marched back to billets feeling refreshed and free from the irritation of active insects, a fresh batch of which would hatch out from the numerous small eggs hidden somewhere in our clothing.

An unexpected sanctuary

Exploring the locality that same afternoon we turned up a narrow path off the lane in which our billet was situated, and traversing this path, enclosed on each side by a high hedge, for some 100yds or so found that it ended at a 5 barred gate which led into a field. On the left just before reaching this gate we saw a small gate set in the hedge and looking over this gate descried a beautiful little cottage with a thatched roof. The garden path led slantways across a tidy front garden up to the thatched porch. Behind the cottage were some tall poplar trees. It seemed as if we had suddenly returned to England. The cottage was the counterpart of many found in the byways at home, and quite dissimilar from any others about that part of France. Its tiny windows set flat in the walls were diamond paned.

Douglas, having a partiality for café suggested that we knocked at the door and asked whether they had any for sale. We did so and a fresh, bright looking little old woman, withal a little bent with age, opened the door. To her we conveyed our wish in bad French. She seemed to hesitate, and then possibly struck with our harmless appearance bade us enter. We were soon seated comfortably by the stove partaking of a very nice cup of coffee. The old woman's grandchild, a pretty little girl of six years or so soon made friends with us. Her name was Julie Dupont.

While we were drinking our café there came bustling in Julie's mother with marketing basket in hand. She seemed surprised and rather taken back at our presence. The old woman evidently explained, we could not follow their rapid talk but their glances told us who they were discussing. When we rose to go we offered them payment which they refused. They also made us understand that we would be welcome at any other time we liked to come. "Encore, monsieurs, encore" We asked whether we might write our letters there during the evenings and were gladly given permission.

On several occasions Douglas and I went to this cottage and spent the evening there. We always received a warm welcome especially from little Julie. For the first part of the evening she would sit on my knee at the table and prattle away to me. I could understand her better than I could the older people. In fact she often put into her plainer childish language what the others failed to make us understand. I would draw rough pictures on my writing pad, and great was her delight to recognise the objects, and tell me the French for them. In this way I taught her a little English, while learning a good deal of French. I can remember the difficulty she had to pronounce my name and the joke the old lady made about it being the same as the Kaiser. Too soon it would be her bedtime, and her mother would say "Couchez, Julie. Donnez le bonheur aux monsieurs." Then kissing her mother and granny and also Douglas and I, would go off quietly to bed. I would then be able to write a few letters. One night as a special treat we asked for some chipped potatoes and the old lady gladly made us some. Every night we had a cup of café before leaving. It was a great boon to be able to sit quietly with these good friends. The only other alternatives were the cold dark barn or the hot crowded estaminets. We had this quiet haven on the two or three occasions when we were resting out of the trenches in the locality, and then we moved to other regions. Early in 1918 the German attack must have swept over this peaceful cottage, in fact I believe that after this attack it must have been in no man's land for several months. I often pictured it standing derelict and ruined amidst all the horrors of that hellish locality. I wondered whether pretty Julie, her … [cheerful] mother and gentle granny had reached safety or had been killed.

A meeting of brothers

One day in this locality I saw some men of the 4th King's Liverpool Regiment, my brother Robert's Regiment, and from them learnt that D company were in billets in a village not 2kms. away. That same evening I set out to find my brother, and by dint of many enquiries found my way to his Company's Mess in a farmhouse. I learnt there that he was home on leave, but expected back shortly. His brother officers treated me very well, inviting me in and giving me a cup of tea. The next night I returned and found my brother just back from ten days leave. He took me along to his billet which was in another farmhouse. I sat on his bed, while he sat on a box, while we exchanged experiences and adventures. My boots were in a deplorable condition, letting in water freely. He was able to provide me with an old pair of his own, which were in a very much better condition.

On this day of reunion between William and Robert in April 1916, all four of the McCrae brothers were in the British Army fighting abroad in the First World War. Each one was in a different regiment. As William tells us, Robert was in D Company of the 4th King's Liverpool Regiment. He was the eldest of them all and was the only officer at this point. He had first disembarked in France on 6 March 1915.[1]

Andrew, a lance corporal, was in Mesopotamia with his regiment, the 2nd Black Watch (Royal Highlanders). He had left the Western Front in December 1915, just the very same time as William had arrived, and had then travelled to what was then known as Mesopotamia in the Middle East where he now was. Prior to this, on 25 September 1915, Andrew had been wounded and awarded the Meritorious Service Medal for 'conspicuous gallantry in the capture of German trenches' on the Western Front.[2]

Alan, the youngest, no doubt keen to join his brothers, had first signed up in early October 1915 to join the Seaforth Highlanders, a regiment that when first raised in 1778 was renowned for so many of their number having the name MacRae, or variations of such.[3] It must have been hard for him to have been at home when all his brothers were in the army. William had been in Llandudno, North Wales for many months and had just moved down to Winchester training camp prior to being sent abroad to fight. Perhaps he just had his final home leave before leaving for France, and Alan had felt he could no longer bear being at home with his three sisters and father. Possibly too, he was very close to William as they were less than two years apart in age. However, with six months still to pass until his eighteenth birthday, he was underage. His father travelled over to France to bring him back to England. It appears from records that he spent the next few months in the training reserve until he was able to rejoin this regiment in early 1916.[4] Alan would therefore have also been on the Western Front at this time when William and Robert met.

This situation, where all four brothers were in different regiments, contrasts with those relatives and friends who were fighting together in what were known as Pals battalions. These Pals battalions were encouraged as official policy at first as men flocked to sign up, reassured by the thought that they would be together in the army with those they knew. Unfortunately, fighting alongside each other frequently led to dying alongside each other, and whole communities of young men from towns and villages were tragically lost as a result. Therefore, the scheme promoted by Lord Kitchener was discontinued after conscription was introduced in 1916.⁵ Edmund Blunden was just one who felt strongly that brothers should not be in the same battalion having experienced the anguish one felt for the other in the event of them being fatally wounded. In Blunden's battalion (the Royal Sussex Regiment), brothers frequently enlisted together.⁶

Holding a line

The day after this we went up into the trenches again. This time the trenches or rather low barricades were lying in a welter of mud and water about the village of Festubert. We held a post in the front line. At night two sentries were posted on the fire-step and couples of us took it in turns, an hour only at a time, to man a listening post 70 yards out in "no man's land."

At the unearthly hour of 1 a.m. Ward and I clambered out of the trench in the wake of our Sergeant Penny, and followed him out beyond the barbed wire entanglements for our turn in this post. We wondered how he could find his way, but presently felt rather than saw, that the mud on the highest points of the broken ground had been trampled firmer than the surrounding ground by numerous other reliefs. He also held in his hand a line, leading from the trench we had just left, to the listening post. When we reached this post we were challenged in a whisper by the occupants, and in a whisper replied giving the countersign. We then took their places in a mere shell hole and they accompanied the sergeant back to the front line. We were left, half sitting, half reclining in the hole. Our feet were in the water at the foot of it, and our heads must have been emerging from the top. Our rifles with bayonets fixed we kept in our hands. We could see little or nothing of our surroundings even when a Verey light went up. The German front line was less than 150 yards away. We could see the flashes of rifles and machine guns fired over the top of his [the enemy's] and our own trenches. We were between, in no man's land. In my hand I held one end of the line mentioned before, the other end was in the hand of the sentry in the front line. Every now and again I felt two sharp jerks on this line and gave two jerks in reply signifying "OK." In the event of us hearing or seeing anything I had to give a series of jerks so that the garrison could be warned and be ready.

The position of the post in the front line was such as to leave it easy prey to a surprise attack or raid during the night. The listening post was to protect it from this eventuality and was in the nature of a sacrifice post. We had little chance of seeing or hearing an enemy raiding party before they would have been on the top of us, and no chance of warding off an attack.

We could not retire on the front line, as that would be cowardice and punishable as such. It was hoped however that the noise made by us when attacked, even if the signals on the line failed (we had a supply of Mills Bombs), and before being dispatched by the enemy would warn the front line in time to save them from a similar fate. Lying there for an hour in silence, we dare not talk as enemy patrols might be about, [it] was no pleasant experience, and I was very glad when I could feel vibrations on the line in my hand which told me that our relief was on its way.

On the last night of our stay in these trenches Bond and Barber were discovered asleep when on sentry in the front line. It was a very serious matter to fall asleep in this manner. The lives of all the men in the post depended on these two men, as they were in touch with the listening post in front. Worn out by lack of sleep, weakened by hunger we often had a hard struggle to keep awake. These two fellows must have succumbed knowing full well the danger to themselves of an enemy raid, their responsibilities to their comrades and above all that, an ignominious death was the price to be paid for their indulgence. It only shows to what tortures we were put through lack of sleep. The sergeant was very worried about the matter. If he reported them his action would be tantamount to a sentence of death. In the end he told no one and we others all kept it dark.

The consequences of a dirty rifle

Some week or so after this event we were in occupation of the ruins in Richebourg St Vaast being in support to the front line. One morning my name was taken by the SM [sergeant major] for having a dirty rifle. This SM was a Welshman named Davis, a school teacher in civil life.

He had recently been promoted and was endeavouring to run the company on the lines of a class on school. To his credit he tried to be fair and was undoubtedly very conscientious. To this last virtue I owe the fact that he took my name. My rifle was not dirty but the barrel had sweated a little in the intervals between cleaning and inspection. His schoolroom methods were the cause of doing me a great deal of good. When a request came from BHQ [Battalion Headquarters] that day for two men for fatigue he thought fit to punish me and another culprit and sent us along.

Evidently there had been issued an Army Order for the salvaging of the large quantities of war stores which had been discarded and littered the immediate vicinity of the trenches. By our unsuspecting SM we had been nominated for this job which was one of the type called "cushy." Instead of going into the trenches that night we joined BHQ in Cuinchy and were given a place to sleep, along with the runners, signallers and BHQ cook, in what had been a cattle shed of a farmhouse. The HQ officers had a dugout in the cellar thereof.

The next day we spent with a few other salvage men, picking up discarded ammunition, equipment etc. etc. We wandered off in couples, went where we liked, rested when we wished, explored many strange ruins and disused trenches and altogether had a rather interesting time. We picked up almost without having to search thousands of rounds of rifle ammunition, many pieces of equipment abandoned by wounded men in recent fighting and many other articles. We carried the spoils back to BHQ in sandbags.

As soon as it was dark we assembled at BHQ and after counting our spoils and rendering an account thereof to the Adjutant were given a meal by the cook. After this we had to fetch rations and water. There was no pump in our own farmyard and we had to go along the village street to another one. About half a dozen of us set off down the road, each carrying two empty petrol tins. We could see our way fairly well as we were very close to the front line and Verey lights were continually going up, sometimes near and sometimes further away.

There was not a roof left on any house. The bare, scarred walls that remained stood out jagged against the faintly luminous background of the starlit sky. Frequently as a

Verey light had its brief day, rising suddenly from a front line trench, reaching its meridian in the course of a few seconds, and slowly subsiding again, queer vast moving shadows were cast by the same walls around us. It was as if the spirits of the dead inhabitants of the village were abroad watching a scene unfamiliar and violently agitated at its strangeness. There were no doors left in the houses or windows, the space where they had been were mere deep black holes, except where some Tommies had found a precarious billet and then the openings were stopped up with sacking. A man came out of one of the occupied houses as we were passing and as he displaced the sacking curtain over the doorway we had a glimpse of a candlelit interior and a dozen or so men sprawling amidst their equipment on the floor.

Reaching a house which stood on a corner, we went through the doorway, and groping our way carefully over the uneven brick strewn floor made our way out to the yard at the back. In the corner of this yard was a very decrepit pump. I grasped the handle and pumped vigorously. The pump shook in its loosened fastenings but no water came. Turnbull, my salvage partner scooped up some dirty water from a puddle in the middle of the yard and poured it down the pump. This gave the necessary suction and we soon had all our tins full. On our way back to B.H.2 we came under fire from the enemy front line, but as it was not aimed at us, but it was only random night firing, it worried us a little.

Two nights after this I went in search of my company. They had been 48 hours in the front line and were now in the "Rest House" just the other side of "Windy Corner." This "Rest House" was a large building standing alone on the road to Festubert and evidently out of sight of the enemy. Its roof had been blown off but a temporary one had been fixed up by the REs. There was ample room on the two floors for the whole company. Douglas was in the upper storey, just settling down in his usual style for a night's rest. He made me share his café au lait which he had just made. They had had a rough time in the trenches and I was glad I had not been with them.

Allied planes overhead

The next morning at about 9a.m. we were out collecting salvage when we became aware of a steadily increasing deep drone of many aeroplanes [and] looking saw a whole flight of them approaching us from our back areas. Ten, twenty, twenty-five we counted amidst great excitement. They were soon overhead and we could see that they were in battle formation. The main body in the form of a large triangle and two wings curving outwards towards the east. So steady did they keep formation in the sunlit sky that one could imagine that they were all connected by invisible rigid bars. Soon little fluff balls, some white and some black appeared all around and seemingly in the midst of them, and we could hear the pop-pop of the distant bursting shrapnel. The enemy anti-aircraft guns were at work. These balls of fluff were evidently innocuous as they looked because the aeroplanes steadily kept on and disappeared over the enemy country. A few minutes after we heard many deep thuds as they dropped their bombs, and one extra big crash as one had evidently found its billet in an ammunition dump. Ten minutes afterwards they appeared again, they had lost their rigid formation, and were pursued by more fluff balls. Progressing steadily they soon again passed our heads and went back from whence they had come. They had likely done some damage to the enemy, but likelier still done a great deal more harm to the helpless civil inhabitants in the occupied territory.

A small piece of 'freedom'

On the afternoon before the Battalion were relieved Turnbull and I decided that we would clear off early and endeavour to reach the village where we were to billet before dark. It would be much more pleasant walking in daylight over the rough roads. We packed up our kit and thinking to make good our exit as Fritz was shelling the vicinity and we expected the S.M. would be like a sensible man in his dugout, we emerged from our shelter. We were however espied by this gentleman who asked us where we were going. He did not stop us but told us to clear off, looking as if he would have liked to have joined us.

About 3 kms. or so on the road we were passing the quarter of the Garrison Artillery and envying their comfortable dugouts and shelters, when a big Artillery man standing at the door of his shelter called out to us. 'Hi Tommy, would you like a cup of tea?' Nothing loath we followed him in and he gave us tea and half a loaf of bread each. We sat down and had a good feed of bread and jam.

We had not had so much bread during the whole of our four days in Cuinchy. We were thankful for the thoughtfulness of our benefactor but could not help wondering why it was that the Artillery, living in comparative comfort and freedom from most of the dangers which beset the infantryman, had such good rations that they had enough and to spare. The PBI [Poor Bloody Infantry], bearing the brunt of the discomforts, work, and peril too often were short of rations. When we reached our billets we were able to select a decent place in the barn. I reserved a place for Douglas. We were asleep long before the rest of the company arrived.

Dinner with officers

While out at rest on this occasion Douglas and I visited Béthune. It was the first town of any size we had been in for a considerable time, but we were rather disappointed with it. It had been knocked about badly in places by enemy shell-fire. Seeing some of my brother's regiment about I soon found his Mess. He invited me to dinner. I accepted, bidding Douglas farewell for the time being. I felt a little awkward at first dining with officers, there were three others besides my brother; but they soon set me at ease. There was a piano in the room and we had some music after dinner. I reflected afterwards that an officer's life was decidedly more comfortable than a ranker's, and the dangers being about equal I would rather be an officer.

The divisional artillery

Our own Divisional Artillery had now joined us. Douglas and I after some search found a friend of ours named Brud Goulding. He was the brother of two girls to whom Douglas and I had been attached to at Llandudno.

We found him in a gun pit with several others of the gun crew. The so-called gun pit was a pit only in name.

The gun being placed on a piece of level ground, and |a rough shelter of brushwood and corrugated iron built round it to serve the double purpose of screening the gun from enemy observation and sheltering the gun crew. This shelter was entered through a canvas covered doorway and a hole was left in the back through which the muzzle pointed. The gun which was an 18 pounder took up most of the space inside. Brud welcomed us and we all sat around on various parts of the gun, or on ammunition boxes. The only light was a flickering candle. We were shown the small spot light a few yards up in front of the gun fixed on a tree trunk. This was for use when night firing. For our special benefit the gun was fired. It was trained on and engaged in harassing fire on a distant road behind the enemy's line. The shell was placed in the breach and clamped in. The gun layer saw that all was correct and I was asked to pull the string. I gave a sharp pull and immediately there was a deafening explosion and the recoil hurtling back in its slot fairly shook the ground. I wonder whether the shell killed any Germans.

Fatigue

A short time after this we moved into the same camp that we had occupied when with the Guards. The second night No.7 platoon were detailed for fatigue. It was an RE carrying fatigue. We first marched to a point on the La Bassée road where there was an RE dump on the left-hand side of the road. Spread over an acre or so were heaps of picks, shovels, drums of barbed wire, sandbags, trench boards etc: From the middle of this dump a light railway track or trench tramway started and took a course leading gradually away from the road in the direction of Neuve Chapelle. We soon had trucks loaded with barbed wire and started out to push them up to the village 2k distant. This was quite a novel experience rather like playing at trains. Just before reaching the village the tramway ran into a cutting and it was here that we unloaded. While engaged in this task we became aware that some excitement was brewing in the front line 700 or 800 yards distant.

   Rifle fire began to increase followed by heavy machine gun fire. Soon there was quite a fusilade and many Verey lights were sent up. Bullets whistled round us and shells began to come over and burst near us. As our duties were now completed, we placed our rifles on the trucks and half pushing, half riding clattered away down the incline to our starting point, getting well out of the range of bullets, although an occasional shell emerged from the storm area and overtook us.

We had no sooner reached our billets and were looking forward to our postponed sleep when we were ordered out to "Stand-to". After five minutes of confusion, men struggling into their equipment in the dark, sergeants calling out orders and hurrying men on, we assembled on the road and stood in silence listening to the bombardment which was still going on. What was going on up there in the trenches 3km away? Was an enemy attack developing? Why otherwise were we standing out in the road waiting?

The faint greyness of approaching dawn became apparent. It was April and therefore about 4am. The favourite time for an attack. Was the enemy at that moment carrying our front line? What would the next few hours mean to us? Would we counter-attack? As the light increased so did the noise of bombardment fall away, until, when it was broad daylight there was silence. An uncanny silence. What did it portend? Had the enemy overcome the resistance of the men in front of us? Perhaps he was at that moment advancing towards us. We were relieved however, soon to receive the order to dismiss. Evidently everything was OK and we settled down for an hour or so's sleep. The whole affair could be classified as an attack of nerves each side thinking that the other meant business.

Cloth caps and helmets

Two days later we assembled to again take over trenches. We had just had a new officer put in charge of the platoon. He was a comical looking man 30yrs of age. His face was round and florrid. He had little chin and his eyebrows, set far above his eyes appeared to be endeavouring to take cover beneath his hat. When he spoke in a thin high-pitched voice, he used his lips to excess, mouthing each word well. On this occasion he carried a shrapnel helmet in his hand, his cloth cap being on his head. Shrapnel helmets were only just being issued at this time. We wore cloth caps but usually found a certain number of helmets in the trenches. These were handed over from one relief to another as trench stores. We were supposed to wear one while on sentry, but usually only put it on hastily on the approach of an officer, removing it when he had passed.

Marching up La Bassée Rd it became apparent that the enemy were shelling the vicinity of the Croix Rouge. One or two shells came over further. Mr.Piper promptly changed his headgear sticking the helmet on at a rakish angle. Finding a few moments afterwards that no more shells were dropping near, and that the helmet was sliding all over his head while he walked, he replaced it again with his cap. Another shell coming over he repeated the performance and continued it several times much to our amusement.

The exercise of daylight relief

When we neared the Croix Rouge we opened out into artillery formation. A salvo of shells was coming over every few minutes and bursting around the Croix Rouge along the road to the left between that spot and the beginning of the CT. When our section arrived at the corner opposite the Croix Rouge we found Mr Piper there with his helmet sliding all over the place, and red as a beetroot, directing a few men at a time along the shell swept side road. Evidently Fritz had an inkling that we were relieving. It was a daylight relief. Mr Piper's trouble was that he could not send us along the side road quick enough to prevent too large a party of men gathering at the dangerous corner, Sections were continually arriving. As we crouched there under the lea of a low wall, waiting for our turn to be sent along to the CT we suddenly heard the swift swish of approaching shells. We instinctively crouched yet further down on our haunches. Following immediately on the sound came a nerve racking bang-bang-bang as the shells burst about us. One shell fell into the ditch on the other side of the road, luckily it was a dud. We only heard a thud and saw a little smoke. The next moment Mr Piper pushing back his helmet which had slid over eyes called out "Next four" and pushed 4 men including myself round the corner. We sprinted for the CT 200yds away and gained its comparative shelter in safety before the next salvo arrived. While we were still panting after our run and were waiting for the rest of the platoon the Non Con (nonconformist) chaplain spoke to us. He was waiting until the fireworks were over before endeavouring to get back to his comfortable billet miles back.

We proceeded up the CT and looked over the same post where we had received our initiation into trenches.

Two new recruits

The post was much changed and formed part of a more or less continuous support line some 300yds behind the front line. D[ouglas] and I with two new arrivals to the Battalion occupied a low dugout. Davies and Fraser were the names of these new men, Davies was a short thick set man of 25 years of age. His large heavy, swarthy face, with sleepy half closed eyes, seemed to overhang his short body. He stood usually with his head inclined forward and his large jaw obscuring his neck gave the impression that it was absent. His voice was very rich and mellow with great penetrating qualities. He was exceedingly fond of hearing it. In civil life he was a solicitor and evidently rather felt his present position. Having been prevented by his fond mother from joining the army before, he had been unceremoniously called up under the Derby scheme[7] and placed in the ranks. His education and brains, he certainly was clever, would have fitted him better for commissioned rank. Alas he was killed several months later and never attained this ambition.

Fraser, his companion, not exactly his friend was a tall youth of 21 years of age. He was as uncouth in looks and uncertain in character as Davies was neat in one and strong in the other. His eyes set under shaggy eyebrows were too close together. His mouth was large and drooping at the corners. He was always in trouble, always grousing and always cadging.

A dugout to lie in, night fatigue and some post

Our dugout was a very low one, there scarcely being room to sit up in it. There was just room for us all to lie down.

It started to rain early the first morning and continued all day. Soon the water was collecting in the trench and trickling into the dugout, which was an inch or two lower.

We did our best to stop this but were only partially successful. The floor of the dugout soon got very sloppy. We remained cooped up inside nearly all day, only emerging to cook our meals or go on sentry. After a few hours of the ceaseless heavy rain, water began to trickle through the roof at several points. I hung my mess tin on a nail under one drip which was falling down my neck, but later had the misfortune to knock it and received the lot at once instead of in instalments. We beguiled the weary time talking and arguing. Davies was most obstinate in argument. It was very miserable cooped up in this damp hole.

At nightfall we were ordered out on fatigue. It was still raining intermittently and we wandered about for miles along the wet glistening roads in the usual follow my leader style. Mr Piper was the leader but had evidently lost his way. We were supposed to meet an R.E. who would show us the work to be done. In between showers the moon showed itself seemingly immovable in a sky of hurrying grey clouds. We saw many strange sights. Deserted villages, their rough misshapen ruins softened in the mellowing peaceful light of the moon. Lone farmhouses likewise deserted by their original inhabitants, but peopled at least in their cellars by some branch or other of our army. There was little movement about them but we could see chinks of light and hear gruff voices. Other long strings of men in single file passed us at times, all draped in their glistening waterproof sheets, like so many misshapen ghosts. Most of them struggling under heavy loads, cursing, stumbling about on the uneven roads. Now and again a few limbers clattered by us, splashing us with mud, taking up shells to the gun batteries which we now and again caught sight of standing in secluded corners. Four or so dark cubes of shadow camouflaged with hanging netting containing each its gun. The symmetrical gaping muzzle sticking out in the direction of the enemy. Possibly a streak of light from within showed that the gun crew were awake by the side of their silent gun. It certainly was quiet. We heard scarcely a shell during the whole time we were out.

We returned to the trench rather wetter than we emerged. It was the eve of my 20th birthday, or rather had been as it was now past midnight.[8] Soon after the return to our dugout Sgt Pelling came sliding and stumbling along the trench with the post bag. "Hi, McCrae" he called "Is it your birthday or something? Four parcels for you. What the devil are you going to do with them all? Don't forget your sergeant if you have any grub to throw away, I have fallen over three times in this damned mud bringing them along."

There inside the dugout, in the light of a candle end stuck on a piece of wood above my head, I opened parcels and letters and fairly revelled in news from home and the good things inside the parcels. There was a large seed cake from Nettie. Another cake from Father – a box containing sardines, tinned salmon, chicken in a jar and many other dainties. The four of us lived like lords for the next three days. There was little left to carry out when leaving the trenches. The next morning was bright and clear. Soon after stand-down I had my seed cake on the firestep cutting it with my bayonet cleaned thoroughly for that purpose. The CO appeared at that moment round the corner of the fire-bay, and I had to stand aside to let him and his orderly pass. He stopped and admired the cake, asking me my age. I did not have the presence of mind to ask him to have a piece.

When we had been 4 days in this trench we were relieved and the company assembling near the Croix Rouge we marched back along La Bassée Rd. This road ran straight as a die for several kilometres in front of us. We could see, about 2 km in front of us a red light which marked a bar across the road where a sentry stood.

As we approached this barrier so the double line of trees on the side of the road gradually resumed their full beauty. When passed the red light we turned to the left and were safely in the back area.

Back in South London, there would never be a time when his sisters and father would not be wondering about their siblings and sons. With the apparent close-knit relationship they had, and none of the children yet married, it would be reasonable to think letters would arrive from one or other of them quite frequently. For their part, families at home did everything they could to keep in contact, especially at key times such as birthdays and Christmas, and at times of sickness. I try to imagine the scene as William's sisters and father write their letters, carefully considering each word, providing them with news of their lives at home in

London, giving encouragement, but reluctant to give any information that may cause them concern —all the time an underlying dread of what might happen, unwritten and unspoken. Little 12-year old Agnes, wondering when she will see her older brothers again, perhaps describing to them how she is trying especially hard with her French lessons at school, and maybe even trying out a few words of that language as she wrote to them.

Her older sister Isabel is almost about to leave Eltham Secondary School as she is now 16 years of age. She will begin work as a clerk, one of the women replacing the hundreds of men who had had that occupation, but who for now are otherwise occupied. Nettie, the oldest sister, is working hard running the household, for both those present, and those who are absent. This has been her role now for three years since her mother died prematurely of tuberculosis. With her father, she is ever aware of keeping cheerful and positive for the sake of the younger ones. Perhaps together they discuss the newspaper reports late into the evening, after they have gone to bed. Perhaps wrapping a parcel, some home-knitted socks or a freshly baked cake. The kitchen table is cleared for the purpose: brown paper, string and sealing wax. The rain pattering against the window. Hoping their loved ones are at least warm and dry. Trying not to imagine further.

Chapter 5

The Raid

It was the night of Sunday, 7 May 1916, and the 15 RWF were about to undertake a raid on a German trench near Laventie on the Western Front.[1] They were to assemble at 11.30 pm. Days earlier William had stepped forward in the call for volunteers to join the raiding party. His story tells of his experience and his reflections of the raid from his own perspective as someone who took part.

The task in hand

We were billeted in the school at La Gorgue. No 7 platoon had a classroom on the first floor and Douglas and I bagged a position under the windows which were actually still glazed. La Gorgue stood on the bank of the canalised river Lys; on the other bank and gained by means of a bridge over the locks was Estaires, a village of the same size. Three kil. [3 km] away along the river was the town of Merville.

One day as we were finishing our dinner of stew in the classroom, S.M. Davies entered by the door directly opposite to where we were sitting on the floor underneath our window. "Just pay attention all of you" he said in his sharp staccato Welsh accent, "The CO has been asked by the O.C. Brigade to arrange for a raid on the enemy to get information and to show him that our tails are up. No man in all the Battalions of the Division has yet entered the trenches of the enemy. The CO is very keen that the London Welsh should be the first. He has called for 10 volunteers from each company to take part in this raid. Now then, who will come forward?" Complete silence followed his statement and then some whispering started. No-one seemed to jump at the offer. The SM said "Come now, surely you are not going to let the rest of the company show No. 7 platoon up? I have already 8 men from 5, 6 and 8 together and only require two more. His mouth was pursed up in a scornful manner. He had not been called upon to volunteer however.

  I was heartily fed up with the life we had to endure and thought "Well why shouldn't I go? Even if I am killed it would be a short cut out of my misery. Who knows? I might get a 'blighty'." I did not like to shout out in front of them all "I'll make one". It savoured too much of mock heroics. I was not actuated by anything approaching bravery. I said to Douglas in an undertone "I wouldn't mind having a cut at Death and Glory". He seemed to be rather surprised but nevertheless rather proud of me, and obtaining confirmation of my willingness shouted out, "Major, Mac'll go". "Right" said that gentleman "That's one, what about the other?" No-one replied for a few minutes and then up spoke Duke, a dark skinned Italian looking Cockney. "If none of these b----- will volunteer I'll go myself although I've a wife and three kids at home." Another man, Roberts, coming forward at last [so] Duke had not to make the sacrifice.

Training

The next day the raiding party took up separate billets in the village of Laventie. This village although only 4k or so from the line was not very much damaged. Most of the inhabitants had cleared out however.

  B Coys [Company's] bombers, 12 in number had a bedroom on the 1st floor of a small cottage. It was a bright little room, the wallpaper was still almost intact. We spent a very happy 8 or 9 days in this village, training for the raid.

  During the day we had the usual drill in order to make us fit and a good deal of practice bombing. At night small parties of us went up into the trenches and patrolled no man's land at the place where we were to cross in order to get some of the idea of the terrain.

  We had a good deal of time to ourselves. Everyone knew that they were on a dangerous job, but for the time being we were in comfortable billets and having good food. Our state of mind can best be described by the quotation "Eat, drink and be merry for tomorrow we die." We certainly were merry. The amount of chaff accompanied by noise and laughter that was bandied about [in] that little room especially before going to sleep at night was astonishing. We alluded to ourselves as the "Suicide Club" and made many jokes about getting killed. We were all as lighthearted and happy as a party of schoolboys on a picnic.

In search of a torch

One night Roberts, the other volunteer from No.7 platoon and I were sent to Estaires to fetch some electric torches for use during the raid. We procured the torches alright, but trying to find a nearer way home we nearly got lost. We came eventually to a place where the road forked and did not know which way to go. However there was a signpost and I shinned up it, [and] striking a match was able to find the correct road. We walked on in silence each content with his own thoughts. It was round about midnight and we had the road to ourselves. The spring was now well advanced and the scent of blossom from the surrounding orchards hung heavy in the still air. Above us the stars twinkled. Although all about us was calm and peaceful, Verey lights on the horizon and the distant rattle of a machine gun reminded us that there was still a war on.

Suddenly our reveries were rudely broken by a hoarse shout from the shadow of a large farmhouse on our left "Halt! Who goes there?" In our usual offhand manner we replied "15th RWF" without slackening in our stride, just as we had always done when challenged. Much to our surprise however the sentry, with a furious "Halt" advanced out of the shadow and arrested our progress by holding us up at the point of his bayonet. He was an outsize Maori belonging to the New Zealand contingent which had recently arrived in France. He hurled several questions in quick succession at us without pausing for a reply. "Why didn't you stop when challenged? Who are you? Where did you come from? Why are you wandering about so late?" I replied as best as I could. "We belong to the 15th RWF and have come from Laventie":- I got no further as the sentry broke in "Now you say that you are from Laventie when I see that you are on your way to Laventie." This knotty question took a great deal of explaining ... He was very suspicious, taking us for spies. Ultimately he called out to his Sergeant who ... took us into the guardroom and examined us in the light of a solitary candle. After some hesitation he accepted our explanations and we were allowed to proceed. He warned us however always to stop when challenged by the Maoris. They … had just come from Gallipoli where it had been quite usual to find spies in the British zone. Shortly after this adventure we entered Laventie and were soon curled up and asleep in our billet.

The day of the raid prayers and weapons

The second Sunday spent training at Laventie came round. We, the actual raiders, were kept in ignorance that the raid was fixed for that very night, possibly to prevent us getting the "wind up." However during the day it became apparent to us that something was afoot. The activity of the officers. An order that we were not to leave the vicinity of our billets. A visit of inspection by the Brigadier. We learnt afterwards that the knowledge kept from us was known in the Battalion early in the day. Quite possibly it was also known to "Brother Bosche." His spies were always active. Early in the evening Roberts and I attended a service in the Y.M.C.A. which was situated, just across the road from our billet, in a large barn. The Padre evidently knew that the raid was billed for that night. In a curious detached way I realised this might be the last religious service I might attend in this world, and heard as if at a great distance the deep slow voice of the Padre actually praying for us. "Lord God we would remember particularly before you tonight the men present and their comrades who have been called to take part shortly in a hazardous and dangerous undertaking. Sustain them in their time of trial. Their lives are in your hands O God. If it be Thy will that any fall Receive them O Lord into Thy Everlasting Rest." After the service the Padre came over to us and shook us both by the hand and gave us his blessing. What a curious reversal of all that religion stands for that we taking part that very night in a bloody raid, nothing short of murder in cold blood should be prayed for and blessed by the representative of the Prince of Peace. It was not that the Padre was a hypocrite. It was not that the Christian religion was fundamentally wrong, it was only weak. So weak that previous to the war it had been unable to influence the wicked policies and statesmanship of the leaders of most of the democracies of Europe. Whirled along in the maelstrom that followed, of a continent gone mad it was doing its best under the circumstances to keep the name of Christ before the unfortunate victims of the same corrupt statesmen and kings, the gun fodder, the poor deluded men who were fighting to defend their countries against whom? The Germans. So these same politicians and their instruments the newspapers said. But last time it had been the French, the time before the Spaniards. Was it really a fact that the Germans, the men in the trenches undergoing trials like our own, were there by choice and really coveted the lands of France or the British Isles or even our colonies? Did they really thirst for our blood? No. A thousand times no. Deluded by their politicians, Emperor, and generals, backed up by their press, in the same way as we were deluded by our own. Thinking of us in the same way as we were led to think of them they sought to kill us as we sought to kill them.

On our return to the billet we were informed that we would parade at 9pm. We did not need to be told what it was for. At 9 o'clock, as it was just getting dusk we assembled at the back of the billet. We had dispensed with the heavier parts of our equipment. Each however carried his rifle, and a fearsome weapon fashioned out of our entrenching tool handles. A huge iron kind of cogged wheel being fastened to one end, [it was] a most bloodthirsty club. The rest of our material for the raid had already been carried up into the trenches and awaited us there.

Fifty men

The roll was called and all being present and reported so to the Captain, we moved off along the road leading out of Laventie to the N[orth]. We were nearly 50 strong. Capt. Davison was in charge and there were two subalterns Pope and Tracey both quite boys as indeed we all were with several exceptions. Pope had only recently joined the Battalion. He was a girlish looking youth, with a complexion which was envied no doubt by many of the fair sex.

SM Bowers was the next in rank, a big surly man about 50 years of age, who had serviced in the Regulars fighting in the Egyptian and S. African campaigns as a string of ribbons on his breast justified. There were also 3 corporals, all bombers.

A hundred yards from Laventie the road curved round to the right and we now marched directly towards the trenches as to our left and right we could see the Verey lights rising frequently, like little balls of incandescence which hovered for a few seconds in the sky, and then disappeared below the horizon, their reflected flickering light lasting a few seconds more.

Left right, left right, we marched on, the regular beat of our feet the only sound we made. The bantering tongues were silent at last. No song broke from our lips, each man, awed by the proximity of a dangerous, hazardous undertaking communed with his own thoughts. A dryness became apparent in my throat. I was almost afraid to swallow in case my neighbours heard me. Looking into the dark shadow of a small wood on our left I seemed to see the face of my mother who died several years back. She seemed to be very near to me watching, waiting. Left, right, left right, we kept on our way, drawing nearer and nearer to the unknown. What did the next few hours hold in store for us? Mercifully for those at least who were to perish in pain and agony we knew not.

When within ½ a mile of the front line we entered a C.T. and now in single file and no longer in step, we wound in and out following its zig-zag course. The Verey lights now cast a pale ghostly radiance over us. The silence we had kept on the road was maintained except for a grunt, or muttered curse as we stumbled over some unseen obstacle. Arriving in the front line I found that we were to go over from the trenches held by my own company. Douglas quickly found me and kept by me as long as my duties would allow. At parting he wrung my hand and said in a choked kind of voice "Good luck! Mac I hope you come back safely"

All in order

We all now blacked our faces and hands with burnt cork, and taking from our heaped up store the articles which we had each had allocated to us, lined up in the trench ready to start. We had practised the procedure back in the safe area of Laventie and all knew our separate jobs.

The officers leading, we walked out of a gap in the trench and through a passage cut for that purpose and marked with white tape, in our barbed wire entanglements. Following the officers were four men carrying planks, behind these were four more carrying big wire cutters, next came some men with huge straw mattresses to throw over the German wire when cut, and so facilitate negotiation of that obstacle. Then came the bombing parties headed by an N.C.O. as chief bomber. Close behind him his carrier, with a canvas bag of bombs, whose duty it was to keep the bomber supplied. Then followed the second bomber and his carrier. Each party also had two men carrying more bombs.

Pete [Roberts] and I were absolutely out of it being the spare men to the whole gang, and we were the last to leave the shelter of the trench. We both carried our loaded rifles, the only men in the whole party to do so, the others depending on bombs, and clubs and revolvers.

I had my rifle slung over my right shoulder. In each hand I carried a short scaling ladder about 6ft long. Each pocket of my uniform, cleared of its usual contents to avoid giving information to the enemy should I be captured, contained a Mills bomb. At a loss [as to] how to carry my club, as I wore no equipment to fasten it to, I solved the difficulty by carrying it suspended by its string from my teeth…. As I followed in the wake of Pete I could not help but think of the sight I must have presented to an onlooker if there had been one. Pockets bulging with engines of destruction, cap placed on my head, peak to the rear. Face black as a sweeps, a murderous club in my teeth. The last fact particularly tickled my fancy. I had often read in bloodthirsty tales of the villain armed to the teeth dashing off to attack the hero. Here I was actually in the same condition.

Beyond the wire

When just clear of our wire the men in front of me stopped. I halted also, and laying my ladder down carefully, and taking my club from my teeth, I lay down. Lying there for some moments I was able to take stock of my surroundings. Behind me [were] the uneven bunched-up barbed wire entanglements. I could even see parts of the white tape which was to show us our way through when we returned, if we ever did. Immediately behind this was the dark mass of the parapet. I could imagine, although I could not see, the many well-known faces which I knew would be peering over to watch us. Above was a clear sky with stars shining brightly. On each side the blackness of night. In front, darkness except the vague outline of Pete sprawling on the ground. As I looked at him he, with very little noise, got up. I did likewise and we went forward again for a few yards and then lay down in the same manner as before. Thus we progressed by fits and starts sometimes going 20yds sometimes 10, sometimes only 2, and lying down in between for long intervals in the grass.

When 150yds out from our front line, we came to a stream or ditch which ran parallel with the front line trenches, dividing no man's land into halves. The banks of the stream were a couple of feet above the surface of the water and were 3yds apart. We crossed by means of a bridge formed of the planks which the leading man had carried out and laid in position.

On the enemies side of this stream it became more than ever expedient that we should be silent, and we went on very carefully.

We then had a long, long wait. I was lying in the grass, this time by the side of Pete. When we halted, as far as possible, he kept a look out to the left and I to the right, both of us also keeping an eye on our rear. It was quite possible that a German patrol on its way back to its trenches might stumble on us. At this time, as I learnt afterwards, our foremost men were up to and stretched along the front of the enemies wire. Pete and I were perhaps 10 or 20yds in their rear, but were in communication with them through the intervening men. We had no idea we were so near until a whispered message came back to us "Keep very quiet, there is a German working party wiring on our left." The officers evidently did not like attacking while the force of men were on our flank. We lay there it seemed like for hours. The long grass formed a soft couch. There seemed less firing than usual. Of course the men directly behind us in our front line had been warned not to fire. To the right and left however we could see frequent flashes from rifles, followed by the noise of the discharge which sounded like a double knock. Verey lights went up at intervals occasionally. Occasionally Fritz sent one up from the trench immediately in front of us, and after, as we thought, showing the whole of us lying out beyond his wire, came sizzling down amongst us to finish its burning in the grass. These lights made so many shadows in their flight that provided there was no movement in our ranks, detection even at so short range was difficult.

To our left we could faintly hear the German wiring party. They were keeping quiet, but we could hear the clink-clink of the wire being uncoiled. It all seemed very peaceful. Was it possible that we were engaged in a bloody raid? I did not seem to have much fear but my throat was still very dry. Tink, tink tink, still that sound came from the left. Strain our eyes as we could, nothing could be seen in that quarter. At last however, we were aware that the wiring party had returned to their trench.

The attack

A thought struck me suddenly. Here was I within a few yards of the enemy, waiting to attack him and I had not cocked my rifle, although of course 10 cartridges were in the magazine. Slowly and silently, I dare not make a noise, and I pushed forward the safety catch and drew back the bolt. I had got the bolt back to its full extent, and was about to close it again so pushing up a cartridge into the chamber, when suddenly hell let loose. Immediately in front of me 3 bombs burst simultaneously with a vivid flash and deafening angry crash. The three bombing sections headed by the two junior officers and the S.M. had with some difficulty cut a path through the enemies wire, scrambled up onto the parapet and opened the attack with these three bombs. There followed screams of pain and guttural shouting, evidently someone had been wounded and orders were being given. Within two seconds of the explosions of our bombs, crash! crash! The enemy had replied, hurling their stick bombs at us, wounding the S.M. who sank, with a grunt to the ground. Several Verey lights flew up with a hiss from the enemy trenches, shedding their sickly light on attacker and attacked alike. The Germans appeared to be ready for us. The quickness with which they replied to our first bomb. A perfect fury of bombing then began. Half a dozen or so of the raiders stood on the parapet and hurled bombs at the Germans they could see grouped in the trench, which seemed a very deep one, doing a certain amount of execution as the yells of pain showed. Many stick bombs were thrown at us in reply. Pope and Gates, the two sub[altern]s., together with two bombers, disappeared during the confusion into the cavernous depths of the trench. Whether they went by their own volition, or whether they fell in wounded or killed, no one at the time knew. (Sometime afterwards we learned that the two officers and one bomber were prisoners, the remaining man having died of wounds.) Two men fell wounded and rolled to the bottom of the parapet, then another one followed suit killed outright, half his head being blown off.

I did not see all these terrible happenings myself, neither did anyone else. I have pieced them together as far as possible from the somewhat conflicting reports which were made afterwards. It was impossible for anyone to have a clear cut knowledge of what occurred in the confusion, noise and terror of those few minutes. Luckily my role was a waiting one and I lay still. The suddenness and nearness of the first explosions seemed to stun me. My heart stopped beating and I was frozen stiff with horror and fear. I could distinguish little in the multitude of dark shadows cast by the Verey lights, but the jagged quick flashes of exploding bombs stood out vividly. Pieces of bomb, hummed, ricoche[te]d and jazzed about us, sometimes thudding into the earth very close by.

The retreat

After some minutes (it seemed an age to me lying there in the grass, expecting to be killed any second) of this inferno, I became aware of a slight slackening of the noise, followed by the quickly nearing rush of running feet. In a moment, silhouetted against the flashes behind, I beheld dusky figures almost on top of me. I learned afterwards that the captain, having gained a start as far as a group of willow trees close to the stream, had sounded three blasts on his whistle which was the prearranged signal to retire. I did not hear the whistle however, and therefore my conduct during the next few moments showed me up for the coward I was. A panic seized me. What was happening? Were the Germans chasing us off? Almost before the first flying figure had passed me, I was up and grasping my rifle and bludgeon, leaving my ladders on the ground, I had joined in the route as it appeared to me. In the next few seconds I experienced the wild, panicky fear which is the lot of a vanquished fleeing army. When brave and cowardly alike race away together, unreasoningly directionless, urged on only by their own all pervading fear, rather than the swords of the pursuing hosts.

Two or three score men were we, with only one thought. To get away from the horror and death of that German trench and reach the shelter of our own. Running, stumbling, jostling each other in our haste, pursued by German machine gun bullets which now swept "no mans land" with a hail of lead, we came to the stream. No stopping to look for the plank bridge. We took flying leaps across. I landed sprawling nearly on top of another man on the other bank, at the foot of a dwarf, bushy willow tree, one foot in the water, picked myself up and went rushing off again. In another half minute, during which we must have missed death many times by inches, we reached our own wire entanglements. No stopping to look for the gap marked by white tape, in fact we were 50yds to the left of it having taken a diagonal course across "no man's land" in our mad flight.

Most of the men made a mad rush at the wire and nearly all were trapped up, and fell entangling themselves.

Profiting by the sight of sprawling, squirming figures which I could see in the dim light cast by the numerous German Verey lights, I picked my way over and through the wire, only tearing my flesh and clothing a little in my haste.

Bullets were whizzing by us, chipping pieces out of the wire, thudding into the parapet and ricocheting off it with shrill wails. Safely over the wire I suddenly saw the figure of an officer, crouching hatless, revolver in hand, in the shelter of a jutting out piece of parapet. "For God's sake" he shouted "What is happening?" He was an artillery officer on duty in the front line. Giving him an incoherent answer I was too short of breath and too anxious to gain the shelter of the trench to answer him at length. I leapt for the parapet and vaulting over, nearly impaled myself on the bayonet of friend Douglas, who with other members of his section was crouching on the fire step keeping his head well down out of danger.

I sank on to the fire-step too exhausted to answer their eager questions. My rifle, which I still held, was in the same condition as it was when the first bomb exploded, the bolt drawn back to its fullest extent. It was now 2 o'clock and dawn was very near. We had actually been two whole hours out in "no man's land", only the last few hectic minutes of which had we been engaged with the enemy.

Other raiders had arrived back simultaneously with me at different parts of the trench, and they continued to come in. Some were wounded, nearly everyone was scratched by barbed wire. Corporal Brown, tottering on his feet so exhausted was he, arrived haggard and white faced. "We have got the SM back in front of our wire, but are too exhausted to carry him any further. I want a couple of men to come over and help." He and another man had carried the SM, no mean weight back from the scene of the raid. They had rested and sheltered during the worst of the machine gun fire in a hollow by the stream. Two men from the trench garrison responded, and followed the Corporal over the parapet. Soon I could hear shuffling and the rescue party appeared on the parapet and laid the SM down on his side on the top.

His eyes were closed and he looked all crumpled up and lifeless. We lowered him as gently as we could into the trench. He opened his eyes, his face drawn with pain and groaned. Then in a very weak voice said "Steady boys" His wounds, the worst of which were in the stomach were dressed by the stretcher bearers and he was placed on a stretcher and carried down to the "Dressing Station." He died the next day.

A good rum ration was served out to us and we needed it. We had not had any before the raid.

Daylight

About an hour after daybreak Capt. Davison appeared from an adjacent dugout, his face covered with grime and told us to make our way back to the billets. It was a beautiful spring morning. The sun was shining brightly but the air was fresh and cool. We were a rough looking crew. Our blackened faces were now streaked with dry sweat. Our uniforms were dirty and torn. Some had lost their caps, others a puttee or some other article of clothing. Most of us were in the silly laughing stage of drunkeness.

Pete was rolling drunk, taking a zigzag course from side to side of the narrow trench. He sang in a cracked voice, and upon meeting anyone informed them "I've been over sh top, over sh-top with the besh of luck" Arriving back at our billets we found that the cook had prepared our breakfast. He had evidently had his share of rum, although not taking part in the raid." Plenty for all. My brave boysh. I've stopped up all nigh' getting it all ready for you. I couldn't shleep knowing you were going over the topsh" were some of his remarks, as with no steady hand he served out bacon and slopped tea into our dixies and on to the ground indiscriminately. The truth was that he had been up all night drinking.

That there was plenty for all of us was occasioned by the fact that eight men or so on our ration strength would not want their breakfast having been killed or wounded, or taken prisoner.

After breakfast we went to sleep just as we were, fully dressed and dirty and dishevelled. Several hours later we were awakened by the noise of someone, swearing lustily, falling up the stairs. It was Roberts just returned blind drunk from the trenches. After the raid an officer had taken him into his dugout and plied him with whisky and rum ad lib.

We learned afterwards that later he had been wandering about in the trenches exhibiting his torn trousers and scratched knees to all and sundry, giving voice to such remarks as "Look at this, done on the wire of the b--- bosche. We bombed the b------ Hurray. We killed the s--- He! He!" Two friendly RE's had brought him the last part of his way home. We did not relish this interruption of our well earned sleep as we had to listen to his ravings, and all had to look at his scratched and dirty knees before he consented to go to sleep.

Conflicting accounts

In the afternoon the captain came round and questioned us all concerning what we knew of the raid. From our confused, rather vague and conflicting impression, a

1. New recruits in Llandudno. William McCrae is back row, far right.

2. Tea at a farmhouse, Lake Gerionydd. William McCrae is fourth from left.

> Just to show you what kind of company I am in. They are a very mixed lot, but we get on fairly well together.
>
> Kind regards to all the Policy Dept
>
> W. McCrae

> Mr W. C. Woodroffe
> Policy Dept
> Royal London House
> Finsbury Square
> London
> E. C.

3. Back of a postcard to Mr Woodroffe, Policy department.

4. Postcard. Mrs Yeoman's, Redcliffe House, Church Walks, Llandudno, 1915. William McCrae is middle row, second from left.

5. 15th (1st London) Royal Welsh Fusiliers parade, Llandudno. (*RWF Trustees*)

6. 15th (1st London) Royal Welsh Fusiliers metal shoulder badge. (*RWF Trustees*)

7. 15th (1st London) Royal Welsh Fusiliers cloth shoulder badge. (*RWF Trustees*)

8. No. 7 Platoon, 15th (1st London), Royal Welsh Fusiliers, outside Hut 30, Winnal Down, Winchester, summer 1915. William McCrae is seated, front row far right.

9. British soldiers eating hot rations, Ancre valley, during the Somme offensive. (*IWM Q1580*)

10. Men of the 15th Royal Welsh Fusiliers resting before the attack on Mametz Wood, July 1916 (*IWM Q723*)

70 sop, for queuesson amongst the rest of us, he would grow on & finally monopolize the stage whether he knew anything about the subject or not. In short he was a bore of the 1st water. Being very thick skinned it was practically impossible to put the extinguisher on him. The sundry remarks & corrective hurled at him at times were quite unavailing. His conceit was superb. He was a nice fellow however, & in spite of his irritating talk, very companionable. For the next two months we spent a great deal of time together.

We manned the post next to the one I had been in the day before, & was situated as per attd sketch.

The CT which began at the Flying Pig, & is empt. & ran along the west side of the canal bank. Had several saps leading from it to the right, which ended in small posts which were on the eastern edge of the bank. These posts were only occupied at night. Our sniping post was built into the end of the last sap of all. The view we had from the single sliphole was an interesting one. We could see the parapet of the German line proper situated at the top of the opposite bank. There was also a sap or loop which ran from the main trench down to within 5 yds or so of the water. The rear was something like that contained in other sketch. The cup shaped hole in the sap, had been at one time used by the Germans to sally out of their trench to obtain water from the canal. This had been quite a facile & safe job while

the trenches opposite were being held by the French territorials. Evidently during that period the combatants had treated eachother with a great deal of laissez-faire. In any case the old Frenchmen, too scared to look along, or to even look over the top, would certainly not had the nerve to shoot anyone. The first morning that these posts were manned by our snipers two German essaying to fetch water after it was light were killed. Just to the left of the gap there was a sentry post we could not only see the small mirror stuck at the end of a stick which was embedded in the parados but could see the reflection of the German sentry therein. It was most uncanny to watch him through our telescope. We could see him moving his hands about, & sometimes eating, sometimes talking. Whenever by "glancing up" into his periscope or mirror, we saw, as if in a frame the reflection of the upper portion of his face & the fair hair of his cap complete with little coloured buttons. His eyes seemed as if they were looking directly at us down the barrel end of the telescope. We were, however, quite invisible to him, & could watch him without apprehension. For long periods we would watch the gap, as at infrequent intervals we could plainly see through the brushwood, men passing along the trench, sometimes singly & sometimes in parties. Unfortunately at least for our point of view there was only one loophole & by the time we had removed the telescope & put in the rifle our quarry had disappeared. We were also up against a difficulty, & owing by the fact that the gap being too far to the left of us & & &

11. William McCrae's original narrative, pages 70 and 71 showing sketches of trenches.

12. Yser Canal, 1917. (*IWM 2635*)

13. Douglas Ward and William McCrae, Poperingue, Belgium 1917.

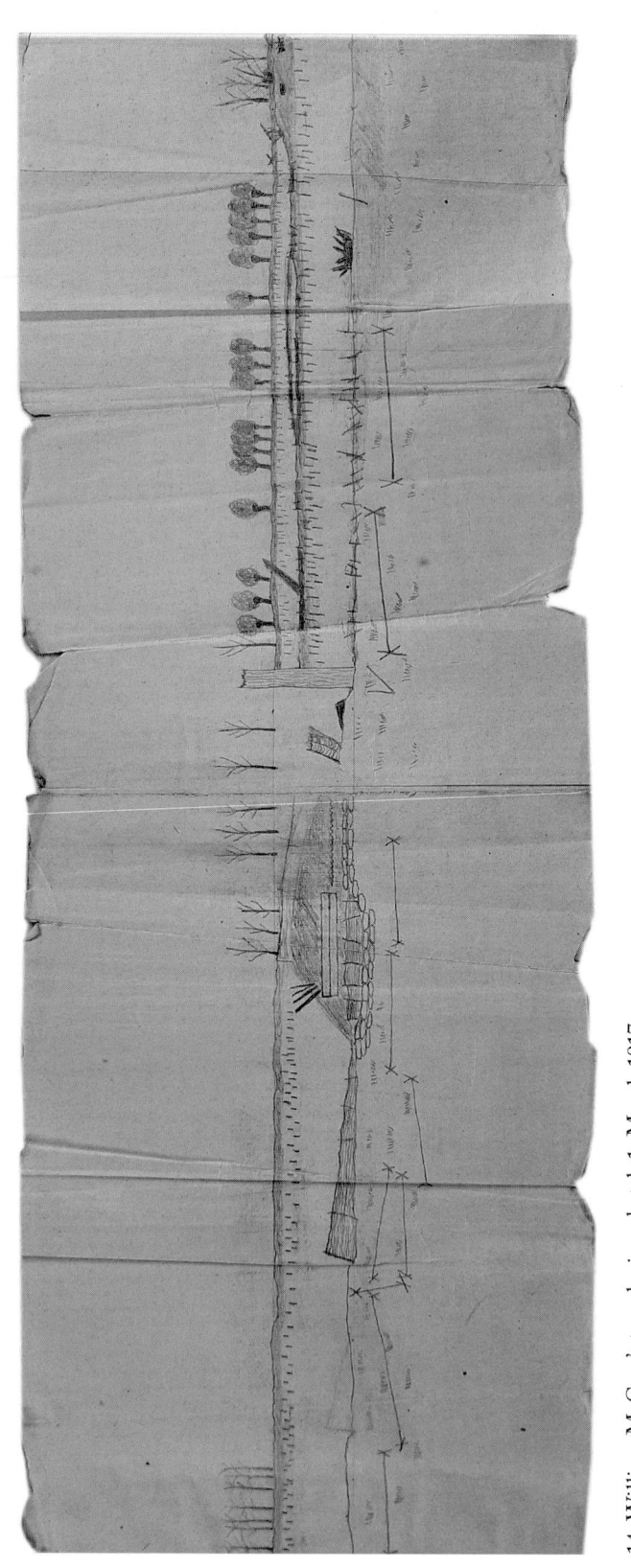

14. William McCrae's trench view sketch 1, March 1917.

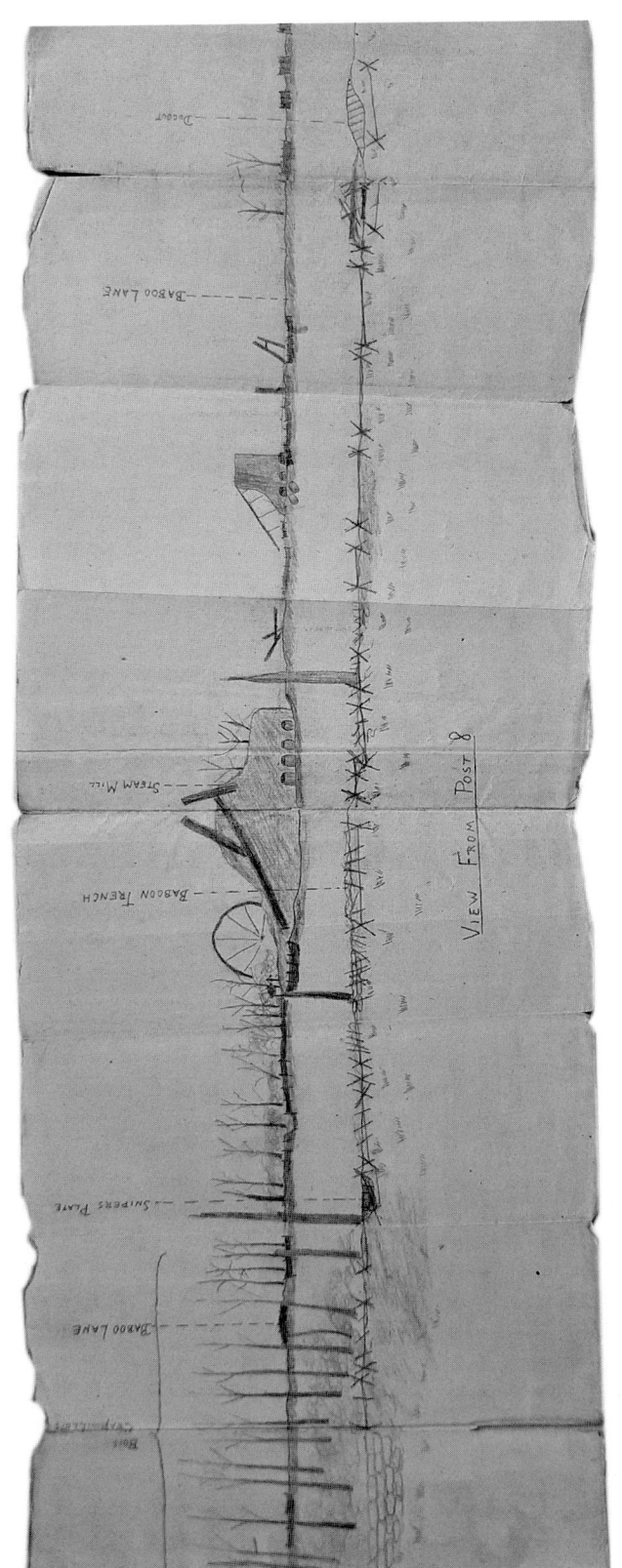

15. William McCrae's trench view sketch 2, March 1917.

16. Survivors of the 15th (1st London) Royal Welsh Fusiliers, end of 1917.

17. 18th Officer Cadet Battalion hockey team, January 1918. William McCrae is front row, far left.

18. 18th Officer Cadet Battalion practising at the firing range, Prior Park, Bath, 1917/18. (*With grateful thanks to Prior Park College Archives*)

19. Prior Park clubroom, Ref. Bath Chronicle Booklet: No. 18 Officer Cadet Battalion, 26 November 1916–20 February 1919. (*With grateful thanks to Prior Park College Archives*)

20. 18th Officer Cadet Battalion detail, early 1918. William McCrae centre.

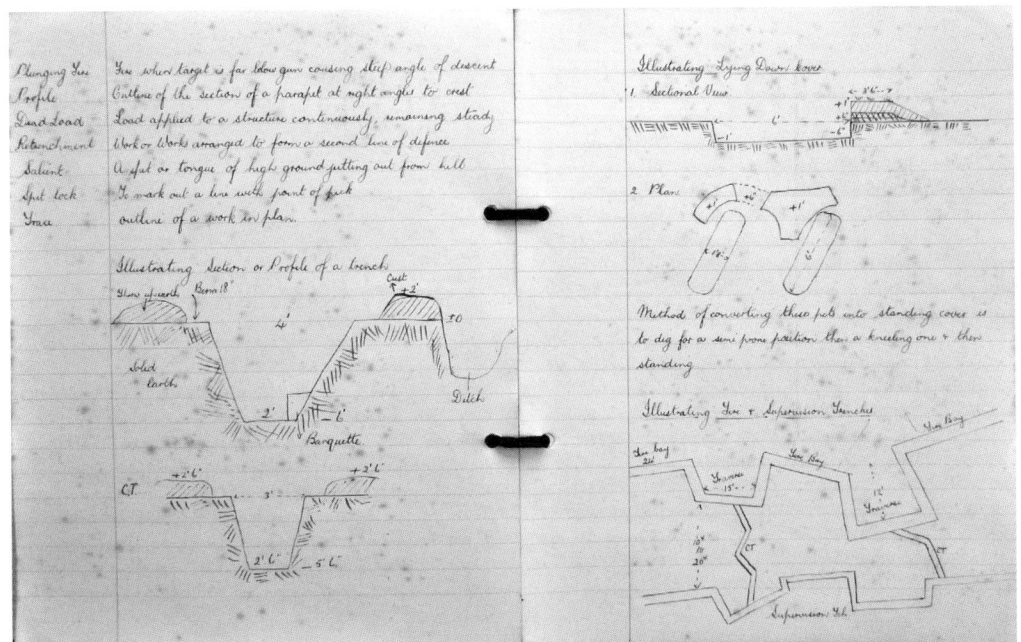

21. William McCrae's handwritten officer training notes (1917/18) showing illustrations of trench design.

22. Second Lieutenant William McCrae, Earston, North Shields, March 1918.

23. Sniping School, Fort Mahon, France, 1918. William McCrae is front row, far right.

Peace in sight at last.

Austria-Hungary has again issued an appeal to all belligerent nations to enter into negotiations of peace.

Austria-Hungary's Allies too have on several occasions declared their readiness for peace, and their point of view remains still unchanged. What are the French, English, and American governments going to say to this? Up to the present the offers of the Central Powers have been rejected by them. Why? Didn't the soldiers at the front want peace? Who then was against it?

What torrents of blood have since flown! Is that going to continue? Or do you want to have this awful bloodshed stopped at last? It's about time, one should think. Let your rulers know that you too want peace.

Once the negotiations have started, they are sure to lead to an end. Then you won't need to charge any more the Hindenburg line, where the Germans, stronger than before and ready for fresh fighting, are awaiting your attacks.

Your fate rests in your hands. Do you want to return home for the winter, or are fresh streams of your blood to flow in the desperate struggle for the strong German positions?

24. German propaganda dropped from aircraft into Allied trenches at Hebuterne, June 1918.

25. 1/5 Lancashire Fusiliers after the Armistice, Hautmont, November 1918. William McCrae is back row, second from right. (*Photo courtesy of The Fusiliers Museum, Bury*)

[Photograph taken at HAUTMONT shortly after the signing of the Armistice, Nov., 1918.]

Back Row—Left to Right—2/Lt. S; H. Bradshaw, 2/Lt. J. Acton, 2/Lt. G. H. Tongue (Sig. Off.), 2/Lt. J. H. Clarkson, 2/Lt. W. McCrae, 2/Lt. W. Ilett.

Second Row—Left to Right.—2/Lt. R. Stirrup, Lt. Bourne, Capt. the Rev. C. A. H. Lowe, 2/Lt. W. MacArthur (T.O.), 2/Lt. Mitchell, 2/Lt. W. Stringer, Capt A. O. Hallick (Bde. T.O.), Capt. B. Lowe, 2/Lt. R. Starkey Smith.

Front Row (seated)—Left to Right.—Lt. M. G. Clarke, 2/Lt. E. Riley, Capt. R. E. Combe, M.C.; Major F. Grey Burn, M.C.; Lt.-Col. G. S. Castle, M.C.; Capt. and Adjt. J. Rouse, Capt. H. R. Waugh, M.C.; Capt. A. W. Haywood, M.C.; Capt. J. Fanstone (R.A.M.C.).

Absent from photograph.—Capt. S. North. M.C.; Capt. Dean, Capt. and Q.M Bussey, Lt. and Asst.-Adjt. R. Quiggin, 2/Lts. Whitworth, Mountford, Moore; Lts. Money, Edwards, St. Barber, Allen, Watkins, Brooks, Caldwell, M.C.

report was made out and submitted. No one for instance had seen what had happened to the 2 officers and 2 men missing. This report set out our accomplishment in no uncertain terms. It was claimed that we had entered the German trenches, found them well manned, had bombed the occupants, killing and wounding up to 50 of them and had retired. My own impression from my own experience, and from what I heard from my comrades was far different. We had certainly bombed the Germans and possibly killed and wounded several. No one in the darkness and confusion could estimate the number. As for entering the enemy trenches, the only men to actually do so were taken prisoner. The bombers who returned had evidently done their bombing from the parapet. If the raid was the success that it was claimed to be, how was [it] that the victorious raiders left four men wounded and prisoners in the hands of the enemy, and returned without a prisoner themselves? Our casualties were 3 killed, 3 wounded and 4 missing believed at the time to be dead. Later we heard that they were prisoners and wounded.

First the CO and then the Brigadier inspected us, congratulating us on our so called success, calling us brave fellows and shaking us each by the hand.

The next day Roberts, whose scratched knee was very much inflamed went to hospital and eventually got back to England.

Most of us had similar scratches from rusty barbed wire, but had washed and dressed them with iodine. Roberts was too drunk and lazy to do this until septic poisoning had set in.

The next day we all rejoined our companies which had come out of the trenches for a rest.

Burying the dead

There only remains two further incidents to recount in connection with this raid. The first was the burial of SM Bowers who died while on his way to the Field Hospital at Merville, and Private Kemp who had died while being carried across no man's land. Two raiders from each company were told off to attend this funeral. I was one of those from B company. We marched to Merville and entered the British Cemetery. The sun was shining brightly, it was one of the first warm days of summer. Little white crosses in orderly rows marked each the final resting place of some obscure soldier. We paused to read the inscriptions but found they were monotonously similar. 216949 Private J Matthews 5th KRR. Killed in action 20 Dec 15 R.I.P. was typical of many.

Each dead man lay under a few inches of soil at the foot of his cross, still in a line as straight as that in which he had often stood with his comrades under the eagle eye of the BSM. We did not pity the dead inhabitants of the Cemetery. They were at last at rest, had passed through the awful moments, or hours or days of agony after injury and were lying at peace. Not one of us knew but that we might be called upon to undergo the same ordeal within the next few hours.

At the other end of the Cemetery we came to the improvised mortuary and looking inside saw the two coffins which contained the remains of our fellow raiders.

They were lucky in being enclosed in coffins, most bodies were buried wrapped in a blanket.

We escorted the dead on their last short journey from the mortuary to the graveside, a file of men with reversed arms on each side of the cortege. Coming to the graves the bearers lowered their burdens into them, and we stood round, each man with his arms resting on the butt of his rifle, while the Divisional Chaplain read the funeral service.

All around us was the fresh green of early summer. The lazy drone of insects filled the air. From afar we could hear the noise of a gun firing. Up above a couple of aeroplanes could be seen and several solemn faced observation balloons, motionless, looked down on the scene. Next to the newly prepared graves were the clean white crosses of men buried within the last week or so. Following on behind them, row upon row of crosses which gradually became less white until those in the final or rather first row were quite weather beaten and old. There they stood a monument to the colossal stupidity of mankind.

We are now in a position to ask of what use was their sacrifice and the only answer possible is "Useless".

The Padre finished the reading of the service and the bugler sounded the "Last Post."

We then left the graves to be filled in by the gravediggers and were soon in the streets of Merville laughing and chatting and expending the few francs in our possession

in chocolate and cigarettes. We had learnt to think little
of death, what we feared most was the manner in which it
claimed its victims.

Bravery

A few decorations were given on account of bravery in
the raid. Capt. Davison received the DSO [Distinguished
Service Order], Private Clarke, a bomber, the DCM
[Distinguished Conduct Medal], Corp--- and Pte---- the
MM [Military Medal]. Far be it from me to say that they
did not deserve them, but it is my opinion that the 4 men
that were wounded and taken prisoner must have been the
bravest and in the van of the attack.

This raid is well documented in the 15 RWF war diaries, within which a narrative was recorded after the returning members of the raiding party were interviewed.[2, 3]

There are also several other accounts, and much of what William relates, as a member of the raiding party, is corroborated. Llewelyn Wyn Griffiths, then a junior officer in the 15 RWF, was returning to the trenches, after twelve days leave 'with a chill in his heart', on that sunny afternoon of 7 May 1916. Having been released for a while from the grim conditions of the front, he had become acutely aware of what he then saw as 'the unrelieved stupidity of this way of manifesting one nation's protest against another'.[4] His company was manning the trench from where the raiding party set off, and his job was to ensure the Allied wires were cut at the agreed spot, in order for their men to go, and importantly, to safely return. He was of the opinion that the raid had not been unexpected by the enemy, and he relates the sadness of the men after the effort of what they saw as failed exercise, that came at such a cost in the loss of some of their party.[5] Reference to the raid is also made in Dilworth's biography of David Jones, whose narrative does diverge at times from the other accounts, such as in his reference to the taking of prisoners. Jones was not one of the raiding party.[6] However, Hughes notes that the raid had been considered a success overall, with the corps commander recommending it to be mentioned in dispatches and referring to the 'fine fighting spirit of the 15 RWF.[7, 8]

Chapter 6

Craters and the Colour Blue

For a short time following the raid the 15 RWF were able to rest and take advantage of the warm weather and sunshine, before heading back to the trenches in the Neuve Chappelle and Givenchy region. They were to stay in this area until they began their training for taking part in the planned offensive in the valley of the River Somme.[1]

A brief respite

We had a quiet, enjoyable spell out of the trenches on this occasion in La Gorgue. The weather was bright, warm and sunny. The hours spent on parade drilling and route marching were few, leaving plenty of time for lying in the shade on the banks of the river Lys, or bathing in its cool waters. The Divisional Concert Party was now in full working order and gave us several excellent concerts. A Lance Cpl named Rowlands who was attached to the Divisional Cyclists took a prominent part in them.
   He was a clever musician, had several letters after his name and had an excellent tenor voice. I had been very friendly with him at Llandudno but had seen him seldom afterwards. He informed me, after one of the concerts that the song "Pack up your troubles in your Old Kit Bag" which we had heard that night for the first time, had been composed by himself, the words being written by another member of the troupe. The printed copies of this at one time popular song which I have since seen do not bear the name of Rowlands. I have never seen Rowlands since and rather think that he must have been killed later.[2]

Concert parties were one of the main forms of entertainment helping to raise the morale of the troops when they were together away from the front line. The men would also sing as they marched, often to the same songs as those performed in the concerts. Refrains such as 'It's a Long

Way to Tipperary' and 'We're Here Because We're Here' and 'Keep the Home Fires Burning' are still familiar. Llewlyn Wyn Griffiths refers to the importance of singing to the Welsh battalions, and how it helped them in times of danger. He describes an incident when Welshmen were waiting to go back into the trenches, when they began singing a hymn in harmony in their native language. The non-Welsh-speaking brigadier general asked why they had to sing such a mournful refrain, not realizing how important this link was to their lives back home. A Welsh speaker himself, Griffiths realized how much this Celtic language marked a strong bond between them, and also enabled his countrymen to speak freely amongst themselves.[3]

A patrol into no man's land

Our next spell in the trenches came round only too quickly, and we were again in the line. This time in a quiet sector. The only incident of note happened one night and was of rather amusing character.

As I had had some experience of patrolling no man's land obtained while training for the raid I was detached to take parties of No.7 platoon out on patrol to accustom them to that duty.

One such party of 5 men or so was headed by Douglas who had recently, while I was occupied with the raid, been made an acting unpaid Lance Jack. Heaven only knows why as he was a wash out at the job and lost his stripe some months later on that account. I instructed them before we started out stressing the need for silence, for keeping touch one with the other. Had told them to progress as much as possible by short walks or runs from one cover to another and to remain absolutely still in whatever position caught [them] when a Verey light was sent up. A man standing upright especially if he remained still would be difficult to spot in the flickering light. Movement of any kind however would give him and perhaps the whole patrol away.

Having warned the sentries for some distance each side of our post in the front line that a patrol was going out, we discarded our jangling equipment, and taking only a bandolier of ammunition and our rifles and one or two Mills bombs in our pockets, we emerged from the trench and crossed our wire, which was in the form of a rather low straggling band a couple of yards wide. We went on into no man's land 100yds or so and then returned. I could not get Douglas to walk upright, he persisted in crawling on the least provocation. If a rifle was discharged in the enemies line he would drop down on his belly and squirm along. He could not understand that although walking a few yards at a time exposed a larger surface to risk from a bullet, the ground was more quickly negotiated, and the walker crouched in comparative safety of the next shell hole, long before the man who crawled. The crawler too stood more risk of getting entangled in stray wire etc which lay all about.

Regaining the outside of our wire, I had seen the 5 men safely across and was just waiting in a convenient shell hole while Douglas negotiated the wire before doing so myself when a machine gun a mile or so away south (it might have been away in Alsace for the danger it was to us) went rat tat tat. Douglas dropped on his knees, he could not get any flatter owing to the barbed wire. I said "Hurry up you fool, how much longer have I to wait here?" He muttered in reply something about being entangled. His own fault entirely as who in their senses would try to crawl through wire entanglements waist high. I clambered out of my shell hole and endeavoured to disentangle him and had just succeeded when pop-pop-pop a machine gun really near this time was sweeping the locality in which we were crouching. I plunged back into my shell hole. It was too small to hold all of me and lying on my back I could see my two feet, silhouetted against the star lit sky and protruding well out of the hole.

I reflected that if it chanced that I was hit it would be in the foot and a "blighty one" perhaps. The short burst of machine gun fire was soon over and I emerged. I was surprised to see Douglas in the same position as that in which I left him. I was going to say something very rude to him when he said in a very small voice "Mac I believe I am hit". Without another word I half dragged him through the wire into the trench. He had been unable to get flat owing to a strand of wire under his chest and had not had the presence of mind to leap for the trench. His behind being presented to the enemy, a bullet had passed between his thighs inflicting no further injury than a small flesh wound. I went down to the dressing station with him and it was the last I saw of him for a fortnight.

'At rest'

When next out at rest No7 platoon were ordered to Estaires to unload coal from barges. This work lasted 3 or 4 days and was very arduous and dirty. The barges were moored to the bank of the canal, and we had to walk to and fro' over planks carrying the coal in primitive kind of carriers, which were like shallow boxes with four handles fitted to each. We were allowed to visit the baths every night after we had finished work.

A crater at Duck's Bill

We next went into the line in a sector near Neuve Chapelle, notorious to all troops who visited the locality. It was known as Duck's Bill, deriving that name from its peculiar shape. It was a very narrow salient jutting out towards the Germans, and was a very hot spot for mines and snipers. Some weeks previously, while a company of Bantams was relieving another company of the same brigade who were holding the line at the top of the "Bill", the Germans had fired a mine under them, killing many of them and making of this tip of the "Bill" a huge crater.

No 7 platoon were stationed in the front line just where the trench first curved sharply out into no man's land and had 2 sections actually manning the crater.

As this was a most unpleasant post each half platoon took it in turns to be there for 24hrs.

My half platoon had to relieve the other half towards the evening of our second day in the trenches. We were led by Sgt Pelling along a very narrow shallow trench which wound in and out. In places, where the debris from the mine had fallen into the trench it was so shallow that we had almost to crawl on all fours. We hazarded one or two quick glances over the top, but any undue exposure of our persons was immediately followed by the vicious spit of a bullet too near to be comfortable. After progressing for some 100yds or so, we had to crawl under a huge log of wood, which had fallen, after the explosion astride the trenches, and soon after entered the crater. The last short piece of trench had been dug after the explosion, and sticking out of it, impeding our way somewhat was more than one fully clothed limb of a dead bantam. We gave a pull at a boot sticking out of the earth, but desisted when we discovered that it was still fastened to the foot of its dead owner. The smell was frightful. There must have been many more bodies buried in the yellow brown earth thrown up by the explosion and which lay everywhere. The actual crater was the largest I ever saw. A circular area of ground measuring quite 100yds in diameter had been blown up; and the displaced soil had ultimately fallen so as to form a vast rim 12ft high and many more feet thick, to the basin-like hole in the centre. In the centre of the crater was a lake of water 50ft in diameter and deep enough to drown anyone who had the misfortune to fall into it. Above this water the earth sloped up sharply. We made our way round the crater by a zigzag path which had been formed by many feet pressing the soft clay into a hard mass, and relieved the garrison who were disposed in three small posts. One near the entrance and the other two on the further lip. The post I went to was one of these last. It was just a small area within a few feet of the lip of the crater, levelled to form a kind of platform. The soft newly erupted soil sloped steeply away at the edge of the platform to the lake in the centre. We squatted as best we could in a disconsolate group and took it in turns to watch through a box periscope.

We could see little through this instrument however, and a quick peep over the top only showed us more yellow earth and the enemies wire so near as to almost take one's breath away. Looking through the periscope during my time on sentry I was startled to hear a shot and at the same moment have broken glass fall over my shrapnel helmet and shoulders, the periscope twirling round with the force of the impact. A German sniper had knocked the top of the periscope right off. We had to manage thereafter with a small mirror attached to a bayonet.

Box periscopes and periscope rifles were widely used by the British Army from 1915 onwards to view enemy movement. Although it was estimated that many men's lives were saved due to the use of this equipment, the enemy snipers targeted them indiscriminately where they could, as William discovered. Soon though, with more camouflage and careful positioning, the Germans found them harder to spot. As sniping became more widely accepted and widespread in the British Army, periscopes were used as a lure to enable the Allies to pinpoint the position of the enemy snipers and their loopholes.⁴

As darkness fell we gradually lost sight of our two companion posts and then of the crater itself. It became almost pitch black, the moon being new, and the sky overcast and misty. So dark was it that we could not see each other except when a Verey light swished into the air and hung for a few seconds over us.

Our rations were brought up to us by a carrying party, and by their language we knew that they had had an exceedingly difficult passage along the narrow trench and round the crater.

They had not long gone and I was standing on sentry with Douglas looking over the top at what looked like a black wall, which turned a dirty grey sometimes when a Verey light went up somewhere in the neighbourhood, when there was a sudden bang-bang, bang-bang. Our artillery had opened on the German front line on our left. Both sides likely were nervous of a raid taking place in the unusual darkness, for within a few seconds of the first salvo there was quite a bombardment going on. Standing there, in between as it were the opposing armies, we were looking on a lane of darkness on the left of which were continual stabbing flashes of bursting German shells, and on our right a similar line where our shells were bursting on the German trenches. The noise was terrible. The Germans sent up many red and green lights as signals to their artillery. Our position seemed a perilous one as except for the rim of the crater we were shelterless. The narrowness of a trench adds to its security in a bombardment. We were crouched down on a bank almost in an open position. As a matter of fact we were safer than if in the front line trench, the crater being too near to each front line for either artillery to drop shells too near us. We did not feel very secure however. Shrapnel and nose caps were whizzing about, flopping into the soft ground or splashing into the water behind us. There was the acrid smell of high explosive. We were glad when the firing slackened and then gradually ceased altogether.

The next afternoon we were relieved from our posts in the crater and went back to a support trench which was situated just behind the front line. Here we had small dugouts or shelters. We were in the trenches for 6 days this time instead of the usual four. Authority had decreed that during the [summer] we could stand 6 days of it. The weather rather suddenly turned sunny and warm. Where had lately been pools of stagnant water were areas of thick mud, where there had been mud was hard, dry soil. Flies and insects of all kinds quickly appeared. In those places where bad smells had been prevalent, and they were many, worse smells saluted our nostrils drawn out of the earth by the sun.

This area was extensively mined and there was always the threat of the firm land we stood on becoming a heaving mass, rising and rising towards the sky taking us with it, finally to fall broken lifeless and be buried in the mines havoc like so many of the Bantams had been in the recent catastrophe.

The fourth day a party of us were returning to the front line having been sent down to BHQ to fetch some barbed wire. The CT we were traversing was in a very dilapidated condition and consisted for most part of a barricade or parapet only, the side facing our territory being quite open. We walked along the duckboards slowly as we were heavily laden and it was very warm. The sun shone overhead. A lark, almost an invisible speck in the blue arch of the sky, sung away happily as if there was no war on. There was the continual buzz of insects. Far up above two of our aeroplanes droned their way to and fro'. Upon nearing the front line we suddenly heard the sound of two rifle shots jarring on the midday quietness. Douglas grunted to me ... "Snipers active up in Ducks Bill. Wonder if they have pipped anyone".

Shortly after William's battalion had left this area, on 21 June 1916, the 2 RWF took over this part of the section at Duck's Bill. A German mine exploded directly under their B Company in the early hours of the next morning. Over two-thirds of the men were lost, including two officers and the company sergeant major. Despite this, men of the battalion led by Captain Stanway, moved forward and repulsed a German raid. This explosion left a huge hollow in the land that was to become known as the 'Red Dragon Crater' in honour of the Welsh regiment that not only lost so many men but defeated the raiders.[5]

At the same time as this mine exploded, men from the No. 254 Tunnelling Company, Royal Engineers were digging a mineshaft towards the enemy lines. This shaft was severely damaged, and the men were buried alive. Some were rescued, but one man, Sapper William Hackett, even though he would have been able to escape himself, would not leave one of his fellow tunnellers who was still trapped and wounded. Rescue efforts continued over the following four days but with no success. Sapper Hackett received a posthumous Victoria Cross for his sacrifice.[6]

In his book *Undertones of War* Edmund Blunden refers to the time when on 7 August 1916, as a field works officer, he was given the task of restoring the sap that had been heavily damaged as a result of the explosion. He was allocated one hundred men from his battalion (the 11th Royal Sussex) to complete this task.[7]

In 2006, a memorial was erected for the tunnellers. This followed the Red Dragon Survey which attempted to detect any traces of the British tunnel that had been damaged, and unsuccessfully attempted to find the remains of Sapper William Hackett VC of 254 Tunnelling Company, and Private Thomas Collins of 14th Welsh Regiment (Swansea Pals).[8]

The colour blue

Ten minutes later as we were approaching our own sector, rounding a corner we came upon a small cavalcade proceeding in the opposite direction. A little party of the kind only too common. Two men carrying between them a stretcher. Upon the stretcher lay huddled a man covered for the most part with his greatcoat upon which were great patches of dried mud. His head was swathed in bloodstained bandages which came down over part of his face making recognition difficult. The stretcher bearers when they reached the spot where we were standing aside to let them pass, gently lowered their burden on to the ground in order to take a breather. Their casualty was a man named Church who was in our own platoon. Church whose quakings and fears during times of danger had earned him the name of "Windy". He had always been the awkward man of the platoon. He never could keep in step. The state of his equipment and rifle were always calling down the wrath of the SM upon his muddled head. In spite of a certain inherent laziness in his character he did at times try to smarten himself up, but seemed physically and mentally incapable of succeeding. He seemed always to be in trouble. This time he had stuck his befuddled head over the top and a German bullet had cut a groove across it. He was still conscious and I said to him "Hullo Church, on your way to Blighty at last". He smiled his slow smile and said that he hoped so. "Hold tight old chap", said the SBs [stretcher bearers] as they lifted up the stretcher "We must get on". We stood and watched them out of sight, all I believe, rather envious of Church who was, so we thought, going out of the trenches, into the comfort of a hospital, possibly even getting right home. He lay there in his stretcher gazing up with his one free eye his other being covered by the bandages, into the blue dome of the summer sky which matched it in colour. Did he hear or see the lark? Within an hour he was dead.

Chapter 7

The Somme and Mametz Wood

During five bloody days in July 1916, the 38th (Welsh) Division of the British Army attacked a wood over a ridge held by the Germans. Four thousand of their men were killed or wounded.[1]

The original orders, issued by general headquarters for the first day of Allied attack in the Somme on 1 July 1916, excluded any consideration of capturing Mametz Wood. It was felt to be too hard a task. The German second line was only 300 yards from its northern edge, making it easy for them to reinforce positions within it.[2] Attacking formations were therefore to move east and west of it. The wood was huge and dense and, at 186 acres, the largest, not only in the Somme but also across the whole of the Western Front. With a mix of lime, oak, hornbeam, hazel and beech,[3] it had been cultivated in the past, but in recent times had been left to grow wild. The undergrowth was thick and impenetrable.

A change in pace

The long spell in the trenches at last came to an end and we were relieved. After a few days at La Gorgue the whole division moved back for "Divisional Training" before taking part in the Battle of the Somme.

Our battalion moved back, route marching 20 or 30k a day for 4-5 days, and at last reached our destination, a village far removed from the trenches. Our billet was a mud and lathe barn open on all sides owing to the falling away of the mud. The weather was exceedingly hot and we were not allowed to rest as we had hoped. Starting out early each morning we had to march 6k to the Divisional training ground where we drilled and manoeuvred all day, returning to our billets at 4 or 5 pm. This Divisional training ground was an area some square miles in extent and mostly composed of fields of growing corn which we had perforce to trample on ruthlessly.

I suppose our beneficent Army Command paid the owners for the damage we did. Possibly, however, owing to lack of farm hands it was never intended to harvest it.

The life was a hard one but I suppose it made us fit and well after so much time cooped up in trenches. It was a rest in one way however. We were so far back from the firing line, even the guns could only be heard faintly and in the dead of night, that we could almost forget its horrors in our peaceful rural surroundings.

THE SOMME 1916

At the end of June we once more set out for the firing line. We knew that we were going to take part in an attack, but to our minds at the time anything seemed preferable to going back to the ennui of trench warfare.

On July 3rd we arrived at a village not many miles distant from Albert. Everywhere was bustle and activity. The roads were filled with traffic. Limber and lorries taking rations and ammunition up to our attacking troops. Messengers on throbbing motorcycles threading their way in and out of the slower traffic. Battalions of men on their way up to take part in the battle, all spic and span. Other depleted and badly battle soiled battalions on their way back to rest and reorganise. A constant stream of Red Cross motors passed each carrying its tragic load.

We only spent one night in this village and early the next morning started out to take up our position in the battle line. The din of the not very distant gunfire was continuous. The roads seemed freer of traffic than they had been the previous evening, although the Red Cross cars were still about in great numbers. The weather was warm and sunny. Far away to our left we could see the Dome of Albert Church with its curiously bent over figure of the Virgin, which hung precariously from the top. It was said that the war would not end until this figure fell from the shell torn tower to which it was so insecurely pendant. Without much hope that its fall would have any such sequel, we most of us voiced a wish that it would ...[4]

As William indicates there was little time for rest, and the men were likely exhausted by the time they arrived in the valley of the Somme. Prior to the seven-day route march down to their attacking position for the offensive on Mametz Wood (see plate 10), the men of the 38th

(Welsh) Division had been undergoing rigorous training in the St Pol region which had been specifically chosen as a terrain that was similar to that of the forthcoming offensive.

On 4 July 1916, the spell of hot and sunny weather broke, with a deluge of heavy rain and thunderstorms. This made the remaining eighteen kilometres they had yet to march, far tougher than the preceding days, slipping, sliding and wading through the mud. Some of the camps were flooded and the communication trenches waterlogged.[5] This also made it difficult to get into position in the advanced trenches where they relieved the 1st Warwicks.[6] Having marched a total of thirty-four kilometres in three days [7], they were exhausted by the time they arrived [8]. They moved into line from Bottom Wood to Caterpillar Wood, which faced the southern edge of Mametz Wood, on 5 July 1916.

William describes this march and his impressions as they approach the Somme, encountering particularly those who were coming away from the battlefield, and the extent of the artillery in the Fricourt Valley, as they gradually moved into position.

Preparing for battle

We were dressed in what was called fighting order. Our packs and greatcoats had been left behind. On our backs in place of the pack we carried the haversack, which contained our hold-alls, caps, iron rations, towel and one or two private belongings for which we could find room. Our waterproof sheets were folded and underneath the flap of our haversacks. Our mess tins fastened on the outside. We carried of course our entrenching tools, water bottles and ammunition pouches. Each man had been issued with two extra bandoliers of .303 ammunition. As the pouches were already full these had to be slung over our shoulders. We also all had tin hats for the first time.
Before long we were passed by a battalion who had just left the battle zone. Dirty, unkempt, and disorderly they straggled past us. What struck us most was the expression on each face. They had been through hell and looked it. Each face was uniformly pale with a curious grey pallor. The eyes were bright and sleepless, set in rings of dark. The mouth was drawn. Each man seemed a little bewildered, wondering if he was really alive, had really left [the]

inferno behind and was plodding along under God's warm sun. They shouted many words of encouragement to us, less from a feeling of kindness than from the joy and relief at coming out of it. Some carried German spiked helmets, others wore the German round cap, carrying their shrapnel helmets in their hands.

Fricourt Valley

After several hours march, we entered Fricourt Valley. For many months this valley had contained both front line trenches, which had each been overlooked from the high ground opposite. Communication and Fire trenches zig-zagged all over the place. The thrown-up chalk of which the soil was largely composed, showing their positions clearly. It was curious to look down into these trenches, now deserted which had been for so long the lurking places of the opposing forces, and to see the sign boards and direction posts still standing in them. During the opening days of the Somme offensive our troops had pushed the Bosche over the brow of the hill upon which Mametz village stood, and he was now holding the next ridge upon which stood Mametz wood and Contalmaison.

The most impressive sight in Fricourt Valley was the artillery. Guns seemed to be everywhere. To the left of the road, which ran along the lowest contour was a long line of 18 pounders standing wheel to wheel for about half a mile. On the right of the road were many groups of 4.5 howitzers. Piles of ammunition stood behind each gun, and when we arrived the personnel were busy unloading more shells from a constant stream of gun limbers, which rapidly clattered up, and as rapidly clattered back empty to fetch another load.

Orderlies and runners were dashing about everywhere. Signallers were laying telephone wires as rapidly as they could from the guns to the Artillery forward observation posts on the ridge above. One or two guns were firing ranging shots, otherwise things were fairly quiet, there being a lull in the fighting.

We marched to the south eastern end of the Valley, and in the shelter of what had once been a small wood rested and had our dinner served out of the field kitchen.

Relieving the Warwicks

Early in the afternoon we again moved off and took over positions from another regiment. These positions were removed by some 100yds from the actual front line, and were in the nature of reserve posts. We approached them in single file, skirting a small wood and mounting up the side of a ridge. The positions were in very hastily dug trenches, which were only 18ins or so deep, and had evidently been dug with entrenching tools to afford cover from shell fire. There was little or no field of fire in front as the view was obscured by a hedge. We settled down here as best we could and as all seemed quiet expected to get some rest. However, when darkness fell Jerry commenced dropping shells close to us, evidently aiming at the wood we had skirted, and which was 100yds in our rear. All night long he kept plugging away at it and pieces of shrapnel were flying about our ears the whole time. There was no sleep for any of us. A ration party had to go down to the road for the next day's rations and Preble was wounded in the arm by shrapnel. He was well out of the miseries that the rest of us were to endure.

The shelling ceased at daybreak and we had a little peace. It was strange to look on the landscape in the calm freshness of a summer dawn, and reflect what confusion, darkness, noise and danger it had held so recently. The nearness of some of the fresh shell holes testified to what danger we had been exposed. We remained here during the day. The officers however went up to reconnoitre the battlefield from the Mametz ridge.

A key account of the events during this time comes from Llewelyn Wyn Griffith. Prior to June 1916, he had been an officer in the 15 RWF, the same battalion as William. His new position as Brigade Staff Officer overseeing the operations of four battalions including 15 RWF, gave him a clear perspective of what happened over the next few hours and days, as described in his book *Up to Mametz and Beyond*.[9]

An attempt was made to attack the wood by the 115th Brigade on 7 July, although it was aborted at an early stage when the impact of enemy machine-gun fire was realized. The advancing infantrymen had little or no cover or smoke screen to mask their movement and were engaged at point-blank range when trying to cross open ground toward the wood. They were also hit with enfilade fire from enemy machine guns situated in isolated copses on the flanks of Mametz Wood. Fortunately, the brigade commander, Brigadier General Evans, was able to make a telephone call to headquarters to explain the situation.

Brigade headquarters was at this stage approximately seven miles away from the front, making functional phone lines essential to operations. Unfortunately, all too often these lines, laid on open ground, were in danger of being sabotaged by the enemy, accidentally cut or blown up by enemy artillery.[10]

The next day, 8 July, the staff captain was evacuated with shell shock, and Llewelyn Wyn Griffith took over his work. The plan was for the two remaining brigades of the division to attack Mametz Wood the following day, with the 113th Brigade, which included the 15 RWF, attacking to the west.

It was however postponed for twelve hours, at which point it then links in with William's account of that day, 10 July 1916. Zero hour was 4.15 am.[11]

Becoming a runner

As soon as it had become dark, we moved off to take up assembly positions for an attack at daybreak.

By a stroke of luck, I was detailed for special duties.

At this period battalions were organised slightly differently than they were later, and it was necessary at a time like this to have auxiliary runners at BHQ. A message was sent round for 3 men per company to act in this capacity. The job turned out to be quite a soft one in comparison with that of the men left in the company. I said goodbye to Douglas, and B company disappeared into the darkness.

The dozen runners of which I was one moved off last of all with BHQ. We were under the leadership of Lt Piper whose antics I have described before. We went up the hill into Mametz village where we came under the fire from the enemy and entering a one-time German trench to the right of the crossroads at the centre of the village, were soon at BHQ. There was a dugout 30ft deep which was occupied by the CO Adjutant, Lt Piper and a few signallers complete with telephone. We runners were left outside in the open trench. It was quite a good trench however, 7ft deep. We sat about on the fire-step dozing for several hours. Everything was fairly quiet. An occasional shell burst somewhere and there was some rifle and machine gun fire. An hour before dawn however the bombardment started with a crash. Our artillery had to prepare the way for the waves of men which were later to advance, by cutting the German barbed wire entanglements, knocking their trenches to hell and generally putting the wind up the Bosche.

Artillery bombardment

It is hard to describe the noise the like of which we had never heard before. Once started it went on continuously, an awe inspiring, ear splitting volume of sound. It banged, it roared, it screamed, it thundered. Swelling in sudden tremendous gusts of fury yet never seemed to lessen. All the noise producing elements of heaven, earth and hell seemed gathered together in one common gigantic chorus. Looking to our rear the sky was lighted up with continuous flashes, and we remembered the long line of guns in the valley behind and could visualise the sweating, swearing gunners feeding them. To our front we could see the quick bright flashes of bursting shells, and sometimes the slow, stately progress of a Verey light through the air showed us ragged clouds of smoke. There were also coloured lights, signals by the enemy to his own artillery which was also in action. In the midst of the awful clamour we would hear the crump-crump of his shells close at hand, hear the swish and hum of shrapnel, and smell the pungent odour of high explosive. When the barrage had gone on for nearly an hour, zero [hour] was close at hand. I thought of those waiting men 500yds or so in front and thanked God that I was not with them. At zero [hour] the guns suddenly redoubled their fury and there was a perfect frenzy of sound beating the air. Stealing through the swirling smoke of the battlefield, dawn came creeping slowly. To the din was now added the rattle of machine guns which told us that the advance was now in progress. We peered out of our trench down into the smoke choked valley beneath us. What was happening down there in that inferno?

As the light strengthened, we began to see more. To the left stood out the jagged ruins of Mametz. In front was a valley scarred with trenches. On the opposite slope we could see the smoke-wreathed ruins of Contalmaison to the left, and covering the right half, as far back as we could see, the dark forbidding Wood of Mametz. Shells were being poured into this wood and the smoke from the explosions in the form of a short, jagged cloud was issuing from the back of it. Little could be seen of the actual combatants but here and there little groups of khaki figures could be seen moving about.

By the time it was broad daylight the artillery fire had slackened somewhat, but the rattle of musketry still went on.

William considered himself to be fortunate in being given the role of a runner, taking messages back and forth. This, he believed was a lucky break and kept him out of the intense fighting, but the responsibility was not without its dangers.

Griffiths refers to a conversation he had with a signals officer where they discuss whether the runners were getting through. The signals officer emphasizes that only urgent messages should be sent, with the loss of seven of his men already that morning. They describe how more than one runner is sent each time, each taking a different route to increase the chance that the message would get through. The signals officer also refers to having a telephone down at Queen's Nullah, and how, if they can reach there, a message can be sent back to headquarters.[12]

In fact, Llewelyn Wyn Griffith's 19-year-old brother, Watcyn, was also a runner on that day, losing his life delivering a message that Llewelyn had written himself.[13]

The Battle of Mametz Wood has been greatly scrutinized, studied, and written about both from a military history point of view, and in compelling accounts that are now part of the literary canon of the time. The grim fascination that this event holds for so many continues, despite the length of time that has since passed.

Using the careful military accounts and diaries of officers and generals, these few days in July 1916 have been pored over and dissected: the Welsh army fighting in unfamiliar terrain, dense woodland with the enemy already 'dug in' and established. With commands generated from some distance away, instructions were out of date the minute they were written, due to the rapidly changing conditions, and the method by which they were communicated. With the tenuous telephone links with headquarters, runners were at this point the most reliable means of communication. As Hicks relates, the information is only as good as when the runner had left the advanced position.[14]

But how much would an ordinary private soldier have known of this at the time? They were part of the machine, each cog needing to work as instructed to make this machine move along. Unsurprisingly, runners such as William were forbidden to know what the message they were carrying contained. Their duty was to deliver whatever it took.

Queen's Nullah

About an hour after daybreak, the Adjutant emerged from the dugout and called for two men to take a message to the CO. As it was my turn I had to go with another man.

We went along the trench until we came out into the centre of Mametz, and then turning to the right took the road leading down the hill into the valley. Up the road was coming a continuous stream of wounded. There were the walking wounded, their wounds roughly dressed with bloodstained bandages, limping happily along to hospitals in back areas. Davies of my platoon was one of these. As soon as he saw me a broad grin spread over his begrimed features "A blighty one this time" he said (he certainly did get home, but a year later was killed with three other men when a shell hit the dugout they were in). There were worse cases, who were being helped along by others, whose white, drawn faces told of the pain they were in. Worse cases still, muffled up figures on stretchers whose eyes were tight closed, unconscious, or at any rate too badly hurt to care where they were going and groaning in their pain. In the midst of all these wounded marched a string of German prisoners, two men with their bayonets fixed, acting as escort. There seemed little need for the bayonets. The prisoners looked a dazed dispirited lot, glad to be out of the inferno of our barrage. One short stumpy German bobbed along in the rear, his head a mass of bandages.

The enemy from the slopes on the other side of the valley was still peppering the locality with machine gun fire. He was also firing shrapnel into the valley.

Regular lines of fluffy black balls suddenly appeared in mid-air and there were nasty crumping sounds.

Reaching the bottom of the hill we turned to our right, entering what was a small ravine called "Queens Nullah" situated on the edge of Mametz Wood the undergrowth from which invaded the Nullah at several places. There were many shelters and dugouts built into the sides of this hollow. It had evidently been a German artillery position. There were numerous piles of shells lying about. In every one of these shelters were two or three bloodstained figures who having been hastily bandaged, had been placed in them to await their turn on the stretchers. Some were groaning, others squirming about in their pain. Some were both silent and still, unconscious or more likely dead. In one dugout was a ghastly trio. Three bloody figures maimed and disfigured lay half in and half out. They were evidently by their convulsive movements and awful groans very badly wounded. Outside this dugout was the unconscious figure of a wounded German. He was dying, a ghastly pallor spreading over his face.

At the south eastern end of the Nullah was our Doctor outside a dugout marked with a red cross. He was in his shirt sleeves, hatless and working like a navvy assisted by two men. He had a rude kind of operating table upon which casualty after casualty were placed for examination and dressing. At this spot a part of Mametz Wood joined the Nullah and a constant stream of messengers and casualties arrived, crashing their way through the dense undergrowth. The bombardment had now lessened even more. But bullets were still flying about freely, and above the Nullah, as regular as clockwork appeared a line of those fluffy black woolly balls, and there was the nasty swish of shrapnel. We learnt that our men were three parts through the wood, but were having a hot time from enfilade fire from the left where the next Division had failed to take Contalmaison.

The journey back

Our message delivered, we decided to cut straight back to our trench up the slope. We found that it would have been better to take the road which was sheltered in parts. There were many obstacles up the slope. Several trenches with barbed wire entanglements had to be negotiated. In front of one of these trenches in amongst the wire lay five or six bodies. One huge fellow must have been six foot in height and 14 stone in weight, lay sprawling. His face turned partly upwards was swollen and black. We took him at first to be a member of a black regiment not knowing the effects of a sudden shattering death. Flies buzzed about his eyes and settled on his swollen distorted lips. These bodies must have laid here for several days. The smell was appalling.

Hidden by smoke

Soon after our return we witnessed a further effort on the part of the Division on our left to capture Contalmaison and the ground to the left of the wood, and so relieve our division from the pressure on their left flank.

The hill opposite our viewpoint was similar in contour and about the same height as the South Downs. The portion to the left was quite open and we could see almost on the extreme left, the misshapen ruins of Contalmaison. The right of the hill was covered by the dark mass of Mametz in whose sombre shades God knows what hideous things were happening. It was on the open slope to our left that we could see an attack developing in the bright sunlight. Shells were bursting all over it, the smoke from each swelling suddenly out and then drifting away. In this drifting smoke we could see pigmy khaki figures, running forward in short spurts. One little party with a Lewis gun we saw for some time. They were evidently making some headway. A German shell would burst close to them, and we would lose sight of them in the smoke and think they had been wiped out. When the smoke cleared away however we would see them again. Men were being killed in dozens across there, but the smoke hid such things from us. The whole operation looked absurdly harmless.

I made another journey into the Nullah about midday. Everything was quieter. The Doctor less busy. The casualties I had seen earlier in the dugouts were still there. The difference was however that now the tortured bodies were still. They were all dead. There had been no time to trouble about the hopeless cases, all hands being wanted to evacuate the other wounded. These poor mangled men had been hastily examined, their wounds dressed and then had been put to one side to die.

A change in position

Late that night we were relieved by a brigade of the Welsh Regiment. We marched back through Mametz, and along to the southern end of Fricourt valley. Here in the shelter of what had once been a small wood the battalion bivouacked. Owing to the proximity to the front line for so long, little was left of this wood except at places tangled undergrowth. I rejoined my platoon here but as it was near dawn, we had little chance to sleep. The next day passed quietly enough for us. Our field kitchens arrived, and we had hot tea and stew. In place of our usual bread ration we had biscuits. During attacks priority of transport had to be given to ammunition, and there was seldom any bread to be had.

The Welsh brigade were not having a quiet time, however. We could hear the noise of barrages and occasionally machine gun fire. The actual field of battle was screened from our view by the Mametz ridge. We saw one of our monoplanes which had been hovering only a few hundred feet up suddenly turn its nose to the ground and fall like a stone.

From various rumours we heard it appeared that the troops who had relieved us were fighting like tigers. The Bosche had, I believe delivered a counterattack on the exposed flank, Contalmaison still remaining in their hands. This brigade was largely composed of miners from S[outh] Wales. The stream of casualties which passed our bivouac seemed to increase, and we heard that many wounded were waiting up in Mametz Wood to be carried down. In the afternoon the Divisional RAMC passed our camp calling forth many comments from us. A little later the "Pioneers", a battalion attached to the Division for labouring, trench digging and the like, also passed. All had been pressed into service as stretcher bearers to cope with the ever-increasing casualties.

As the long summer day drew to a close, we packed up our belongings and made all ready for an early move up to the firing line. When darkness fell the passage past our camp of lorries, ammunition waggons, [and] limbers increased tenfold and we were soon moving in their midst up to Mametz again.

When we reached the crossroads in the centre of Mametz we branched off to the north, and soon afterwards entered a trench which ran round the eastern boundaries of the village. No7 platoon [William's] was to be in support to the front line which was some 400yds away across the valley. Evidently, we had lost a great deal of the ground gained so recently at such a big cost.

German trenches

Our position was in a deep, well-made German trench excavated out of the chalk of which the soil was mainly composed. It must have been some kind of German communication trench as it had no field of fire on its western side, rising ground and the ruins of Mametz obscuring the vision on that side. However, it made an admirable support trench for us as it commanded a great deal of terrain in the direction of Contalmaison.

There were several deep dugouts in this trench, all of which had been partly demolished in the first attack several days before, but we were able to find shelter in them. Entrance was gained from the trench and there were staircases leading down into the bowels of the earth. At 30ft or so below the surface there had been chambers hollowed out, but in each case, these had been demolished. We found ample shelter sitting on the stairs. As they were German dugouts they were built on the western side of the trench and sloped down away from the enemy. I always had the idea that if a German shell found the entrance it would continue in its flight right down to the bottom killing all the occupants. We were in this position 48hrs and when not on sentry spent most of our time in the dugouts. Soon after we arrived it commenced to rain and the bottom of the trench was soon covered with thick, chalky mud. Boards were placed on this mud to facilitate our movements to and fro', and in one place a couple of dead Germans served the purpose. It was gruesome to step off a board on to the soft giving back of a German lying face down in the mud. Sleep was next to impossible, owing to the fact that we could only sit on the narrow stairs, and owing also to the noise of almost continuous shell bursts in the village directly behind us. The rainwater began to encroach on our staircase step by step until we were all sitting in the wet.

On the second night the Division was relieved. We had gained some ground from the enemy, inflicted heavy losses on him notably on some Prussian Guards, but at an awful cost in lives to ourselves. The Division which had gone into the battle at full strength were now so weakened that it was useless for further attacks, and it was replaced by a fresh Division. A few days later this relieving Division, after losing some ground and many of its personnel, was in its turn relieved. So it went on. Gradually the British Army advanced, and at the cost of prodigious sacrifice, a sacrifice little justified by the results obtained, eventually forced back the Bosche some few miles. An attacking force advancing against prepared positions such as we were, was bound to lose far more men than the defenders. The Germans always looked after their men better than we did. They had deep dugouts in which to shelter during bombardments. We did not to the same extent. Later they had pill boxes off which our shells would bounce. Of course, this fact acted both ways. We took many prisoners in these same dugouts and pill boxes, the enemy often remaining in the shelter too long.

Exhaustion

When I think of that march back from Mametz I can still remember vividly the agony and yet the joy of it. We were absolutely worn out through lack of sleep and hunger. We were in a state of nervous exhaustion which had followed our terrible experiences. Mile after mile we kept on marching or rather straggling. A crescent moon hung in the sky above and a white mist covered the ground. Tramp-tramp-tramp-tramp we struggled on, thinking each minute that we would have to give up in the next, but still doggedly and silently sticking it. We had a feeling of light-headedness, of detachment from our poor worn out bodies. Above all, however, we had a feeling of relief, mingled with a strange wonder that we were actually free from what had seemed a never-ending hurricane of hurling steel. Our ears seemed to be learning afresh to hear the common sounds of the countryside. Our eyes, which had seen so much that was ugly, so much that was terrible, dwelt with a feeling of rest, on the soft shapes of unspoiled trees and whole farmhouses standing out of the white mist. Our nostrils stung for so long with the acrid fumes of high explosives, nauseated by the smell of carrion, breathed in thankfully the cool fresh air.

In this manner, not quite knowing how we managed it, we reached the village from which we had started 5 nights before;[15] and after a drink of tea we lay down on the cobble stones of a stable without even removing our boots, and were soon asleep.

We had only slept 4 hours when we were aroused as we had to make an early start. The first part of our journey we rode in lorries, but when they had taken us 15 kilometres we had to continue on foot.[16] Then commenced the most agonising march we had ever made. It was yet early in the morning when we dismounted from the lorries, and all day we marched under a broiling hot sun. Village after village we passed through, hoping that each one was our resting place for the night. We would espy in the distance a group of trees or a church tower and know that we were approaching a village. Our flagging spirits would rise and we would step out briskly, only to resume our weary, dogged slouching when we saw that we were not stopping. We had of course the usual ten minutes halt every hour, and so tired were we, that upon receiving the signal to halt we would fall down on the side of the road and go fast asleep. When the ten minutes had expired the officers had to shake and even kick some men into consciousness. Most of us had the experience of falling asleep while yet we were marching. Slouching along, head down, we would fall asleep and immediately wake up with a start, as we realised that we were in imminent danger of banging into the bent figure in front.

Sniper on the Ypres Salient

The scene described by William of the men of the battalion marching away from the battlefield was also viewed from afar by Llewelyn Wyn Griffith:

> The battalions of the brigade were marching in columns of four along the road, and from a little distance it was clear that there was a lack of spine in the column. No ring of feet, no swing of shoulder, no sway of company; slack knees and frequent hitching of packs, a doddering rise and fall of heads and much leaning forward. Fatigue and exhaustion in a body of men.[17]

Regrouping and roll call

Ultimately, we did stop at a scattered hamlet. No7 platoon were billeted in a dilapidated cottage which stood on its own in an orchard. Trees and hedges stood all round making it quite a sylvan retreat. In this spot we spent three peaceful days. Parades were few and of short duration. We were allowed to rest. Every night we slept the clock round and even in the daytime we had a doze or two.

Our first job was to clean ourselves and our equipment. A seven days growth of beard had to be removed from our faces and a corresponding amount of grime. Far as we were from the usual haunts of troops, we were unable to have baths, but we could take our clothing off and kill some of the vermin with which they were infested. Our field kitchens had not arrived, and we had perforce to cook our own scanty meals. We were paid the usual amount, ten francs, but all we could buy in the hamlet besides beer was the unsweetened French chocolate.

The arrival of a week's accumulation of parcels helped us a great deal.

On the second day of our stay the battalion paraded for a roll call in the middle of a splendid avenue of trees which led up to a chateau where the officers were billeted. Under our feet was the soft carpet made by the accumulation of leaves for years. From this soft bed, which was interspersed with writhing tree roots, rose the gigantic gnarled trunks. Above was the double line of dark heavy foliage divided by a stretch of blue white-flecked sky. Shining white in the sunlight at the end of the avenue was the façade of the chateau.

Each platoon's roll was called by an NCO. As our Sergeant called a name to which there was no answering 'Here', he would pause and ask whether any of us knew what had happened to the absentee. "Yes, Sergeant" would answer someone, "I saw him carried away wounded," or "I saw him killed by a shell". After roll call an inquiry was held into the movements of all men who had absented themselves from the firing line in Mametz Wood. Quite a number had carried down or accompanied wounded pals down to the dressing station and had in some cases failed to return to their platoons. This had led to a serious depletion of men in the firing line. The men guilty of leaving their platoons without authority received a homily from the CO but no further action was taken against them.

By the time the 38th Division was relieved on 12 July 1916, 4,000 men had been lost. Over 1,000, including four out of the five commanding officers, were lost in the Royal Welsh Fusiliers alone. As Glover and Riley (2008) point out, the British Army, unlike the Germans, did not realize the challenges of fighting in such an arena, the thick undergrowth and fallen trees providing at times a visibility of only a few yards.[18]

The lack of experience of fighting in a wooded area, for both commanders and commanded led to inappropriate orders being issued. Events were rapidly changing, and it could be seen that to continue would lead to further unnecessary bloodshed, but the officers in the front line were obliged to obey orders. The rigid timing used in other military theatres, did not work in this situation and at one point led to the artillery firing on their own men. Once in the wood it was impossible to keep formation. Many lost their sense of direction in amongst the tangles of scrub and brambles. No one knew where anyone else was. Leadership was at times impossible; no one could hear commands above the noise of the artillery. As William describes from beyond Mametz Wood: 'The whole operation looked absurdly harmless.'

Harmless and hidden

Despite their achievement of pushing through such an alien military landscape and gaining ground of about a mile,[19] the reputation of the Welsh Division suffered badly. Much of this was due to the reporting of Brigadier General Price-Davies of 113th Brigade, who was initially highly critical of his soldiers.[20] It was not until subsequently undertaking an attack through two smaller woods, High Wood and Delville Wood, that the achievement of the Welsh Division began to be appreciated.[21] As Hicks states, despite their comparative inexperience the 38th (Welsh Division) had courageously fought a highly trained enemy and successfully taken Mametz Wood; they still to this day do not gain the credit they deserve for such a feat.[22]

The memorial of the 38th (Welsh) Division of the British Army was dedicated on the site overlooking the wood on 11 July 1987, seventy-one years after the battle. On a small hill set above the road the Red Welsh Dragon faces Mametz Wood, strong and defiant, its front claws entwined in barbed wire.

That so many accounts and depictions of the battle, not only in prose, but also in art and performance, continue to explore those few days, touches on the impact and trauma that it caused. As Robinson (2017) states, Mametz Wood has come to symbolize the Welsh sacrifice in that Great War.[23]

The climax of David Jones's epic poem, *In Parenthesis*, comes when a soldier, John Ball is wounded, and many of his fellow men are killed.[24] Although the wood is not named, David Jones himself was wounded in the leg in Mametz Wood. Jones was an infantryman in the same regiment as William, the 15 RWF.

Robert Graves, in *Goodbye to All That*, refers to the attack and describes how after the battle, he bivouacked outside and entered Mametz Wood to collect greatcoats off dead German officers to keep himself warm.[25] This experience led to his famous poem 'A Dead Boche', describing what he saw, in Mametz Wood, as 'a certain cure for lust of blood'.[26] William's description of what he initially assumed to be a member of a black regiment sprawled across the entanglement of wire, not realizing at the time the effects of 'a sudden, shattering death' and seeing how 'flies buzzed about his eyes and settled on his swollen, distorted lips' constructs a similar picture.

In 1974, Colin Hughes put out a request in local Welsh newspapers for anyone who had been at Mametz to contact him. He was overwhelmed by the response which resulted in an archive of correspondence, currently held at the University of Cardiff.[27]

With the marking of the centenary of the First World War, and the events within that time, came a play entitled *Mametz* by Owen Sheers based on the accounts of Llewelyn Wyn Griffith and David Jones.[28] An exhibition entitled 'War's Hell!: The Battle of Mametz Wood in Art' took place during the summer of 2016 at the National Museum in Cardiff. Included in this was the painting by Christopher Williams, *The Welsh Division at the Battle of Mametz Wood*, commissioned by David Lloyd George in 1916. The Battle of Mametz came to represent the bravery and sacrifice of the Welsh troops in the First World War.[29]

William's words add to the many of those already written about this short but deadly time during the summer of 1916. The marching towards the next battle, the freedom from the mind-dulling tedium juxtaposed with the horror of the trenches, the lines of men walking towards the battle and the striking difference from those coming away horrendously changed in demeanour whether outwardly injured or not. His experience as a runner, delivering messages, the contents unknown to him but each one influencing the future direction of his fellow men. He reflects on the way as the days pass, how division replaces division on the front line, as each becomes exhausted and the manner in which it just carried on, the Allies pouring men into the conflict.

The march away, the exhaustion, the solace of the post from home, and intriguingly, the roll call, several days after moving away from the battle. 'The men guilty of leaving their platoons without authority received a homily from the CO but no further action was taken against them.' These reassuring few words suggest at least this time perhaps, there was a compassionate and understanding attitude towards those that had found themselves in such a desperate situation.

Chapter 8

A Respite of Sorts

Reverberations across the Channel

Back in South London it is very likely that William's father and sisters would have heard the Allies' seven-day bombardment ahead of the Somme advance on 1 July 1916, such was its intensity. When the wind was blowing in the right direction the noise was heard as far north as Hampstead Heath, and in parts of Essex and Kent sash windows shook in their frames.[1] Little was to prepare those at home however for the resultant scale of death and injury that was to come. Heralded as the 'Great Push', it was seen back in England as the assault that would at last enable the Allies to break through the German defences.[2] Instead, with little gained, there were more than 57,000 casualties on that very first day.[3] The impact was immense, especially for some communities who lost so many of their men, all fighting together in the same battalion, as a result of Kitchener's recruitment strategy.[4] Close-knit neighbours would dread the news of injury or death of their loved ones. Only officers' families received telegrams informing them of their loss. For the rest, buff-coloured envelopes with the initials OHMS (On His Majesty's Service) were delivered in their thousand, along with the rest of the post. There was no indication on the front of the envelope as to what the news was inside, but the one that was dreaded most of all contained army form B.104-82B that began, 'It is my painful duty to inform you …'[5]

In June 1916, the War Office had agreed that the forthcoming Somme offensive could be filmed. Two official cinematographers, Geoffrey Malins and John McDowell, returned to London on 10 July with 8,000 feet of film. Released in August 1916, the resulting silent film ran for seventy-seven minutes, with musical accompaniment.[6] It depicted the build-up to the battle, marching infantry, wounded soldiers being treated and unflinching images of dead soldiers. A scene during which British troops crouch in a ditch and then 'go over the top' had to be staged for the camera behind the lines, as the filming equipment was too heavy and unwieldy to be able to capture a real-life attack. People were astounded to see such footage. Such was the impact; audiences were often heard to be cheering the soldiers on as they were seen to go to battle and crying out when the images of dead soldiers appeared. It was shown in cinemas across the country. Over twenty million people in Britain were to see it in the first six weeks of its release.[7]

Moving north-east

While the Battle of the Somme was to continue until 18 November 1916, the decimated 15 RWF continued to move north-east beyond Auchonvillers.

At the end of our stay in this hamlet we moved once more into the locality of the firing line, reaching the village of Authie after two days marching. Here we were billeted in the backyard of a farm. My section were allocated the pigsty to sleep in. It was a low shed with a dirty uneven earthen floor. There was a door, but it only covered part of the doorway. We had no greatcoats or blankets, our waterproof sheets alone had to duty as bedding. By lying curled up, and drawing the bottom of the sheet over our lower limbs, and covering the upper part of our bodies with our tunics we managed somehow. The nights were exceptionally cold for the time of year and I can remember Kirby, a late addition to the platoon, swearing heartily at the cold in the middle of the night, his teeth chattering in between his oaths.

Outside our billet the road forked and on the apex of the acute angle so formed, stood a small wayside shrine. Behind this shrine the ground banked up steeply, and by clambering up 15ft or so Douglas and I found a quiet spot in the long grass at the top. We could see a good deal from our retreat of Authie and during our three days in this billet we spent a great deal of our spare time up there, resting and writing letters. It was here that Douglas broke the news to me that René[e], the girl I had left behind me, had taken up with another man. For some time I had received no letters from her and had remarked on the fact to Douglas. The regard I had had for this young lady 4 or 5 years my senior could only be classed as a mild attack of calf love. Eight months absence from the light of her smile, (she had one tooth missing and two others badly decayed) during which I had passed through so many hardships and dangers had sufficed to show me the affair in its true perspective.

Long as I ardently did for the cessation of hostilities and a return home, a return to René[e] was not included. Douglas showed me a photo of my successor in the affections of René[e] (D was engaged to her sister) and I was immensely tickled to find that I had been thrown over for a bald headed, home service RE at least ten years my senior.

When our stay at Authie was at an end we moved off one morning through Authie St Leger and past Couin, halting in a valley a mile or so east of the last named. We were here 4 kilometres behind Hébuterne from which sector our troops had made an unsuccessful attack on the "Serre" ridge.

To our surprise we learnt that we were to bivouac in the open.[8] However we arranged ourselves in parties of six and by tying 4 waterproof sheets together we managed to rig up quite a decent shelter. The remaining two sheets we used for lying on.

Isolated and out of the war

The next morning No7 platoon were detailed to go up to the trenches as a working party. Our route lay across country thro' fields and fields of self sown corn, and was marked out by short white pots stuck in the ground at intervals. We wound up and down over the rolling low hills, past Bayencourt, past Sailly au Bois, a village on a hill, up to Courcelles where we entered a CT called Railway Avenue. We had to carry trench stores up to Auchonvillers along this CT. Soon after noon we retraced our steps over the downs back to camp. The heat was very oppressive, the sun beating down with great force.

I had felt very seedy since reveille and was steadily getting worse. Upon our return to camp I found that a rash had broken out on my body and I at once reported sick. The MO [Medical Officer] diagnosed my complaint as German measles and I was ordered to pack my kit and get ready to go to hospital. I did not feel very ill and the prospect of a holiday from all the hardships and misery nearly made me better. Corporal Humphries of the SB's [stretcher bearers], an old friend of mine accompanied me down to the road. He told me that I had a chance of getting to Blighty. On the road I found a motor ambulance waiting and after receiving a warning from the driver to keep clear of his blankets which were folded up inside, we drove off.

I did not want his old blankets. The knowledge that I might get to Blighty was enough to keep me warm. My comrades who I had left behind would have welcomed the gift of a German Measle or two.

A few minutes later we reached the Field Hospital in Couin Wood and I was examined by another MO and placed in the isolation tent, where I remained alone for some hours. This tent was separated from the others and a deep trench had been dug round it for drainage purposes. I seemed to be sitting on an island, around which the usual bustle of military life went on. The guns boomed, men walked about swiftly on various errands. I alone seemed to be out of the war.

A night-time journey

By this time I was somewhat feverish and light-headed but was quite content to rest on the wooden flooring. At last, as darkness was falling, an orderly came for me and I was escorted to another ambulance car. This time the driver was kinder and before shutting the door on me bade me make myself comfortable with the blankets. I did not avail myself of the privilege, but lying down on the shelf on one side of the car I scarcely moved for a long period, during which the ambulance throbbed and bumped its way over many kilometres of primitive road. Reclining there in a kind of torpor I was yet conscious of the various sounds outside. Now we would slow down to pass a crowd of soldiers on the march. I could hear their clanking equipment. Sometimes gun limbers passed us with a clatter. Then a heavy lorry loaded with stores would rumble past. At times we would halt for a few minutes while the driver had a colloquy with a traffic man at some cross-roads.

After such a stop I was sensible of a sudden change of direction as we swung round a corner. Shut up in that dark Red Cross car I was content to lie without worrying where

I was going, or how long the way was. I was going miles back, to some hospital where I might get a real bed to sleep in. Eventually might I not end up by getting home?

Once the car stopped for some considerable time. The driver appeared at the door with a lantern and asked me how I did. He also brought me a cup of tea for which I was very thankful. I could not eat the bread he also offered me. He told me that we still had 10k to go.

A different world

At last we were at the end of our journey and I stepped out of the car into a strange world. A quiet stillness pervaded the cool midnight air. No angry guns banged and spluttered about, but I heard the shrill peeping whistle of a French locomotive on the nearby railway. I stood at the gate of a canvas hospital. Great shadowy white marquees stood round amongst the trees. Presently a figure approached down the duckboard path and the night orderly took charge of me, and loading himself up with my rifle and equipment escorted me into one of the marquees.

In the pale light of a lantern I saw a double row of recumbent figures, one on each side of a gangway which lead from one doorway to the other. There was one vacant place in a corner and this was allotted to me. My bed, in common with the others was a stretcher raised from the ground on wooden supports, and thereon were four blankets neatly folded. The orderly said "I expect you will be very glad to get into bed. Can you manage by yourself while I go and see if I can get you a drink?" I would have been very ill indeed if I could not have undressed myself, with the prospect of a comfortable rest and sleep in the inviting stretcher, and declining his help was soon in between the blankets.

The orderly returned in a few minutes bringing me a mug of milky tea. The memory of that first half hour in bed will remain with me always. Stretched out on my back with my head pillowed on a rolled up blanket I was content to be there quite still, my tired aching limbs at last in complete repose, and feel the grateful luxurious feeling of warmth created by a sufficiency of blankets, gradually pervade the whole of my chilled body. Inside the tent the other patients slept on. Although both doors were open no sound came from the surrounding camp, but in the distance I could hear sound of shunting carriages on the railway, and at times the shrill, piping locomotive whistle which had greeted me on my arrival. Gradually I became drowsy and ultimately dropped off into a deep sleep.

The next thing I remembered was noise and bustle around me and I awoke to find that it was early morning. The orderly was insisting upon every man sitting up and washing his face and hands in the bowls he provided. This habit of waking up patients at an unearthly hour and forcing them to wash was I believe constant to all hospitals in France. What the actual sense in it was I don't know but the cause was Red Tape. The night orderly, who was due to go off duty at 8am, had to hand over his patients to the day orderly duly washed and with their fasts broken.

To achieve this he had to perforce to start at 5.30am or so in order to get everything done. Breakfast was not ready until 7.30 but then there was little chance of resuming sleep after having thoroughly awakened oneself by the application of cold water. It seemed to me that it was an iniquitous and even harmful arrangement. Patients were deprived of two hours of wholesome restoring sleep at times when for the most part they had many hours arrears to make up. I wonder who issued the Army Order which made this silly arrangement imperative. Washing, whilst sitting up in bed, in a bowl containing about an inch of water was no mean feat. Sponges or flannels were not provided and it was most difficult to prevent drops of water trickling down my neck.

I was able to take stock of my fellow patients who were now all awake, some more so than others. The noisiest of the lot was a Scotsman belonging to the 11th Hussars. His protest and remarks to the orderly about the early wash, all made in broad Scots were intensely funny and made us all laugh, however queer we felt. It is strange that Scotsmen should be generally accused of absence of humour. Generally in my experience when a party of men drawn from all parts of the British Isles were thrown together as in the present instance, it was the Scotsman who was the life and soul of them all. This man, who was convalescent could talk the hind leg off a donkey. His repertoire of episodes in his history was inexhaustible and I suspect not always true, but they were all funny and told in his droll way were very entertaining.

Just before breakfast we were visited by the sister. She entered the tent quite unexpectedly and said "Good morning boys and how do you all find yourselves this morning?"

The effect she produced on me was like a tonic. After nine months in France during which the only members of the weaker sex I had seen were for the most part old looking and wizened female farm labourers, ... the entry of this young ... fresh complexioned countrywoman, who bustled in with this greeting in pure English on her lips, was like a breeze straight from Blighty. Even Scotty as we called him was rather subdued, and could only make one or two fairly audible facetious remarks in an undertone to his neighbour.

Sister said "How many eggs this morning?" (If our morning temperature was 100(degrees F) or over we were given an egg for breakfast). We all claimed that our temperatures were fantastically high. She only laughed and proceeded to visit each one of us in turn, ascertaining our temperature from the orderly who had previously taken them all, and asking each of us the question "Did your bowels move yesterday?" The fellow next to me named Day was a Lancashire lad from the famous 29th Division, who had seen service with the Division in Gallipoli as well as France. When asked this question by sister he only stared at her bewildered. Discreetly she moved off to the other end of the tent and he leaned across to me and said "What the hell does she mean?" I enlightened him using a slang phrase he was well acquainted with and on the sister returning and repeating her question he was able to answer her.

I spent three days in bed in this tent. I did not feel very ill but my temperature rose a little towards the evenings and made me uncomfortable. Apart from that discomfort I was well content to sleep at any time, or listen to the tales of Scotty, or my other nine fellow patients. From Day I learnt many incidents concerning Gallipoli and from his description had to alter my views of this ill fated expedition altogether. It was with surprise for instance, that I learnt what few hundred yards depth of the beach we had held. It had always been my idea, no doubt encouraged by the official or Government inspired reports that we had held a few miles.

Scotty regaled us with many a tale of the Hussars life which was mostly spent in the peaceful back areas. The duties of the Hussars were not as arduous as to preclude what he called a little "Square poaching" now and again. We were given very good food. For the first two days however I was unable to eat solids. Afterwards I made up for lost time.

On my fourth day in hospital, the whole outfit moved 40k to another site near Amiens. As I was considered a little better I was told that I would have to get up, one or two others had to remain in their stretchers and be carried thus in the ambulances. After breakfast that morning I did get up and carefully dressed myself and went for a walk round the camp. I had before seen Davis, another patient, fall clean over in a faint on getting up through weakness, and was very much afraid I would do the same. I walked very slowly on that account, making up my mind that I would sit down on the ground at the first sign of giddiness.

At 11am we were packed into ambulances and were off for our long ride. Arriving an hour or so at our new camp the convalescent cases were told off to help put up tents, marquees etc: I and some of the others who were not quite so advanced were glad to be in the shade of our marquee which had speedily been erected, and before long were ordered back into bed.

Convalescence

The next day I was much better, indeed had got rid of all the unpleasant symptoms of the measles except for a stuffed up nose which persisted for a week or more longer, and was able to get up and enjoy the perfect weather which we were being blessed with at the time.

The field hospital was situated in the beautiful grounds of a chateau which was unoccupied. One of the chief features of these grounds was a long avenue composed of huge trees, each one of which would by itself have earned the name of "Monarch of the Forest". Overhead the foliage met obscuring the sky. The pathway underneath between the two rows of giant tree trunks was cool and but dimly lighted. One's feet made no sound on the yielding carpet of fallen leaves which had accumulated for years. Close to this avenue was a field covered with dwarf brushwood and here the wild strawberry grew in profusion. Many a time did we raid this field collecting the small juicy fruit. Returning to our tent afterwards with the spoil we would add a little water to some Nestle's milk and thoroughly enjoy our Strawberries and Cream.

There was an S. I. Ward in this field hospital, that is a ward reserved for men who had self-inflicted wounds. It was strange to see a score or so men all wounded and bandaged, under an armed guard, doing odd jobs in the camp. On looking closer however, one would notice that they were all wounded in the hand, arm, leg or foot. The majority had in fact injured their right hands, evidently wishing to render themselves unable to handle a rifle.

Back to the battalion

I spent three happy weeks in this camp[9] and it was with great regret that at last I left it and was taken with a lorry load of other fit men 10 kilometres into Amiens. This was the first time I had been in a French town of any size, but unfortunately I did not see much of it as we were deposited at the "Gare" and were kept prisoner there. Two Redcaps keeping a sharp eye on us. After a long wait I received my movement order, and mounting a cattle truck, was soon jolting and shaking on my way north where it seemed my battalion had been moved during the time I had been away.

Arriving at long last at Poperinghe I had to walk miles past the various camps until I at last found the 15th RWF, and after reporting at the OR [operations room] was soon being welcomed back by my platoon. The battalion had only recently moved up to this area and had not yet been into the line. We were comfortably housed in wooden huts, a great improvement on the barns we had been accustomed to further south.

Gas attack

One night soon after my return, I woke up at night to find myself persistently coughing, something was irritating my throat. In an adjacent hut another man evidently had a similar attack. After I had spent half an hour vainly striving to stop the coughing, there was movement apparent in the camp, Sergeant came rushing round shouting "Stand to." We all hastily donned our clothes and equipment and fell in outside. The Germans had let loose a cloud of chlorine gas across Ypres salient. My lungs weakened possibly by my recent illness had been among the first to react to the creeping, silent menace. Situated as we were some 10k or so from the line the gas was too weak by the time it reached us to do much harm, but [we] could distinguish the faint smell of chlorine.

We stood there in almost complete silence, listening to the distant beat of the bombardment which had evidently answered the SOS which had been sent from the front line. This was our first experience of a gas attack and we wondered what special kind of hell was being perpetrated up there in front of us, what scenes of horror, agony and death. Within half an hour of the first alarm we were dismissed, a message having evidently been received by the CO that it was purely a gas attack, there being no expectation of it being followed by an attack in force.

Of course, William was extremely fortunate in that this was his only experience of needing any care from the huge network of field hospitals, and other medical and nursing facilities, set up across the Western Front to cope with all the casualties coming back from the front lines. Clearly the greatest danger was receiving an wound from enemy fire. Each man had a first field dressing stitched into the lining of his jacket to be used in the field in the case of injury.[10] Wounded soldiers would have been taken to one of the Casualty Clearing Stations and then, according to the severity of his condition, he would have been operated on there and then by a surgeon or transported further behind the front.[11] None of those attending to these men had seen such damage before the First World War, the high-velocity shells, bullets, and shrapnel ripping and tearing at the flesh of the men. Deep and dirty wounds, as many of them were, led to a high risk of anaerobic infection such as gas gangrene.[12]

Alongside the care of wounded soldiers, infectious diseases such as German measles that William was suffering from, were something the doctors and nurses took very seriously. Even though this was one of the milder diseases, it was still contagious and could spread amongst men squeezed together in the cramped conditions of the trenches. Isolation and careful nursing care for those who were infectious was the necessary route for recovery at that time.[13] In *Memoirs of an Infantry Officer*, Siegfried Sassoon describes how he had German measles, spending ten days in No. 25 Stationary Hospital occasionally slipping through the wire fence to walk in the surrounding pine woods.[14]

The possibility that disease could be caused by infectious microorganisms, was still a novel idea at that time. The use of antibiotics was a long way off. However, for some of the more serious diseases vaccinations were becoming available.[15] Vaccinating the soldiers against typhoid successfully prevented large outbreaks as had occurred in previous wars. Wounded soldiers were also being given horse antitoxin, which it was believed, prevented many of them developing tetanus.[16]

William's description of arriving at the field hospital, peacefully calm and away from the guns, being given a warm drink and being able to lie down under warm blankets, demonstrates not only the appreciation he had for being able to rest his body and recover and regain his strength, but also emphasizes the desperately poor conditions the infantry had to endure day after day. The importance of compassionate care and quiet convalescence at that time is clear.

Chapter 9

The Yser Canal

Shortly after William returned to his platoon, in August 1916, the 15 RWF, along with the rest of 38th (Welsh) Division, moved to their next position, to defend the northern edge of the Ypres Salient, on the banks of the Yser Canal.[1] Before they left the training camp to do so, they were addressed by the army commander.

A lengthy speech

We were now in the 2nd Army under General Sir Hunter-Weston familiarly known as Hunter-Bunter. He addressed the massed brigade while we were in camp.
  He spoke in a very fatherly kind of way, emphasising the need for hard work on the new front. Dig, Dig and Dig again was his advice, every spadeful of Belgium which was put into a sandbag was so much progress made towards victory. (We knew later what he was driving at, as when we came to take over the trenches, we found them in a very bad state of repair, and it took months and months with all our hard work, and all Hunter-Bunter's urging to make a well-fortified system of trenches.) He also spoke about the need for good gas discipline, telling us how in the recent gas attack that there had been very many casualties in one Division owing to defective discipline, while a neighbouring Division had suffered scarcely at all.

On such occasions General Hunter-Weston would inspect the troops on his horse, with his name branded across its flank. Two mounted sergeants, one carrying a flag served as his escort. He was well known for being self-important, quite erratic and eccentric, and was never very popular with those around him.[2] Clearly though, it seems, in this instance he did inspire the hard-working infantry.

Marching to the next position

One day soon after this harangue we moved up to the line. Leaving camp early in the morning we marched through Poperinghe and past many camps on the Pop[eringhe]-Elverdinge Rd till we reached International Corner. This was a spot where 4 roads met about 6 km from the line. Owing to their being Belgian, French and British troops in the vicinity there was a traffic controller or sentry for each of the three nations stationed there. We here turned to the right and halting ½ mile further on, had our dinner off the field kitchens. Moving off after the meal we reached the Elverdinge-Ypres Rd and turning along it to the right, march[ed] in artillery formation thro[ugh] the deserted village of Brielen. Many houses in the village were still partly standing but the inhabitants had left, and it looked as if it was considered unhealthy by the military as no [one] seemed to make use of even its cellars.

Near the S[outh] end of the village was an avenue of trees, splintered but still alive, leading up to a white faced chateau which was partly hidden by the foliage … [It] had three domes in its roof. It was in fact "Le Chateau du Trois Tours".[3] Soon after passing this chateau we turned at right angles to the left and some ¾ miles further on crossed the Boesinghe-Ypres Rd and reached the Western bank of the Yser Canal.

The northern sector of the Ypres Salient and 'Blightly Bridge'

As I was destined to spend nearly a year at this part of the front it will be as well to describe roughly the lie of the trenches and fortifications of this northern sector of the famous Ypres Salient.

From this spot, which we had reached just by No. 4 bridge [across the Yser] … the western bank of the canal, which in places was 30–40 ft high and 200ft or so thick, stretched to our right and left. Running roughly parallel with the canal and some 200yds to the west of it was the B[oesinghe]-Ypres road. A road of the usual type, wide, with cobbled centre and lined with trees on either side. Following the canal and road 3 kilometres due south one reached the centre of Ypres, whose whitened ruins were plainly visible, notably the famous square tower of the Cloth Hall. Travelling 2 kilo[metre]s in the opposite direction due N[orth] one came to the spot where the opposing trenches, which had from the coast followed roughly the line of the Yser canal, suddenly bent outwards towards the east and curving ever further and further from the N and S line of the canals, past near St. Jan and St. Julien until the peak of the salient was reached due E[ast] of Ypres on the Menin Rd. South of the spot the line curved back again to Armentieres.

Across the canal to the front line

Straight in front of us at this spot was a gap in the canal bank leading to a wooden bridge wide enough to take a cart, which crossed the lowered water of the canal. From the other side of the bridge started a communication trench, which was largely only a barricade with a duckboard track on the southern side of it. This CT led due east to the front line distant about 2km, and it was the section extending north of it to where the trenches and the canal converged that was the new Divisional front.

We met guides at this spot and were led along a duckboard track which wound along between a stream which was evidently a service stream for the canal and the bank of the canal itself. Built into the bank were many dugouts and shelters, many of them made of stout, black, corrugated steel covered with sandbags. The bank behind not only screened them from enemy observation but protected them from shell fire. Shells either struck the east side of the bank or just grazing the top, fell clear of the dugouts on to the road 100yds or so away.

This bank, as was also the other bank, (in this case of course on the canal side away from the enemy) stretching for 3 miles or so into Ypres and possibly further south, were veritably teeming with members of all branches of the British Army.

At times it reminded me of a rather primitive town, with only two long streets. Dugouts were dry and for the most part safe from shells. There was a plentiful supply of clean water obtainable from the stream. Altogether an ideal place, when, considering the many shell torn unsheltered positions we had been in when in the same relation to the front line as we were here. After 15 minutes' walk, we reached a point where the canal and road which had run parallel so far, gradually slanted away from each other. The road, its direction well marked by its mature trees, proceeding in the direction of Boesinghe. Light was by now failing and after another 5 mins walk, we turned to the right and passed through a gap in the canal bank and crossed over the water by means of a rickety plank bridge. This bridge was screened on the left side with canvas, which … was full of holes, showing that it was in view of, and often shot at by the enemy, from further up the canal. It was the most northerly usable bridge, although the derelict planks of other broken bridges could be seen in daylight, further on. This bridge was known as "Blightly Bridge" and we were warned not to linger on it. On the other side of the canal, we entered a CT and after winding in and out for 10 mins or so, reached the front line, where we took over positions from the outgoing troops. They warned us to be very careful in daylight, as the enemy snipers were very active.

Taking stock

When light the next morning we could better take stock of our position. The trench was in a very poor condition. For a great deal of its length, it was merely a sandbag barricade. Here and there, there was a short parado. The barricade or parapet was very low and uneven. To walk along the trench upright was to find oneself suddenly with head and shoulders exposed over the top. Hung on the parapet at dangerous spots were a number of notices such as "Sniper active", "Duck your Nut", "Pocket your Pride" and "Bend your lordly head". The troops in this sector before us had evidently deemed such notices sufficient, but we were soon set to work to improve the trenches. In the daytime we filled sandbags to be placed in position during the night. This ground had been well fought over in various battles of Ypres. Half way across no mans' land was an old trench called International trench owing to the number of times it had changed hands.

It was not surprising therefore that in digging up soil to fill sandbags, we first came across scraps of clothing and soon after an obstruction in the ground. At the same time our nostrils were assailed with the pungent odour of a man a long time dead. We hastily covered him up again and sprinkled the ground with disinfectant.

To our rear was an area a thousand yards deep of broken ground, somewhere in which the support trenches were situated. Behind this was the canal bank, with the green tops of the trees on the road showing above it. To the left the front-line trench bent back to reach the canal bank, and it appeared to us that our backs were exposed to enfilade fire from the Bosche in that direction. To our right our vision was bounded by the CT and rising ground, but slightly to our right rear we could see some of the ruins of Ypres. A quick cautious glance over the top gave us an interesting view of the Pilckem ridge.

An enemy sighting?

Our second night in this position was marked by a prolonged trench mortar bombardment on part of the line to our right. The detonations were terrific and nerve racking to us although we were not within range. One trench mortar must have fallen clean on top of an officer in A Co[mpan]y. One or two scraps of clothing and a yawning hole in the ground marked the spot where he had been standing.

The next night I was on sentry with a boy named Barber. We were standing on the firestep together gazing in rather a bored way over the top. Suddenly a burst of heavy rifle fire broke out on our right. That was startling enough, but we soon realised that it was only the CO of the 16th battalion [RWF] having one of his private strafes. He would line up his whole front line garrison some nights and give them the order of 15 rounds rapid. Then followed the "mad minute". What actual damage this hail of lead, directed at the enemy, did is problematical. The likelihood is that it did no damage, but successfully put the wind up fatigue and ration parties of the enemy who were unfortunate enough to be in the open behind the trenches. The usual reply of the Bosche was to send over a few whizz-bangs.

Soon after the firing died down Barber startled me by saying "Look Mac, there are some Germans in front". He had seen their white faces in the light of a Verey light which had gone up on our right. Our sentry post was overlooking a sap or old CT which evidently had led out to International trench full of dead bodies. The entrance to this sap was in the traverse on the left of our fire bay. It was quite a likely thing a Bosche bombing party, using the cover of this old CT, and taking advantage of the noise of the strafe on our right flank, had approached and were waiting the signal to raid our trench. I strained my eyes in the direction Barber pointed but could see nothing in the darkness. "Are you certain that you saw them?" I said. "Yes", he said "I saw four or five of them just the other side of our wire". "Alright" I whispered, "you go and get the section to stand to and I will go a yard or two up the sap and wait your return." Placing a Mills bomb in my pocket and extracting the safety pin from another which I grasped in my right hand, and taking my rifle, bayonet fixed in my left hand, I advanced several yards down the sap, thinking that if a raid was about to be made, I could possibly be able to keep them off until my comrades would be able to get into position in the fire bay behind. I then stopped at a spot where there was a turn in the trench and thrusting my head round the corner kept my gaze fixed on the few yards of trench I could see in the dark. My bomb I held in my hand ready to fling immediately. I remained in this position for what seemed to me an age, although it could not have been more than two minutes as the rest of the section were quite close in dugouts. Several times I could swear that I saw a shadowy figure creep round the corner, which was the limit of my view, and instantly drew back my arm for a throw, only to discover that it was a figment of my imagination.

At last I heard a sound behind me, and turned to see the crouching figure and pale long face of Sgt. Pelling "Seen anything, Mac? I have the section standing to behind me," he whispered.

"No, Barber did all the seeing," I replied.

"Keep down here," he added "for a second or so longer. I am going back into the trench to fire a Verey light."

A few seconds later there was a pop and a splutter and the area I had been at such pains to see became quite clear. Nothing could be seen but the dancing shadows caused by the vivid light. Of course, the light cast by these Verey lights could be very deceiving and some of the shadows might well be the enemy, but if there were any they remained still and did not reveal themselves by movement. The necessity of freezing when taken unawares by a light was one of the first things impressed on us when we started active trench life.

I retired to the trench when I found the whole section on the fire step ready for any eventuality and, finding the safety pin of my bomb I replaced it.

The strain of the past months had begun to tell on the nerves of Barber, as indeed it had done to all of us and possibly his Germans were pure imagination. On the other hand, patrolling no mans' land, even up to the wire of the opposing trench was carried out by both combatants, and it might have been a patrol that he caught sight of for a second before the Verey light dropped.

Moving position

The night after this event we were relieved, or rather we exchanged trenches with A company who were in support. As we were halted in the CT while a heavily laden carrying party past us, there was an outbreak of bombing in the front line which we had just left. I was relieved to think that we were out of it. When we reached the canal bank, we turned N[orth] along another CT and several hundred yards along it reached the support post which was to be manned by our section. The next morning, we found that our post was situated on the canal bank. The continuation of the trench which we were in could be seen zig-zagging along the canal bank for some 500 yards due north, where it evidently joined the front line. This part of the trench was disused at this period. The bank was lower at this spot than it was further south, and the trench was a good mark for the enemies' artillery. The one sentry post which we had to man was overlooking this disused trench. We had two dugouts to sleep in during the day. They were well covered ones but were rather decayed and in danger of falling in at any moment.

Gas alarm and respirators

The next night I went on sentry with Davies just after dark, at about 8 o'clock. The rest of the section were detailed as ration parties to take rations up to the front line, leaving only us two sentries and Douglas who was now a Lance Cpl in the post. The ration parties got lost or something and were away for 6 hours or so.

Davies and I were on sentry, standing on the firestep for the whole time except for a brief spell now and again when Douglas relieved us each in turn. This disused trench had become known as a short cut back from the front line during the hours of darkness, and we had several parties to challenge. Suddenly we heard a distant jangle as of a stick striking a tin tray. This signal was taken up by nearer and noisier gas alarm posts. A strident Claxon horn took up the tale and added to the din. By this time, we had our gas masks on. At this period, we had the masks which were made of impregnated cloth in the form of a kind of ugly hood, the skirt of which had to be tucked into the neck of our tunics. There were two round glass covered goggles for eye pieces. Inhaling was done through the nose and exhaling through the mouthpiece, which was a short pipe passing through the respirator, and having on the outside a rubber valve shaped like a leaf.[4]

The three of us stood on the fire-step like three ghouls, the valves of our respirators inflating and deflating with each breath. Saliva or condensed [air] was soon dripping off the end with each breath. It was a calm, warm night with a very light breeze blowing from the east, just the night for a gas attack. We seemed shut off from our surroundings inside our respirators. Sounds from outside seemed muffled as our ears were of course covered. The desultory exchange of rifle and machine gun fire had died down considerably. It seemed that everyone was waiting and watching, expecting the invisible deadly cloud of poison gas to drift over and surround them. Possibly everyone was too busy engaged in an endeavour to keep the goggles of their respirators clear, to fire their rifles. The perspiration which we were in inside the stuffy respirators soon clouded the glasses, and we had continually to be cleaning them with the two little pockets provided for that purpose. Even when clear we could see little in the darkness. After some 15 minutes spent in this discomfort, we heard a sound behind us, and I got down from the firestep and went back along the trench. When I had gone about 10 yds I saw our officer approaching. He was wearing his respirator. In one hand was his shrapnel helmet, in the other a stick. He was

progressing slowly and stumbling often. His stick he was
using like a blind man. I removed the mouthpiece from my
mouth and challenged him. "Halt! Who are you?" His reply
was unintelligible as he spoke without removing the tube
from his mouth. Upon receiving the report that all was
well with us he stumbled off to visit another section.
  After 10 minutes more of discomfort I said to Douglas "I
don't think there is gas about. Anyway, I am sick of this".
I then tested the gas in the approved way, by letting a
little air into my respirator and sniffing to see if I
could detect chlorine. Smelling nothing, I removed my
helmet and found the air quite sweet and fresh without.
Ten minutes later a runner arrived with the message "All
clear". It either had been a false alarm or gas had been
sent over some distance away.

The first attack using poisonous gas in the First World War came when the Germans released 150 tons of chlorine gas on 22 April 1915, at the beginning of the Second Battle of Ypres. It was aimed at the French and Algerian troops who were manning a four-mile length of trench protecting the city of Ypres. From then on, other gases were used regularly along the front line, such as mustard gas and phosgene, mostly by the Germans, but also by the French and British. Gas drill and protective equipment became an essential part of manning the trenches.[5]

Wiring party

The next night I was sent up to the front line in charge
of a wiring party consisting of half a dozen men.
  I preferred this job to that of carrying party. The
labour involved in progressing along tortuous narrow
trenches, heavily laden was considerable.[6]
  Out in front of our trench, movement was fairly free,
and as the spot we were wiring was a considerable distance
from the enemy, [it] was fairly safe. We took out our iron
screw stakes and placing them in position, soon were
running out drums of barbed wire to connect them up.
Owing to being on the outward bend of a salient the front
line trenches some 500 yards away were almost behind us.
The consequence was that when Verey lights went up in
that sector we were rather afraid of being silhouetted
against them. Added to this was the fact that as this

sector to our left rear was held by French troops, the star shells were French ones, which, being attached to a parachute hovered much longer in the air than ours did. We did not stop work however on their account. We really spent quite a peaceful time out there wiring, only having to throw ourselves down several times when a German m[achine] g[un] spat in our direction. After a couple of hours work, we went back to our dugouts, being excused further duty for the night.[7]

Sniping

For some weeks now I had been awaiting a summons to join the sniping section of the battalion. I was friendly with several members of it and had been promised a place in it as soon as there was a vacancy. On the last day of our stay in this post the SM came up to see me and tell me that I was to report to Mr Lewis, the Sniping Officer that evening. He was loth for me to go and said as much.

The company was gradually losing, through casualties and other things, the majority of its experienced men, whose places were being taken by fresh drafts from home, largely composed of Derby recruits.[8] There was no doubt about it that these men who had practically been forced into the army, were not as good as those who had fairly volunteered.

That evening I said goodbye to my platoon, who were again going into the front line, and made my way across Blighty Bridge to one of the dugouts clustered round BHQ [Battalion Headquarters]. I here reported to the Corp[ora]l in charge and was introduced into the dugout which was crowded with 15 Snipers.

I had not been there more than an hour or so when the Corpl. came in with a message that I was to report to Mr Lewis and to act as his runner. There was great outcry at this, and I was looked on as a lucky dog for getting a cushy job so soon.

The British Army were slow to adapt and adopt sniping as part of their approach to defeating the enemy, and, at this time they were only just beginning to develop it fully. Rather, their military machine had been focused on moving forward in a clear, 'clean' line towards its foe. During the opening months of the conflict, sniping was completely one-sided. In the early months of the war, the British were losing men at an alarming rate to skilled German snipers. In fact, eighteen men were lost in one battalion in one day.[9] The Allies were mystified. They did not at first recognize such enemy action, accusing 'stray bullets' of killing their men, rather than realizing the impact of hidden, skilled marksmen using high-performance weapons.[10]

From the beginning of the war, German civilians were required to hand in any hunting rifles they may have had, to the military. Not to do so was unlawful. Many of their young men had grown up soaked in the culture of the *Jäger*, or hunter. A knowledge of firearms was commonplace, along with the need for patience, observation and the ability to stalk their prey. Trained in the wild woodlands of their country, they were already skilled marksmen.[11]

The Allies eventually came to realize some response was needed, although the number of men selected for sniping across the British Expeditionary Force would depend on the attitude of the lieutenant colonel who commanded the battalion. Details of the number of snipers and their composition were rarely recorded.[12]

The 38th Divisional Sniping Company

The Snipers in the whole Division i.e. 16 from each battalion had just been formed into a separate unit called the 38th Divisional Sniping Co[mpan]y composed of between 200 and 250 men. Half the company would be in the line manning Observation and Sniping posts while the other half were in camp undergoing training. There was a change about every 10 days.
 At this time, the organisation of the company was in its initial stages and although the officers were quartered together in dugouts 200 metres south of Bridge 4, the sections themselves were widely scattered around wherever accommodation could be found for them. As Mr Lewis was some 2 kilometres away from his section, he wanted a runner to not only accompany him up the line on his frequent visits but to carry messages to the section when required.

This reorganization of the snipers was a deliberate change in policy resulting from consideration of German sniping methods. Previously the British snipers would come and go with their battalions to which they were attached, and it would take time for them to get to know the terrain. German snipers would stay in the same place for months, becoming familiar with every inch of the landscape. In the same way, by keeping their snipers attached, in this case to the 38th Divisional Headquarters, they would also stay in the same place, irrespective of the coming and going of the different brigades, helping to make them more efficient in their role [13].

I reported to 2nd Lt Lewis and was told to share his servant's dugout. This dugout was built, as were nearly all along this bank of the canal, of sections of thick, black, corrugated steel … bolted together to form a tunnel shaped abode. The back was built into the canal bank, the front was filled up with sandbags leaving a doorway in the middle, over which a piece of sacking could be hung. The top was covered with sandbags and earth to the depth of 6ft or so and was light shell proof. The floor being made of tongued and grooved wood the inside was quite dry and comfortable. In this, the first of its kind I had occupied, there were two beds made of wire netting nailed over a framework of wood.

A change in circumstances

I had entered upon quite a different life than I had been used to for the last 9 months. The drudgery and the discomfort of the ordinary infantryman's life were considerably ameliorated. I found that the work was interesting, easier and above all more comfortable. One great boon was that mainly we were daylight soldiers, sniping in the dark being impossible of course, and the hours of darkness could be spent asleep in our, for the most part, comfortable dugouts.

I found that Mr Lewis's batman Owen was a proper London Welshman. He had been born in London, his speech was cockney, but his parents were Welsh, and he looked thoroughly Welsh himself with his dark eyes and hair. A good deal of my time during the next ten days, which was the period my job of runner lasted, was spent in his company, and in that of another officer's batman named Davies who was a Welshman straight from his native hills.

The routine

The next day was typical of the following 9. I was ordered to hold myself in readiness to accompany Mr Lewis up the line at daybreak. Owen received orders to call his boss at 5 o'clock and we arranged for the sentry whose beat lay along the duckboard track outside, to call us. Owen said to me "For the love of Mike wake me up in the morning or I will get the sack. I sleep like the dead and I give you leave to shake, punch, half throttle me, do anything you like so long as you wake me up in time to call Lewis." I duly promised little knowing what that promise meant.

The next morning, I was awakened by someone drawing aside our curtain door and shouting out "Mac! Owen! It's 5 o'clock." I answered "alright" and getting up lit a candle. Owen was still sound asleep. I went over to him and shouted "Owen, get up you lazy devil" No answer. I put my lips to his ear and shouted again, still no response. I pulled him half off his bed, pinched him, punched him, shoved him back again and still he lay like a log. I have never met anyone like it before or since. A 5.9 bursting outside our dugout would not have roused him. At last, in desperation, I went outside and filled my mess tin with water out of the stream and trickled the water over his face and neck. He showed some faint signs of waking. I again shouted in his ear, a bellow which ought to have broken his eardrum. He opened his eyes and said "Alright, no need to shout. I'm not deaf." "Not deaf" I said "glad to hear it. I thought you were dead."

He lay there blinking for several minutes more until, seeing that he was going to drop off again I made for my mess tin and threatened him with some more water. He then got up and immediately began to grumble at me. "You needn't have half drowned me, my shirt's all wet." There was gratitude at all the trouble I had gone to. He went out to call Lt Lewis and I proceeded to put on my boots, puttees and equipment. I then went across the single plank that bridged the stream to the Officer's Cooking Galley which was the other side and begged a cup of "gun fire" knowing well that the cooks would be making some for the officers. Ten minutes later Owen came back laughing and quite his usual cheerful self. "Lewis is a lad. He's just put half a bottle of whisky in his tea and will be feeling like going over the top when you get into the trenches." I thanked him for the information but pointed out that if Lewis went over the top, I as his faithful runner would have to go over the top also, and I had had no whisky in my tea. Soon after Lewis put his head in the door "McCwae, are you weddy?" I jumped up and went out to him.

Lewis

At the age of 16, in 1910, Harold Lewis had left his family and a strictly religious way of life in London, to travel to Australia. After spending four years carrying his swag, finding work wherever he could, 'jackerooing' on sheep farms, well-sinking and laying sleepers for railways, he realized that he would not be able to make a fortune as easily as he had hoped. His return to England coincided with the start of the war, arriving back in London in December 1914. He had been at sea for five months, working as a coal trimmer to earn his passage. Leaving Townsville, Australia in July, the first boat he worked on was the SS *Bochum*, a German ship, which was heading for Hamburg. War broke out as they were passing the East Indies, and the ship was then required to change course to join the German Pacific Fleet. For a time, Lewis was therefore the only British person on a ship 'dodging British and Allied warships through the Pacific Islands'. Finally, he was able to secure a working passage on a 'miserable meat packet from Hong Kong to Liverpool'.[14]

His father met him at the station in London, clutching a borrowed overcoat, anticipating this might bring welcome warmth for his son, dressed as he was in his flimsy clothes. On arriving home Harold found himself feeling 'too big and too clumsy …[and] needing far too much to eat'. To him everywhere seemed tiny and overcluttered after his time in the outback.[15]

He signed up at a nearby recruiting office and was initially sent to work in a territorial artillery unit on the Essex marches. The aim was to defend London from Zeppelin attack. Yet he found their artillery did not have the range to reach the required altitude to inflict any damage to the enemy. This did not fit at all into his expectation of 'a thrilling adventure', and when the men were ordered one day to construct gravel paths adorned with perhaps a few flowerbeds, he found he was unable to obey.[16]

Fortunately, his Welsh father managed to procure him a commission in the 15 RWF. After his recent antipodean lifestyle, he found joining the officers' mess at Wrexham depot an ordeal: 'every meal, every parade, every appearance in the adjutant's office was performed in a new and more rigid type of discipline'. He was assigned a batman who brought morning tea, brushed his uniform and checked all was correct. Once established on the Western Front, owing to the rifle practice he had gained from his east-of-England posting, he was made a sniping officer.[17]

```
Lewis was a tall young man of about 25 years of age.
His hair was fair, almost ginger, and inclined to curl,
his eyes a light blue. He suffered from an inability to
sound his "r's". He was a good sort and although we all
at times laughed and mimicked him, we all liked him. This
morning he started off at a good round pace along the
trench boards, a pace not only round but slightly zigzag.
My legs being much shorter than his I had almost to run
after him. For my consolation I had whiffs of the whisky
he had been drinking wafted back to me. As we neared the
front line his speed slackened, and he walked straight.
His friskiness occasioned by the whisky taken on an empty
stomach was at an end.
  Soberly he visited the 6 sniping posts held by his section,
receiving reports from the men in them. Occasionally he
would tell one of the inmates to come out and he himself
would go in behind the curtain and have a look through
the telescope.
  At one post we reached he drew aside the curtain, which
was used to prevent the light throwing the loophole into
relief, and thus rendering it visible to the Bosch sniper.
A voice from within called "Who the hell's that moving the
b--- curtain? Put it down" It was Sammy Shields who was
sitting with his eye glued to a telescope. He apologised
when he saw who it was.
```

The written report

When he had visited all the posts, we returned to HQ and breakfasted. I then cadged a cigarette tin of hot water from the cooks and shaved, afterwards washing in a bowl of clean water obtained from the stream. The rest of the morning I spent sleeping. In the afternoon I was sent up to the front with a message to Corp[ora]l---. On my return I had ample time to write some letters before being sent on my last journey to collect the Snipers' reports. A written report concerning what had taken place during the day was written by the Snipers in each post and handed to the Corporal upon their return, just after dark, to their dugout. It was almost dark when I started out. I passed the large square-built dugout of the Field Dressing Station, with its red cross above the door. Next to it were many more big dugouts in which were housed the many officers attached to Brigade HQ. The glimpses I had of their candle-lit interiors through the narrow doorway, showed me comfortable little rooms complete with camp bedstead, tables and sometimes chairs. I thought that it must be good to be an officer attached to [the] brigade. Runners with red bands on their wrist, brigade clerks … with typewritten sheets in their hands, mess waiters carrying food through the footway beside the dugouts.

As the war progressed and the use of snipers became more commonplace, the value of the snipers' reports of enemy movements was realized. This is reflected in the eventual change of title of those commanding them, from 'Sniping Officer' to 'Intelligence Officer', as their important role in correctly interpreting the men's observations and sending clear accounts to Intelligence Headquarters was recognized.

Sniper conversation

Further on the dugouts became lower, meaner and more scattered. Here was situated a battalion HQ. There was the same briskness, but the footway was narrower and more congested, there was the usual early evening traffic of carrying and ration parties who had come down from the trenches. I then passed the dugouts where the company in support were billeted and then came to the Snipers' dugout.

I had to wait in here until two more men came back from the furthest post, and while I was waiting listened to the Snipers recounting their experiences of the day. "There he was," I heard Sammy Shields say "the big square headed b---, looking over the top. I could see the gold stoppin' in his pianner keys [piano keys, or teeth] as plain as I see this tin of Machonochie (he was eating his supper). Must have been a 'Proosion' [Prussian] officer. I got the pointer of my telescopic sight [lined up] (under his chin) and fired. Blimey, I saw the hole in for'ead before he fell. Several minutes after, Bill here saw through his telescope, the handles of the German stretcher moving along the top of the trench".

I arrived back at HQ and delivered the reports to Mr Lewis. The officers had just finished dinner. I was messing in with the officers' servants and cooks and we had our dinner afterwards. While I was eating mine Davies returned from a visit to a pal of his who was in the Pioneers battalion[18] who were quartered also on the canal back a kilometre south. He was boisterously drunk and his antics … kept us in fits of laughter. In his absence Owen had had to act as Mess waiter and grumbled at him. "Nice thing this is, you going away and having a good time and coming back drunk while I do your beastly work."

"All right, all right Owen bacho, I'm very sorry, I'll go and apologise to officers for being late." He would have done so had not Owen held him back saying "If your boss sees you in this state, you'll get the sack. Where are your teeth?" Davies had an upper set of false ones.

"Teeth, he-he, I lost them, dropped them in the stream, must find them or I'll get the sack."

With this he staggered on to the single plank bridge which led across the stream to the cook's kitchen and remained, balancing himself precariously over the water, cackling to himself and repeating his last sentence, while he lit matches and pretended to look for the teeth. Owen pulled him back to safety and in …[the] struggle he had with him, found his teeth in his pocket, where he had evidently put them for safety. We then put him to bed and Owen had to look after his boss for him, making some excuse about Davies not being well.

Harold Lewis, in his autobiography *Bluey*, mentions his battalion of the 15th (1st London) Royal Welsh Fusiliers. He speaks of his brave platoon sergeant and of his group affectionately: 'We were a happy battalion, though a queer mixture, consisting of Londoners, who had, or were nominally supposed to have Welsh blood, and genuine Welsh from North Wales, gamekeepers and poachers among them. The gamekeepers became sergeants and the poachers first-class snipers and daredevils.'[19]

William captures this mix well in his depiction of Owen and Davies as, respectively, the London Welshman, and the Welshman straight from the hills.

Chapter 10

Sniping School and Observation

'If you who read this know a man who served his year or two in the sniping section of his battalion, you know one whom it is well that you should honour.'[1]

Sniping never sat comfortably with much of the British Army, even up to the end of the war. As mentioned in the previous chapter, how little this type of warfare was established and accepted by the Allies is illustrated by how few medals and awards were received. Only one Victoria Cross was ever awarded to a British sniper in the First World War, to Private Thomas Barrett, of the South Staffordshire Regiment, for hunting down the German snipers who were holding up an advance in 1917.[2] In contrast German snipers were celebrated and honoured, with as many as 15,000 of them being awarded the Iron Cross.[3]

To be invisible was clearly the way a sniper worked. Then again, it could be argued that British snipers were treated this way by their own army. Only other snipers knew and understood what was actually required of them and what it meant to fulfil their role. The infantry found them mysterious and were unsettled by them. They felt that they were more at risk of being killed themselves as a result of the way the snipers worked, and that to kill the enemy by those means could be seen more as an act of murder.[4]

A Hampshire County fast bowler, with experience in big-game hunting, became the key protagonist with the necessary attributes to recognize and develop sniping in the British Army, although to begin with progress was slow. First arriving on the Western Front in March 1915, Captain (later Major) Vernon Hesketh-Prichard was appalled to see what impact the German snipers were having on the Allied troops. Aside from the casualties, Hesketh-Prichard also realized the negative impact such onslaught was having on morale in the trenches.[5]

To begin with, as he travelled along the front line demonstrating his skills, it seems he was single-handedly making the Germans more cautious in their sniping, although there were many notable others who were interested in promoting this approach, such as Major F. M. Crum, 2nd Battalion, King's Royal Rifle Corps. In fact, Pegler points out that the history of sniping in the British Army in its formative years of 1914/15 was mainly down to the effort of individuals.[6] At a time when there were only eight telescopic sighted rifles available to each battalion, which were usually given to the signallers, many officers brought their own rifles, telescopic sights and other necessary equipment such as telescopes and periscopes, to the Western Front [7].

Conversely, not only did the Germans have a good supply of telescopic sights, estimated in number to be 20,000 as early as the end of 1914, but also their snipers were trained in their use.[8]

Hesketh-Prichard worked hard to convince senior officers of the value of his trade. He was lucky that his commander was interested in sniping.[9] The accepted approach for engaging with the enemy at that time was by attacking from the front line, using high explosives and machine guns. In comparison, the "opportunism of sniping" was seen as somewhat underhand.[10]

Hesketh-Prichard also learnt a good deal about enemy methods of sniping by the careful questioning of German prisoners. For example, the loss of so many Allied officers was a result of the enemy being able to pick them out by the cut of their riding breeches.[11]

Finally, Hesketh-Prichard was recruited as a sniping officer for the entire Third Army, although it took some time to become established with staff and the necessary training facilities.[12]

September 1916

[After being] relieved by the other half company [and spending time in] J camp … situated 4 kilo[metre]s NE of Poperinghe, ten days later we went up for our next spell in the trenches. This time the whole ½ company were quartered in dugouts about the spot where only the officers had been before. There was therefore no need for a runner and I was initiated into the duties of a sniper. I was paired with a man named Wilkins. He was evidently the dud of the whole section and was also called "Windy" owing to his liability to get into that state. In the cold, misty light of a September dawn we started out from our dugout.

When we reached Blighty Bridge 4 pairs branched off, crossing it to man posts in the front line. The remaining 4 of us kept straight along the canal bank, which gradually had decreased in height and girth since we had left HQ. It was here little more than 10ft high. At first there were dugouts manned by a supporting co[mpan]y. The last dugouts contained members of a.t.m.b. [artillery trench mortar battalion] who were engaged in building a gun emplacement for the heavy trench mortar, which fired huge shells. These shells were called "Flying Pigs" on account of their fat bulgy shape. We learnt that it was to take some 12 months to complete this emplacement which was mainly constructed of reinforced concrete. The trench board path we had followed to this spot here terminated, and we entered a ct [communication trench] which zigzagged on for two hundred yards or so. We then crossed [a] footbridge over a stream which had at one time entered or left the canal at this spot and reached the front line which here of course was on the canal bank. There was only 1 section of men of our battalion posted here which was the extreme left flank of the British Army. Next to us there came a Division of so called French Territorials, old men of 45 or over, who were given a cushy part of the line to hold. On the other side of these French troops were the Belgians.

A sniper's post

The post we had to man had been constructed by cutting 4ft off the top of the parapet of the trench away to a depth of 3ft or so leaving the outer, or German side of the parapet intact. Corrugated iron was placed over the cavity so formed to make the roof, and a curtain was hung at the back. At the front end of the post two snipers' loopholes had been placed, in the outer shell of the parapet. The original parapet being left as far as was possible, or at any rate replaced if it was displaced. These snipers' loopholes were made of bullet proof iron and were about 18inches long by 1ft high. In the centre was the loophole either shaped like a keyhole or thus [fingernail sketch inserted in script]. This loophole could be closed with an iron shutter. These posts were always made during the hours of darkness and the care and skill used in making them invisible from the eyes of German snipers was considerable. We knew well in what detail the enemy parapet stood out when viewed through our telescopes and knew what to expect if the German snipers discovered our loopholes. The actual holes through the outer edge of the parapet were usually made by pushing a bayonet through the loophole from the inside of the post and twirling it about. The hole was then enlarged, working from the outside and suitably camouflaged. A favourite device, if the outside of the parapet was earth, was to place a macho[nochie] ration or bully beef tin in position over the hole as if it had been thrown out of the trench, the bottom of the tin being first removed and the jagged top of the tin only open far enough to enable a clear view to be obtained through the loophole. If the outside of the parapet was of sandbags the plates were disguised by placing a little earth in some sandbags and rolling or cutting off the surplus material and putting them in front to resemble the ends of the full sandbags either side. Cleverly leaving a little space in between two of them, which space, while affording a view through the loophole, looked just like an ill placed sandbag when viewed from no man's land. Other numerous and equally effective devices were used. It all depended on the locality and the means which were to hand. One very ingenious one was made by cutting the heel out of an old German boot and placing it over the loophole with the uppers towards the enemy.

Initially the Germans were very well supplied with loopholes. The British, in response, attempted to requisition suitable metal from old boiler plates in rubbish dumps, although they were not thick enough to resist enemy bullets.[13] By the time William was a sniper, loophole plates had much improved thanks to Hesketh-Prichard and his colleagues.

Other factors also influenced the balance of advantage in this deadly contest. The building of German trenches was always carefully considered, strategically placed, with a permanency in mind that the Allies did not share. The Germans' understanding was that they would not relinquish land that they now occupied. Despite this careful construction, the top of their trenches appeared somewhat haphazard and untidy, with colour being used to further break up the appearance.

This was intentional, in order to hide the snipers' loopholes through which they shot. Conversely the British trenches were shallow and poorly built, but with a neat array of sandbags placed along the top. An 'ill-placed sandbag' was anathema to some in the British Army. Difficult then, to hide any change in such order with a metal plate or protruding gun, although fluttering rags on wires were sometimes used to disturb the view.[14]

As William describes, the snipers later became far more inventive in hiding their loopholes from the enemy.

Telescope and rifle

Inside our post we lay sprawling on our stomachs side by side. I had the left hand loophole and placed my telescope carefully in position wrapping the end in a piece of sandbag to break up its regular outline. Wilkins sprawled on my right. He had a telescopic rifle. It was a rifle like the … MV111 but as well as the usual sights, had fittings on the side of the barrel to which could be affixed a small telescope. When in the firing position one had to incline one's head further over the butt than for the ordinary sights and look through the eyepiece of the telescope.
Every detail of the field of view stood out very clearly. In the centre of the object glass was a horizontal line, which was just bisected by the tip of a vertical pointer, which was used to get correct aim. These rifles were really wonderfully adjusted and made. It was nothing to see the actual hole made by the bullet in the victim. Their one drawback was that they could not be made or adjusted to be accurate at more than 200 or 300yds

The main rifle used by the British and Commonwealth armies, including the snipers, was the Lee–Enfield, with various adaptations, particularly the SMLE, the Short Magazine Lee–Enfield. The Mark III version was most commonly used in the First World War. Very few were initially available with added telescopic sights. The quartermasters responsible for their distribution did not understand their significance, and they were often given out to anyone who required an ordinary rifle. Thus, Hesketh-Prichard was to discover, many of the men who had ownership of these carefully crafted weapons had no idea how to use them. Also, many of the telescopic sights had not been set properly, and it was to become a key task for sniping officers such as Second Lieutenant Lewis to check and re-align them correctly.[15]

Although the telescopic sights enhanced the accuracy of the shot, one of the greatest difficulties was that these sights were set on the left-hand side of the rifle, rather than on the top as described above by William. This made it impossible to see through the loophole with the telescope, when the muzzle was in position. It was sadly impossible for the design to be altered in their manufacture using the government pattern, so this limitation continued to hinder the snipers throughout the war.[16]

Observing

```
I was the observer. Wilkins the Sniper. If I saw a German
it was my duty to tell Wilkins when he would open the
shutter of his loophole and getting his rifle into position
[and] take a shot at him.
    We took it in turns to be observer as looking for any
period through a telescope was tiring. I soon learnt
however to use the telescope with both eyes open, using
each alternately, and found it far less tiring than if
I had had to keep one eye screwed up. The view from our
loophole was very restricted. We saw perhaps 50yds or so
of the German parapet, which was on the opposite bank of
the Yser [canal] not more than 70yds distant. It looked
something like a heap of rubbish. Tins, weather beaten
pieces of sandbag, old planks of wood and pieces of shell-
torn corrugated iron lay strewn all about. We saw nothing
all day but the smoke of a fire.
```

Hesketh-Prichard found that snipers working in pairs in this way quickly gained an advantage over their German counterparts.[17] Their logbook notes became a useful source of intelligence. If a line was well covered, very little could happen without it being recorded. This helped the success of the discipline grow very rapidly. As William mentions, the men would swap roles every twenty minutes in order to rest the observer's eyes. This technique of sniper pairs was found to be so effective it is still used by the British Army today.

The French next door

At midday Wilkins disappeared for a few minutes. He returned with a half pint of wine which he had obtained from a Froggy [soldier] in exchange for a tin of bully beef. Evidently the French had a daily ration of wine.

Upon his return I went to see the Froggies. I found first a single sentry who was pacing up and down a short piece of trench, his rifle with, what seemed to me a very long bayonet slung on his shoulder. He looked quite an old man and was no doubt in the neighbourhood of 50yrs [of age]. I said "Bonjour,M'siur" He put his finger up and said "Hist!" and pointed significantly in the direction of the enemy. A little further on was a group of several more old men in their faded, shabby blue uniforms, who were conversing in whispers. They seemed quite terrified at their noisy British neighbours in the adjoining post who carried on talking, and even singing at times in the usual manner. As far as I could see, there were no periscopes being used and no sort of watch being kept on the Germans. I could imagine the surprise on the old sentry's face if a party of raiding Germans had suddenly jumped into the trench.

An appraisal of the trench mortar

In the afternoon we were the victims of a tm [trench mortar] bombardment. Wilkins and I should have stopped in our post, but at the first awe inspiring detonation Wilkins jumped for the trench and I followed suit. Jerry was sending over t m at the rate of one every minute or so and they were falling behind us to our right and left.

There is something about trench mortar shells which made them far worse to put up with, than ordinary shells from guns. I always put down the greater fear to the fact that we could see the shells and watch their course, whereas the shells from guns could rarely be seen in flight, and (occasionally in certain positions in relation to the fall of the shell) a howitzer shell could be seen for a fleeting instant just before it struck the ground. As a matter of fact the t m shell was not nearly so dangerous as its brother. For one thing the direction of its flight, and possible fall could usually be observed in time to decamp with all speed from that fatal spot. For another, as it was mainly HE [high explosive]; the burst of which occurred in an upward direction, the actual danger to persons in the vicinity was less than from a shrapnel shell burst which spread more.

I shall never forget the scene that followed. Eight or so Frenchmen and a doz[en] British soldiers crouched, intermingled in the trench, all with white, expectant faces strained upwards. Suddenly we would hear the expected plop of the tm being fired from its mortar and we would sweep the sky with agonised eyes until we could discern a moving black spot. With one accord blue and khaki clad soldiers then would make a helter-skelter rush along the trench away from the likely site of the explosion, and once more crouching, would watch the black shell drop from a great height with seeming ever increasing velocity, and strike the ground with a deafening crash which was followed immediately by the rise of a column of earth and debris quite 30ft high.

We would again wait, and perhaps this time see the black speck rising swiftly from the German lines, mounting up and up and getting smaller and smaller until the force of gravity, overcoming the force of the gun discharge, it would slowly curve round and fall swiftly to earth again several hundred yards to our left. We would then see the column of debris and feel the ground shake under our feet, but it would be a second or two later before we heard the explosion.

The next shell would send us hastening back in a disordered mob to our original position. The bombardment lasted half an hour. Most of the shells found their billet in the open ground to the rear of the trench, and we only got pieces of mud, falling on us, or occasionally a heavy piece of metal would fall near us. The reply of our own tm batteries was very feeble. A few medium ones, called "toffee apples" owing to their likeness to that sweetmeat on a stick only were sent over.

Observation post repairs and a new sniping partner

As soon as it was dark enough Wilkins and I, acting on the instructions of Mr Lewis who had visited us in the morning, jumped on the top of the trench and set to work

Sniping School and Observation 151

to improve the field of view from our loophole which was rather restricted. This took us only a few minutes and we were soon on our way back to our dugout, for a meal and a sleep.

The next day I was sent up to the line with a man named Walker, nicknamed "Johnny". He was a fair-haired, blue eyed youth, the same age as myself. Before the war he had been [an] office boy in a Solicitor's office. According to his own account his solicitor had nearly shut down his business upon losing so valuable a clerk. He had very much the gift of the gab. Could have talked the hind legs off a donkey. Should any argument come up for discussion amongst the rest of us, he would join in and finally monopolise the stage whether he knew anything about the subject or not. In short, he was a bore of the 1st water. Being very thick skinned it was practically impossible to put the extinguisher on him. The rude remarks and invective hurled at him at times were quite ... [forthright]. His conceit was superb. He was a nice fellow however, and in spite of his unending talk very companionable. For the next two months we spent a great deal of time together.

We manned the post, next to the one I had been in the day before and was situated as per attached sketch [see plate 11].

The French and the Germans

The CT which began at the Flying Pig tm emp[lacement] and ran along the west side of the canal bank, had several saps leading from it to the right, which all ended in small posts which were on the extreme eastern edge of the bank. These posts were only occupied at night. Our sniping post was built into the end of the last sap of all. The view we had from the single loophole was an interesting one. We could see the parapet of the German f[ront] line proper, situated at the top of the opposite bank. There was also a sap or loop which ran from this main trench down to within 5 yds or so of the water. The view was something like that contained in attached sketch [see plate 11].

The cup shaped hole in this sap, had been at one time used by the Germans to sally out of their trench to obtain water from the canal. This had been quite a facile and safe job while the trenches opposite were being held by the French territorials.

Evidently during that period the combatants had treated each other with a great deal of laissez-faire. In any case the old Frenchmen, too scared to talk aloud or to even look over the top, would certainly not [have] had the nerve to shoot anyone. The first morning that these posts were manned by our snipers, two German essaying to fetch water after it was light were killed.

'Think you got the blighter'

Just to the left of this gap there was a sentry post. We could not only see the small mirror stuck on the end of a stick which was embedded in the parados but could see the reflection of the German sentry therein. It was most uncanny to watch him through our telescope. We could see him moving his hands about and sometimes eating, sometimes talking. Whenever he glanced up into his periscope or mirror, we saw as if in a frame the reflection of the upper portion of his face, and the front band of his cap complete with little coloured buttons. His eyes seemed as if they were looking directly at us down the butt end of the telescope. We were, however, quite invisible to him, and could watch him without apprehension.

For long periods we would watch the gap, as at infrequent intervals we could plainly see through the brushwood, men passing along the trench, sometimes singly and sometimes in small parties. Unfortunately, at least from our point of view, there was only one loophole and by the time we had removed the telescope and put in the rifle our quarry had disappeared. We were also up against a difficulty caused by the fact that the gap being too far to the left of our field of view for us to use the telescopic sight.

During one of my turns at observation I plainly saw the outline of a portly German standing behind the brushwood gazing through at our trenches. After this I got out of the post, and sticking a quantity of grass in my cap and tying some over the muzzle end of my rifle (it was one of the kind with ear flaps), I slowly and carefully crawled up the bank by the side of the post. The bank was covered in long grass, with here and there the dark splintered stump of a tree. When I reached the top I slowly, very slowly raised my head until I could get a view of the gap, and again, very slowly pushed forward my rifle until I was in a comfortable firing position. I knew how each blade of grass would stand out on the object glass of a telescope, if one was being used on the opposite side of the canal, and had to be very careful and slow in my movements. It was a very great strain, lying thus with eye glued to the telescopic sight and with finger on the trigger. The chance of another German standing for some seconds in the gap, like the last was remote, and I intended having a shot at one of the swiftly passing figures which appeared at intervals. I had to come down after ten minutes in this position as my arms were aching terribly holding the rifle rigidly in position. After a little rest I carefully regained my position and this time my patience was rewarded. Three things happened simultaneously. There was a muffled exclamation from Johnny in the post, I saw a fleeting shadow, and in the same instant pulled the trigger. Too late I believe, and in any case too high. This was the first time I had ever fired directly at a German, and I am thankful to think that I almost certainly missed. I hastily regained the trench thinking that possibly my position on the bank would be discovered after the shot. Johnny said "Think you got the Blighter."

"I'm afraid I was too late," I replied. "A pity too because I fired an armour piercing bullet at him." We were served out with these bullets really to use them against the enemy sniper behind his ordinary bullet proof shield or loophole, but we generally liked to use them against ordinary victims and boast after that we had put an "armour piercing" through him.

"At any rate," said Johnny, "we'll put it down on the report as a doubtful victim, you might have winged him."

Looking through the telescope later I could see the hole made by my bullet in the piece of wood to which was fastened the brushwood hurdles.

During the afternoon we saw no more upright figures passing the gap, but occasionally we would see a rounded hump moving swiftly passed the very bottom of the gap, evidently brother bosche was keeping his head very low and only exposing a less vulnerable part of his anatomy to a sniper's bullet.

Camouflage

As William mentions camouflage such as leaves and foliage was often used by the snipers in order to blend in with the background. The ghillies of the Highlands wore camouflage suits, originally used in combat by the Lovat Scouts during the Boer War.

Harold Lewis, William's sniping officer, refers to a time he was able to secure some camouflage smocks for his men when he was sent on a sniping course near Le Touguet.[18] Major Crum taught his snipers to make their own camouflage with whatever they could find, even if it was just an empty sandbag pulled over their heads with holes for their eyes.[19]

A small Special Works Park section of the Royal Engineers developed camouflage not only for individuals, but also cloth screens to place along the side of the road, and to cover military dumps. French women with experience in making scenery for theatre productions, were employed to help increase the supply.[20]

Hesketh-Prichard also refers to a visit he made to a French camouflage works in Amiens where he found they had made papier mâché heads and shoulders of British soldiers. These were used to draw fire, thus making it possible to work out the direction and location of the enemy sniper. These dummy heads would be raised above the level of the trench using grooved sticks or by attaching them to periscopes.[21]

A great deal of care was taken to ensure that the observing snipers were hidden, and indeed there were certain British observation posts from which no shot was ever allowed to be fired lest the post should be betrayed, thus losing a valuable source of intelligence.[22]

Poperinge

```
The next few days were spent in one or the other of these
posts and at the end of our spell we were relieved by
the other ½ company and this time moved back to H camp.
By this time I had got to know the other members of the
section well. We had a hut to ourselves. The hours spent
on parade were few. We had a football and were able to
play fairly often. Sometimes, obtaining passes from the
CO we would walk the 5 kilo[metre]s into Poperinghe. It
was possible in an estaminet there to obtain some very
nice food. Egg on chipped potatoes was the favourite.
```

This was the first time I had tasted this dish which I believe was unknown in England before the war and must have been introduced into that country by Tommy.

Boxing

In the evening Johnny and I usually went up to the YMCA hut which was a few hundred yards away on the Pop[eringue]. Elverdinghe Rd and wrote letters, supping sumptiously on sweet biscuits and cocoa. Some evenings however Cpl ---- would fetch the boxing gloves from the QMS [Quarter Master Stores] and we would have friendly bouts in candlelight in the hut. Titch, a young London street arab [urchin] and myself were often matched, being the two smallest.

As we, stripped to the waist, wheeled and dodged round each other, clinching often and raining blows on the empty air, there would be shouts of encouragement and much laughter. Evidently we were the star turn, "Go it Titch." "Go it Mac." "Look at that beautiful upper cut." "Mind that candle, they'll be into it in a minute." "Keep them off that equipment." We sometimes managed to hit each other and then the audience howled with glee. Time being called we would return to our corners and receive exaggerated attention, including towel flapping from our seconds. For several weeks neither of us was free from one or two black eyes.

Poperinge was important for the Allies situated on this part of the Western Front. It was the rail hub bringing men, horses, equipment, munitions and much else to supply the war effort on the Ypres Salient. The Young Men's Christian Association (YMCA) that William mentions was located right by the railway station. During the war this organization was present across the Western Front to support the soldiers when away from the front line, by providing them with a place where they could relax in comfort. It catered for soldiers of all religions who were able to come to the YMCA canteens for free tea and coffee, and cheap cake and chocolate. Writing paper was provided, and many men would go there to write letters home. It was staffed by volunteers, 40 per cent of whom were women, and often clergy, who were exempt from service. Many recreational activities were organized for the men, including boxing.[23]

Another establishment in Poperinge famous for the key role it played in creating a safe space to relax and unwind during the war, was Talbot House. Still open today, as a place to stay and a museum, it became well known for being somewhere where 'rank was left at the front door'. An army chaplain, the Reverend Philip 'Tubby' Clayton recognized the need for such a haven and rented the empty property in 1915 from a wealthy brewer, Monsieur Coevoet Camerlynck. Thousands of men visited during the remaining three years of war, grateful for its warm welcome and peaceful garden. A chapel located in the roof space, held many religious services, especially in advance of the key battles fought in that area.[24]

Sniping school

Hesketh-Prichard had eventually been successful in his endeavour to set up and establish sniping schools, initially training officers who could then train the men, and then to men of all ranks across the British Army. The curriculum he developed was to become the foundation for all such training across the world.[25]

Two men, one my grandfather, were picked to attend a course at one of these sniping schools in November 1916, on the Mont des Cats.

```
Johnny and I were sent for a 10 day Sniping Course to the
2nd Army Sniping School on the Mont des Cattes. Mr Lewis
explained to us that as our Division Sniping Company was
in the way of an experiment the CO was anxious that Army
HQ should have a good impression of the Company's skills
etc: and for that purpose Johnny and I, as we were amongst
the better educated in the company had been picked to go.
We travelled to Mont des Cattes by train from Poperinghe
one Saturday. It was only some 10 kilometres distant.
```

Mont des Cats, a small but prominent elevation topped with a monastery, stands out proudly, rising from its flat surroundings. F. M. Crum describes the landscape he saw from the top of this hill when he visited in October 1917, thus giving some idea of how it was when William was there a year earlier: 'away below are Poperinghe, Ypres, Messines, the whole salient spread out like a map; a band is playing popular tunes to some tired Battalion resting in billets, where all are rejoicing at the return of the sun after days of dreadful rain and mud, and far away beyond, the guns are booming.'²⁶

Arriving at the School of Sniping about midday we found that we were the first arrivals for the new course which was to start the following Monday. During the remainder of Saturday and all Sunday men from all the infantry units in the 2nd Army arrived in twos or threes. We were billeted in a huge dark barn. Even at midday it was only twilight inside. Three blankets were supplied to each of us, and we were glad of them as it was November and accordingly cold. My blankets were infested with huge brown fleas and I had a rare job getting rid of them. Lice we had always with us, but it was not often that we had the more active parasite to deal with.

We had our meals in the lecture hall, a roughly built wooden hut.

We had lectures and demonstrations illustrative of sniping and observation. We also spent a considerable time at the firing range which was situated on the side of the Mont des Cattes. In the firing courses I had the honour of obtaining the highest aggregate score amongst the men with ordinary open sights. Considering that the participants were sharpshooters from many regiments and included in their number Canadians and Australians I felt considerably bucked at my success. Of course, several men who were in possession of telescopic sighted rifles had equalled or passed my total.

Hesketh-Prichard recognized how worn out the men arriving at the schools were, and how too, they were in need of a clear mental challenge. He decided that during the training there was no need to have time taken up with drill and discipline. He instigated games such as football and cricket, and even some close combat activities such as ju-jitsu, a Japanese combat sport, to help men work off tension.²⁷ All the training was done in competition with each other in different groups. As well as working on their shooting skills, they also focused on map-reading, the use of prismatic compasses and intelligence work. They were given lectures on aeroplane photos, providing the men with a practical knowledge of what trenches looked like from above.

They were taught the need for very careful observation and how vital it was for them to take immediate action when anything unusual was seen. Instructions were given in how to judge distance and being aware of how changes of light and shade might give their location away, even if they had tried to disguise themselves against the background. Men in camouflage intentionally hidden close to the trainees were often not spotted.[28]

Demonstrations also were given of how in dry weather the dust that can be seen round the mouth of a loophole can give the enemy position away, and in cold weather the smoke can hang a little once a shot had been fired.[29] Hesketh-Prichard noted though how thousands of lives were likely saved on each side by the impact of the wind on the accuracy of the shots. It was something that was almost impossible to judge when in a trench.[30]

With his own background, what Hesketh-Prichard realized was that it was men who were experienced in hunting that would make good snipers. There were skilled British men who could fulfil this need, particularly those who hunted for a living, such as the ghillies and glassmen from the highlands of Scotland, skilled in spotting movement from a great distance. In the Boer War, in South Africa, which took place between 1899 and 1902, a small group of such men had formed the Lovat Scouts, named after their clan leader, Lord Lovat. They became known for their ability to observe and track. Although their skills were not utilized at first in the First World War, they were initially sent to Gallipoli as mounted yeomanry; many were later involved in training snipers once such schools became established.[31]

The British Commonwealth was also a source of many hunting men, including members of indigenous tribes. The Canadians particularly excelled, earning themselves a reputation with the Germans of being an unpopular force to be facing in the opposing trench. Men from the outback and the mountains came. Australians and New Zealanders, with their strong allegiance to Britain, returned to fight, even though they had only recently emigrated. Commonwealth battalions always had a larger proportion of good shooting men than the British.[32]

Exercise in observation

Upon our return to the Sniping Co[mpan]y we found that our section were up in the line and were due to be relieved in a day or so. Johnny and I were just congratulating each other on missing a spell in the trenches when we were warned to join the other ½ company who were due to relieve our own. We were attached to the SWB [South Wales Borderers] section who were short of men.

The SWB section were composed mainly of miners from South Wales. They were keen snipers and observers but had not the power of reporting what they saw, and could not read a map.

Our first day up in the line Johnny and I manned a post in the front line. We felt rather sore at being separated from our own section and discussed our wrongs at length. There was little to be seen through the loophole. Only a stretch of the German front line, and a portion of their CT leading back from it. To pass the time I made a little sketch of what we could see, and we wrote out an elaborate report in the best Sniping School.

We had seen one German, the smoke of two trench fires and several shells had come over. We put it all down elaborately including time, map reference etc:

Our report and sketch impressed our new officer so much that the next day we were sent to an Observation post.

The art of reporting what was seen

The next morning, we were aroused an hour before daylight, and after breakfasting we set out guided by Sgt. Norman. We crossed No. 4 bridge and taking the CT leading due east, walked along it for a mile or so. We then took a disused trench which led up and round a small hill. This trench was in places almost waist-deep in water but as we had been provided with rubber waders we did not get wet. It was just getting daylight as we reached the brow of the hill. Here the trench came to an end. The last yard or so had been widened and roofed with corrugated iron. A sacking curtain was hung over the open end. Inside a board had been fixed to form a seat, and two holes had been bored through the outer shell of the trench to take the telescope.

We found the view from this OP very extensive and spent quite an interesting morning picking out the landmarks and generally making ourselves familiar by the aid of a map with the whole panorama. On our left we had a good view of the Pilckem Ridge and the fortification thereon. In front we could see the German front, support and reserve lines, like as many low, irregular ridges of upturned soil. Joining these we could see other trenches, which by their direction and regular zigzag course proclaimed themselves CT's. Several ruined buildings were dotted about the landscape. One notable one was on the top of the ridge immediately in front of us. Part of the walls still remained and the roof had fallen on them covering them with debris. Collections of splintered tree stumps showed where little copses had stood. Further back we could see lines of more or less whole trees which showed us the direction of a possible road. And behind them still further we could see the wooded country as far back and further as Langemark. To the extreme right of our view we could distinguish the Church tower and other buildings of St Jean.

As dusk was falling we shut up our telescopes and went back the way we had come. This time in negotiating the flooded part of the trench I stepped on a floating trench-board and going into the water rather further than usual I took in about half a pint of water through a leak in my gum boots. Although I took it off and drained the water off, I had an uncomfortable walk home.

During the next few days we spent many interested hours in the OP. We saw more Germans than we had ever seen before. An ordinary infantryman, when things are quiet, sees nothing of his enemy for months together. Even when he goes over the top he sees little of them alive. The bodies of men killed by the artillery are plentiful, but the live Germans were usually hidden somewhere in the smoke of battle and were mainly conspicuous by the spitting of their rifles and machine guns.

Sometimes we saw parties of Germans carrying a tank looking object strapped to their backs. These Spartans had been reported before by some overzealous observer as a Flamenwurfer section (Liquid Fire) [flamethrower] but we knew them to be a party carrying liquid refreshment up to their comrades from the kitchens further back.

Sniping schools had in fact a longer title, that of a School of Scouting, Observation and Sniping, and the way in which observation was becoming increasingly recognized and valued is clear in William's account. As Hesketh-Prichard pointed out, all snipers were given the same equipment of telescopes and notebooks, but there was a great difference in how much was observed and thus reported.[33]

He specifically mentions the sniping company that William was in, in his book *Sniping in France*: 'The Welsh were very good indeed, their 38th Division keeping a special sniper's book, and their sniping officer Captain Johnson was very able. I think that in early 1918, the snipers of this Division had accounted for 387 Germans in trench-warfare.'[34]

In addition, Private Edwin Hurley, of the 10th Battalion, Welsh Regiment attached to the 38th Divisional Sniping Company, was awarded a Military Medal for bravery in the field.[35]

Pillboxes

Possibly we were the first or amongst the first to note and report upon the erection of the so-called pill boxes, which were to be such great obstacles to any advance a year afterwards. One day we noticed on the Pilckem ridge a spot where a great deal of fresh earth had been thrown up. The next morning we saw that it had increased. The day after that we noticed a dark, regular, oblong slit near the top of this heap of earth. Twenty-four hours later this slot had practically disappeared, evidently it had been camouflaged. This was reported upon in our daily report as a machine gun emplacement. We never saw anyone at work on it but could day by day see the progress made the previous night. One day when visibility was partic[ularly] good we noticed in the ruined farmhouse at the top of the ridge directly in front of us, a pair of oblong slits, about 6ft or so from the ground level, which being in the shadow of the fallen roof we had not noticed before.

We reported this as another m[achine] g[un] emplacement and had the pleasure a day or so afterwards of seeing our 6ft how[itzer]s. firing on it. They made one or two OK's, and then displaced brickwork revealed plainly the corner of a concrete work. Evidently the Bosche had used the shell of the ruined farmhouse as a camouflage in which to conceal his defensive work; these two m[achine] g[un] emplacements were evidently two of the afterwards familiar pillboxes.

The carefully recorded observations were, in hindsight to provide useful information as to changes in enemy tactics. The area that he describes is the location of the Third Battle of Ypres, otherwise known as the Battle of Passchendaele. The 38th (Welsh) Division, in which William served, was to play a key part in the opening attack on 31 July–2 August 1917, in the Battle of Pilckem Ridge.[36]

We often saw periscopes on the German front line and further back could often distinguish Germans taking a look over the top. Occasionally we saw a group of Germans observing for 15 min[ute]s or so at a time from the trenches about the Pilckem ridge. The glittering of their field glasses in the sun would make them most conspicuous.

Sometimes we saw the white smoke of a train, which was puffing along somewhere out of sight behind the opposite ridge. We discovered movement going on in what looked like a small wood almost on the horizon. On clear days we would see horsemen, parties of infantry, carts etc. which came into view for a second or so in a clearing. By the use of a prismatic compass and a judicious examination of the contours of our map we found that this must be the village of Langemark.

Every little thing we observed whether important or unimportant in our eyes, was duly included in our daily reports. We would take it in turns to observe for an hour at a stretch, and when not observing could read if we had anything to read or write letters. We were at times so quiet in our little shelter that the rats used to emerge from their hiding places and run about the floor. One old one I can especially remember. Its ears and head generally bore the signs of many a battle fought, and it was very lame. Once I kicked at it with my foot. It reared up on its hind legs and spat and snarled at me.

Staff officers and a brigadier

One day which Johnny and I had off duty, a group of us were seated on the canal bank. This time the other bank of the canal overlooking the water. The dugouts etc. were similar to those on the other bank. I was at the time reading the weekly "Telegraph" which I had recently received from home, when I was aware that my companions had stood up. Unseen by me the Brigadier of another brigade and his retinue of staff officers had approached by the duckboard track and my companions were standing to attention. I sprung up and we saluted. He stopped and glared at me, then roared "Stand to attention properly. Drop your damned paper." Surprised, I relinquished hold of my paper, which I had retained in my hand in case it blew down into the mud, and it promptly fluttered away. "Now salute me properly." I did so. "That's better," he went on. "You ought to be ashamed of yourself a Divisional Sniper too." He could tell this by the green band we wore on our sleeves at the time. He continued on his way grumbling. With a curse at him which included the whole staff of the British Army I retrieved my paper from the mud and went on reading it.

It was incidents like this, which although viewed from the present time seem ludicrous and of small consequence which did more to break our morale than anything the Bosche would do. We were actually in the trenches and here was some upstart brigadier bullying us for not being as smart as on the parade ground.

When next back at H camp for our spell out of the trenches, Johnny Walker rejoined his own section and I was left to make the best of things amongst a ½ company who were almost strangers to me.

About this time, which was the middle of December '16 the British took over that section of the line which ran in front of Boesinghe relieving the aged Frenchmen who had held it hitherto. Our armies left flank now joined up with the right flank of the Belgians. This gave a new interesting part of the line to be manned by us Snipers. As the opposing front line trenches were so …

It is here where, apart from a single loose sheet of paper describing the retreat of the German Army on Armistice Day, William's written account stops. It stops mid-sentence at the bottom of this penultimate flimsy page of handwritten, pencil script.

It was clearly not the end of the intended account, nor was it the end of William's war. In fact, around seven months later, on the very day of the opening attack of the Third Battle of Ypres, when the 38th (Welsh) Division was advancing on Pilckem Ridge, William was on his way back to England, to begin training, following his successful application for a commission to become a temporary officer.

Chapter 11

1917–1918

William's narrative stops a year after it began, in December 1916. Any records he may have made after that time no longer exist. It is my understanding that some of his papers including perhaps original field diaries, were discarded sometime after his death in the 1960s. However, with William's collection of photos, sketches and maps, along with relevant war diaries, other references and archives, I have been able to piece together and track the remainder of his journey through the First World War.

At the beginning of 1917, this part of the Allied front line was established in the low-lying bowl of the salient protecting the remains of the ancient city of Ypres. The Germans occupied the slightly higher surrounding ground. Lyn McDonald describes the area as if it were an amphitheatre, with the Germans 'having a grandstand view of everything that moved on the stage-like salient below', as they occupied the semi-circle of low ridges to the east of Ypres.[1] In the most northern part of the salient, the front line had been pushed right back to the bank of the Yser canal. A tenuous and precarious hold petering out on the eastern side of it moving northwards. As Llewelyn Wyn Griffith describes: 'the canal was shallow … less water than slimy filth, strewn with empty bully beef and jam tins no longer a canal but a drain in which rats alone thrived.'[2] (See plate 12.)

For the Allies looking east they would see occupied Belgium and, further away, the occupied great railway junction of Roulers, which provided the Germans with a direct line of communication back to their homeland, to the Ruhr armament factories and a steady supply of troops. Behind them, beyond Ypres, which they were defending at such great cost, on a clear day they could just see the glinting English Channel.[3]

Unable to dig deep trenches in the gentle folds of the ground, the Germans resorted to building reinforced concrete pillboxes, often within existing farm buildings, all along their line,[4] much as William had seen from his observation post as described in the previous chapter.

The 38th Division continued to hold the line on the extreme left of the British Expeditionary Force, to the north of the Ypres Salient, flanked to their left by Belgian forces. In January 1917 cold weather set in, freezing the ground and the canal. It was impossible to carry out the normal fatigue work of digging unless the Royal Engineers first blew up the surface soil. Every night, bombs were dropped on the canal to keep the ice broken and so prevent the Germans from crossing and pushing further west.[5] The harsh winter conditions caused an increase in the number of cases of trench foot, prompting men's feet to be regularly inspected.[6] Misty days were quiet. A note, in the 15 RWF War Diary on 5 February, reports news of a rupture in the diplomatic relationship between the USA and Germany which 'enlivened our interest in things generally & causes us to speculate brilliantly on the future'.[7]

Towards the middle of February, a slow thaw set in. The men were set to work to improve conditions in the dugouts. In the first two weeks of that month the battalion caught 342 rats in their traps. Six hundred sandbags were filled with empty, discarded tins but seemed to make little impression on the number still scattered around everywhere.[8] Showers of snow and sleet were still being recorded well into April.

The entry in the 15 RWF war diary captures the situation on 7 April 1917: 'Canal Bank. Gas Alarm. Test carried out commencing at 10.0 AM. Quite satisfactory. Weather bright, wind dangerous. Day very quiet. News received of formal declaration of War by U.S.A on Germany. YPRES heavily shelled between the hours of 9.0 & 11.30 PM.'[9]

More about sniping

Having completed his training as a sniper the previous year and having also had some experience in this role, William was made an 'unpaid' lance corporal in the 38th Divisional Sniping Company from the beginning of January 1917. He would continue in this position for another six months.[10]

A few scattered references in war diaries detail the ongoing activity of this group. For example, secret plans for planned bombardments of the enemy were copied to the Sniping Company, and on 5 April 1917 it was stated that 'the 38th Divisional Sniping Company had a very successful day and claim to have shot 10 Germans'.[11]

Generally, observation continued to be central in the role of the sniper. As training for key objectives such as raids on enemy trenches and battles continued, they became invaluable in providing information to those in command. Some would watch from a distance from a place of safety behind their front line, undertaking rear area observation. For example, they would watch enemy railway crossings that already had Allied guns trained on them. When a train stopped, resulting in a good deal of activity at that spot, the observer would call up the guns.[12] Later on in his life, William talked to me about being involved in such an attack on a train.

The value of battle observation, to obtain and report on how each phase of the battle developed, was also key. Hesketh Prichard pointed out that during a battle 'the observer is the eye of the High Command'.[13] Those positioned at HQ needed such information. Being further back from the front line they were all blind to what was going on. The snipers would at first watch from their observation posts, then move forward to a series of shell holes and beyond, sometimes into enemy territory.

They were of course unable to observe when wearing a gasmask and in many of the later attacks the Germans would specifically target suspected observation posts with gas.[14]

As the Great War progressed from the initial trench warfare to more open warfare, snipers also played an increasing role in the fighting, and in 1917 they began working strategically with advancing fire platoons, which aimed to knock out machine-gunners and those directing the enemy from their flank.[15]

It is difficult to find any estimate of how many sniper casualties there were, as their injury or death was counted within the infantry. In 1918, however, it is estimated that snipers had a casualty rate of approximately 50 per cent [16].

Pencil sketches

Tucked in amongst old photos in one of William's exercise books, labelled 1914–1919, there are two folded, fragile, flimsy lengths of paper – pencil sketches illustrating what he saw from the observation posts that he manned. The label beneath explains: 'Views of German trenches, through loopholes in Snipers posts, on Yser Canal, Boesinghe 2m N Ypres. March 1917.' (See plates 14 and 15.)

Skeletal trees, grass, sandbags, dug-out earth, barbed wire, are all carefully depicted. One sketch is entitled 'View from Post 8' with further details in clear capitals: 'Baboon trench', 'dugout', 'steam Mill', 'Bois Crapouillot' and an enemy 'Sniper's Plate', and a record of his exact position: 28NW.B6c61.[17]

Temporarily rejoining the 15 RWF and the Battle of Pilckem Ridge

During the spring of 1917, plans were being made for an offensive on the northern edge of the Ypres Salient, the objective of which was to capture ground at Pilckem Ridge and over towards Langemarque. This was the very part of the front line that the Welsh Division was defending, and every day snipers such as William therefore were observing from their sniping posts. In contrast to the actions of the previous year with the attack on Mametz Wood, this time the men underwent rigorous training, and those who were possibly unfit were examined for battle fitness by the Royal Army Medical Corps.[18]

At the same time, William was in the process of applying to undergo training to become a temporary officer. He had completed a blue form, number MT393, in November 1916, which his father had also signed, as had the headmaster of Roan School at Greenwich, which William had attended, who stated that he had attained a good level of education. A minister of the church he attended bore witness to his good moral character. This was initially signed by the military on 15 December 1916, later scratched out and re-signed in June 1917. Such application forms came in a variety of colours and asked slightly different questions, depending on the type of applicant. William's form states that it was not to be used if he was a cadet of the Officer Training Corps Senior Division, nor if he was a member of a university. It included a question as to whether he could ride a horse, to which a positive reply was given.[19, 20]

William ceased his sniping duties in the 38th Divisional Sniping Company and rejoined his battalion, the 15 RWF, on the 28 June 1917. Perhaps his commanding officers, knowing that he was soon to leave, and having relevant experience, thought he would be better placed to help with training the men. On this same day his battalion were relieved from their front-line posts. They travelled by train and bus over the next couple of days to Fléchin, where they were trained intensively for two weeks, practising their advance over replica German trenches.[21]

It was at this point that the 15 RWF was joined by one of the most famous of Welsh poets, Ellis Humphry Ellis, also known by his bardic name 'Hedd Wyn'. Ellis Evans was born on 3 January 1887 in Trawsfynnydd in Meirionydd, North Wales. His family were farmers and, as the eldest of eleven children, he left school at the age of 14 to work as a shepherd on his father's farm. His love for poetry was already evident from an even earlier age, and he soon became an established poet in his native language of Welsh, winning several regional chairs. He came second in the National Eisteddfod in 1916. Although the Ellis family were at first exempt from taking part in the war due to farm work being of national importance, in 1916 it became mandatory for one of their sons to sign up. Ellis enlisted rather than allow his younger, married brother to go. He went to train at Litherland in Liverpool in February 1917. A month later, along with many other farmworkers, he was given seven weeks' leave to return home to help with ploughing. It was during this time that he worked on his poem 'Yr Arwr', which was to become his entry for the National Eisteddfod. Hedd Wyn reluctantly joined his battalion at Fléchin in France, in late June 1917. Here he finished the poem, signing it with his nom de plume 'Fleur de Lis'. On 15 July, the day the move towards the front line for the major assault on Pilckem Ridge commenced, Hedd Wyn's poem began its journey back to the National Eisteddfod held that year at Birkenhead.[22]

Over the next few days, the 38th (Welsh) Division moved closer to their jumping-off positions, marching for three to four hours a day, camping or bivouacking overnight. As they neared their destination, they practised the attack yet again. Once in position near the Yser Canal, they dug and camouflaged trenches in preparation. The enemy sent mustard gas shells overnight and, as dawn broke on 24 July, many of the men were unable to see, blinded by the effects of the attack, some so badly that they had to be evacuated from the front.[23]

On the 26 July 1917, senior officers were informed of a three-day postponement of the attack which had been due to take place on the 28 July.[24]

The opening attack on Pilckem Ridge, in what became known as the Third Battle of Ypres, or the Battle of Passchendaele, began on 31 July

1917 at 0350, led by the 113th Brigade of the Welsh Division (which included the 15 RWF), and the 114th Brigade.[25]

The attack was costly in terms of life. Hedd Wyn was one of the many to fall that day, heavy artillery and machine-gun fire halting their advance. Draped in black mourning cloth, the National Eisteddfod chair was awarded to him posthumously later that year.[26]

William arrived back in England on that very same day, 31 July 1917, signing Form S.D. 605 which acknowledged his return for the purpose of joining an officer cadet unit to begin his training.[27] Had the attack not been postponed for three days, would he have taken part? What must he have thought of leaving the men that he had lived and fought alongside for so many months? A mixture of feelings perhaps: guilt for leaving them at such a crucial time, but also relief that he was on the way back to England, at least for a while, with a chance of a commission and a change in his fortunes.

By the time William had arrived back in England, his battalion had all crossed the Yser Canal and were now on the east bank. By 0615 that day, casualties were so heavy that there were no officers left to command the 15th Battalion, and Regimental Sergeant Major Jones had to take charge.[28] The Battle of Pilckem Ridge redeemed the Welsh Division's reputation after the misinformed criticism they received after the Battle of Mametz Wood, but they were to suffer great losses in the process.[29]

During this time, Harold Lewis, the sniping officer with 15 RWF, already described by William in Chapter 9, provides us with some insight into the movements of a sniper detachment that he was leading, which it had been decided should be kept in reserve until new positions were established, enabling them to then come in as long-range defence. On 1 August, wearing gasmasks, and therefore seeing little, the line of men staggered through the mud. They were attacked by a German plane from the rear. No one was killed but the group was broken up and Lewis lost contact with them.[30]

Lewis estimated that in his battalion there were just under 100 men left, of the almost 800 who began the attack.[31] Conditions turned the whole area into a sea of mud. The battalion was relieved on 5 August 1917. The remaining, exhausted men were taken by bus to Elverdinghe Chateau, and given hot food, clean clothes, chocolate and cigarettes, which were 'greatly appreciated by both officers and men'.[32]

Back to England and home

It is likely that on leaving his battalion William would have walked or managed to get a lift back in one of the lorries from the Yser Canal to Poperinge, where the nearest railway hub supplying that part of the front line was situated. From there he would have travelled across the Channel and on arriving in England completed and signed the form that was date-stamped 31 July 1917, confirming his application to join an officer cadet unit. A rail warrant was issued to him to travel to the Royal Welsh Fusiliers Depot at Wrexham instructing him to report to the commanding officer. For a short while, from the 15 August 1917 he became a cadet in the 13th Training Reserve Brigade.[33]

It seems very likely that William was able to return home to Eltham in South London for leave at the beginning of August, before he embarked on this next step of his wartime journey. It would have been the first opportunity he had had to see his father and sisters after the death of his youngest brother Alan.[34] Fighting in the 2nd Battalion of the Seaforth Highlanders, Alan was killed in action on 11 April 1917 in a disastrous attack in the First Battle of the Scarpe, also known as the Battle of Arras. Along with the 1st Royal Irish Fusiliers his battalion became visible to the enemy as they crouched in a sunken road near the famous Chemical Works at Roeux, their tartan kilts showing up against the snow. As they advanced, they were shot down mercilessly by a barrage of machine-gun fire. Out of 430 officers and men, fewer than sixty survived. All twelve officers were killed.[35]

His older brother Robert, in the King's Liverpool Regiment, also took part in this same offensive. Being an officer, and therefore perhaps aware of the movements of other regiments in the vicinity he may have been the first in the family to hear of Alan's death.[36]

During this same month, August 1917, in Basra, Mesopotamia, the fourth McCrae brother, Andrew, a lance corporal in the 2nd Black Watch, was diagnosed with a condition known as diffuse alveolar haemorrhage, a debilitating respiratory condition.[37] This was documented as an 'after effect of Sand Fly fever and two summers spent in Basra, Mesopotamia, Exp Force'. Travelling to India the following month he was to spend ninety-seven days in hospital, first in Cumballa Hospital, Bombay (Mumbai) and then Deccan War Hospital in Poona. It appears he spent the rest of the war in this region. At the time of his demobilization in April 1919, he completed a disability claim form. The RAMC examining medical officer in Poona claimed the 'DAH does not trouble him much as he does clerical work, but he complains of shortness of breath on exertion'.[38]

William's eldest sister 'Nettie', by now in her mid-twenties had continued, as she would do for many years, housekeeping and caring for her widowed father and younger siblings. Despite William's father being a manager there are no signs in the census of any live-in housemaids or servants, so much of the work would have fallen to her. Isabel, one of William's younger sisters, had left school by this time and had been working as a clerk for over a year. She was to celebrate her seventeenth birthday while William was with them, a special, poignant time for them all.

Eltham, where William grew up, changed considerably as a result of The Great War. Previously a small village at the turn of the century, new housing, cinemas, shops and churches were now needed to supply the growing population. Munition workers arrived in large numbers to work at the Woolwich Arsenal and room at the local schools needed to be found for their children. Life was disrupted by frequent air-raid warnings.[39].

School

Both Isabel and Agnes attended Eltham Secondary (Grammar) Girls' School, which had only been established a few years earlier in 1906 following the Education for All Act 1902. At the time the school admitted pupils from both the families of the more well-to-do in Eltham for a fee, as well as from poorer families in Woolwich who received free scholarships. Both the sisters had been exempt from tuition fees.

The girls at the school would all have been touched by the war. As with the McCrae sisters, their brothers or fathers were likely away fighting on the Western Front, or even further afield. Earlier in the war, thinking it was a boys' school, the major in charge of the headquarters of the 15th Battalion, County of London Regiment had mistakenly written to the headmistress, Miss Bramwell, hoping the school would encourage their older pupils to consider recruiting for the armed forces. Although they were not able to help in that way, as a result the school developed a link with the regiment, with the girls knitting comforts for the men. In

December 1915, they began to send regular parcels to a Private W. Miles from Woolwich while he was a prisoner of war in Germany. Refugees from across the Channel began to arrive in the area. Some whole families had escaped, while others had had to leave relatives behind. Six young Belgian girls received their education at the school.

A record of a special magazine to celebrate the school's tenth anniversary in 1916 provides a glimpse of the strides the school had taken over that time to promote good education for their pupils, not only academically but also in social service and personal development. They also had a strong tradition of charity work. Many of the young women went on to become university graduates, teachers, civil servants and nurses despite neither they nor their teachers yet being entitled to vote.[40]

Agnes, by this time aged 14, would still be attending Eltham Secondary Grammar, although it is likely she would be having a summer break at the time. Less than a mile away from where they lived, it only took her a few minutes to walk there, dressed in her navy and white uniform, complete with a blue speckled sailor hat.[41]

A school report for Agnes indicates that she undertook public exams, both at Junior School Certificate level in July 1918, where she gained a distinction in English Literature, French (written and oral) and English, as well as at General School Certificate level in July 1920 which she passed in several subjects including gaining a distinction in oral French. On leaving school at the age of 16, she also took up employment as a clerk.

Agnes was to become the only married one of the three sisters. It was to be one of the legacies of the war that so many young women were to remain single, because so many of the young men of that generation had died.

Sir Harold Gillies

During the month of August when William was on leave, a short distance from the McCrae family home, the Queen's Hospital in Sidcup was about to open, with a thousand beds, all to be used for the treatment of injuries to the face sustained in the war. Over the next few years, teams of surgeons and experts in reconstructive work, pioneered and led by Harold Gillies, originally from New Zealand, endeavoured to help the grotesquely disfigured men, most of such a young age, find a route back to some sort of normality. Masks concealed their injuries. As they stared through the inanimate features, at least they hoped, it was possible for someone to look their way without wincing. They would stay for months or years, locked into cycles of pain and recovery as they underwent a seemingly endless series of operations. Outside the hospital, the patients would wear a uniform of cornflower-blue jackets and red ties. Blue benches appeared for them to sit on, the colour warning people of what they might see: these men from the war, set apart.[42]

Officer training

On 7 September 1917, following a spell in the Training Reserve Brigade, William joined the 18th Officer Cadet Battalion in Bath, to commence training to become an officer.

Standing majestically overlooking an eighteenth-century landscaped garden of green pastures and trees, dropping down towards the honey-coloured stone buildings of the Regency city of Bath, stood Prior Park College. With this quintessentially English backdrop, nothing could be further from the world of the Western Front that William had recently endured. It was early September when he first arrived, a chill in the air in the mornings. He would no doubt have delighted in seeing, as the weeks passed by, the beauty of the autumn-coloured leaves and appreciated the warmth and comfort that would be his inside this magnificent building, as time moved on towards the end of the year. He must have especially appreciated his situation after the freezing conditions he had experienced during the previous winter on the banks of the Yser Canal.

Originally built in 1742 as a private mansion by a local wealthy businessman, Ralph Allen, Prior Park became a college in 1830, as it now continues to be, privately educating both boarding and day schoolchildren.[43]

In February 1916, as a result of the need for new officers to replace the large numbers that had been lost, a new system was introduced to provide those from 'the ranks' an opportunity to become temporary officers. They would only hold this rank for the duration of the war. The training lasted for four and a half months and included lectures, drill, practice on the firing range and sport (see plates 17 and 18). It focused on the men learning 'the art of being an officer'; those recruited would have been recommended by their commanding officers out in the field.[44]

Many notable establishments across the country such as universities, colleges, stately homes and former barracks were used to accommodate these officer cadet battalions, and by 1917 twenty-three had been established. In all, 107,929 men went successfully through this training.[45]

Within the pages of a booklet entitled *No. 18 Officer Cadet Battalion November 26th, 1916 to February 20th 1919*, there is a flavour of the life that was led by these men in Prior Park. Photos show the comfortable rooms: the writing room, the club room (see plate 19), the theatre, and the dining room with white linen tablecloths, cutlery and flowers laid out immaculately for the next meal. A list of the many staff who supported this enterprise provides a picture of the extent of the necessary organization. From commanding officers, to chaplains, CQMSs, gymnastic staff and a medical officer, each one is listed. The number of domestic staff included seventeen cooks, an additional seven vegetable women, and forty-nine waitresses.[46]

Listed under the regiment they each went on to serve with is the total of 1,543 men who received commissions after training at Prior Park. Of these, 117 died and 260 were wounded.

There were regular inspections by high-ranking officers and while William was there, on 9 November 1918, the officer cadet battalion was visited by His Majesty, King George V.[47]

Prior to the establishment of the officer cadet battalions, officers were not paid enough to live on and thus were required to have a private income. This financial model was seen as a way of keeping the 'lower class' out. Those training as temporary officers clearly could not afford such a lifestyle on an infantryman's pay. Their allowance was necessarily increased so they were able to exist exclusively on their pay, and various allowances were also introduced for lodging, rations and travel. They also received a £50 kit allowance to purchase their uniforms.[48]

Temporary gentlemen

In 2017, Hentel[49] published a study of these 'temporary gentlemen' which considered how the men responded to this change in rank. She suggests these men had been marginalized in the historical record up until now, but discovered that those who trained to become temporary officers became confident in their identity and believed that they could contribute positively to the war effort. She found that they were happy to adapt and felt they could live up to the hegemonic upper-middle-class attitude that the officer cadet battalions promoted.

In her research she found some of them were proud of the extra insight that their experience as ordinary ranking infantrymen could contribute to their role as an officer. Initially, there was some prejudice towards these men from the regular officers, leading to those who were temporary to name themselves as 'temporary gentlemen'. There was also prejudice from temporary officers from a higher class to those of lower classes.

Siegfried Sassoon refers to the unease that some of the established officer class had towards these men. In his book *Memoirs of an Infantry Officer* he speaks of the Hôtel de la Poste in Rouen, which had become so popular with the officers that it was suggested it should be declared out of bounds to those temporary officers on the way to the front as 'The place, they felt, was becoming too crowded, and the deportment of a "temporary gentleman" enjoying his last decent dinner was apt to be more suitable to a dug-out than a military club'.[50]

The temporary officers were trained to lead men and emulate existing officers (see plate 20). After the war they had a difficult time in gaining employment, no longer a gentleman but changed from an ordinary infantryman.[51] William was fortunate in that his job as an insurance clerk was waiting for him on his return from the army.

Training notes

Still in existence are forty handwritten pages of notes that William wrote in a brown 'improved Patent "IDEAL" Loose-Leaf Lecture Note Book' during his time as a cadet. It covers a wide range of topics including military law, how to maintain discipline, map-reading, and care and maintenance of a rifle. In one of the margins, reference is made to the King's Regulations manual which he would have used alongside: 'KR para 483 to 492'. Under the section on field engineering, careful diagrams are sketched of the structure and layout of trenches (see plate 21).

Another section covers the formation of a battalion with a description of the various ranks within and their roles. From commanding officers and quarter masters and bombing officers, mention is also given to shoemakers, tailors, butchers, and postmen.

Listed too is the Sniping, Scouting and Intelligence Officer who is 'responsible to CO for all intelligence, and keeps in touch with observing officers and battalions on each flank. They were responsible for training the scouts and snipers but similarly helped with the riflemen'. It is possible that William might have been allocated this role once on the Western Front given his previous experience.[52]

Inserted within the pages is a mauve carbon copy sheet of a talk by a brigadier to platoon commanders dated 17 May 1918, emphasizing the importance of fostering the platoon spirit.

After training

William was commissioned into the Duke of Wellington's Regiment on 30 January 1918, on graduation from the 18th Officer Cadet Battalion, Bath. He was posted to the regiment's 3rd (Militia) Battalion at Earsdon, in the coal-mining district of North Shields (see plate 22). This was a training and drafting unit responsible for providing reinforcements for the 2nd (Regular Army) Battalion which saw action in France and Flanders between 1914 and 1918. The 3rd Battalion also provided an administrative base for wounded soldiers in the final stages of recuperation and soldiers who had been on leave from all the various battalions of the regiment, particularly officers. The battalion headquarters was housed in a local village school.[53]

His posting order to embark for active service in France and Flanders in 1918 would probably have been made out to join the 2nd Battalion. He arrived in France on 9 April 1918[54] at one of a number of large infantry base depots on the French coast. It is likely that this would have been the 34th Infantry Base Depot, in Etaples, which was the one particularly linked to the regiment.[55] From there he would be expected to lead a draft of recovered casualties and reinforcements to the Divisional Reinforcement Centre and thence on to the Battalion Transport Lines for joining their respective companies.

Most likely as a result of the loss of a number of men and officers, and a need to bring the unit up to strength, he then became attached to the 1/5 Lancashire Fusiliers, although he remained a member of the Duke of Wellington's (West Riding) Regiment and continued to wear their uniform.[56]

1/5 Lancashire Fusiliers

William joined this battalion on 13 April 1918,[57] which was part of the 42nd Division. Several other officers and more than 100 'other ranks' also joined the 1/5 Lancashire Fusiliers at this time.[58] A rebuilding of their strength after so many had been lost in earlier combat, they were, at that time billeted in Vauchelles-lès-Authie village, very near to where he had been with the 15 RWF prior to their time on the Yser Canal. The headquarters was in the priest's house next to the church.

Training and preparations were made over the next week for the battalion to rejoin the line. It is very possible that William may have been the battalion Sniping Officer, given his previous experience. Further evidence for this is a photo of him in officer uniform, along with other officers from many different regiments entitled 'Sniping School, Fort Mahon, France' (see plate 23). Although undated, this must have been after he joined the 1/5 Lancashire Fusiliers. Perhaps he had spent some time at this location on the French coast, teaching infantrymen sniping skills.

In William's album I also find evidence of his position one day in June 1918 with two sheets of German propaganda dropped from a plane above him while he was in the trenches in Hebuterne (see plate 24).

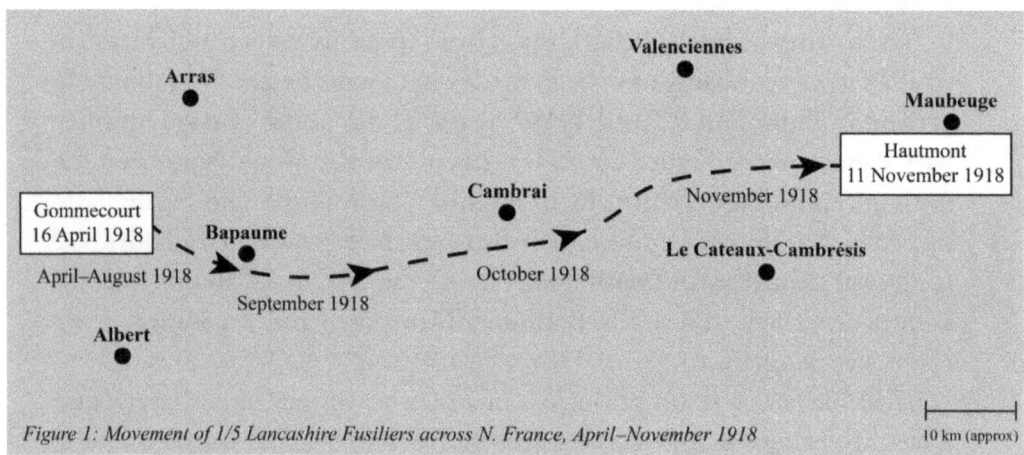

Figure 1: Movement of 1/5 Lancashire Fusiliers across N. France, April–November 1918.

In mid-August the Germans began their withdrawal and the 1/5 Lancashire Fusiliers along with the rest of the Allies began to move forward. They made steady progress in pursuit, participating in key battles such as the Battle of Albert (21–23 August 1918), and the second Battle of Bapaume (31 August–3 September 1918) during the fighting on the Somme. On the Hindenburg Line it was in the Battle of the Canal du Nord (27–28 September 1918). In Picardy they were in the Battle of the Selle from 17–23 October, where they successfully reached three objectives before the New Zealand Division passed through to continue the attack. The route they followed is shown in Figure 1.[59]

The maps

Amongst William's collection, I also found nine military maps of Belgium and France. It is clear from the dates that these were the ones he was using during these last few months of the war. Two of these are particularly pertinent.

The first, heavily used, torn at the edges and frayed on the folds, is inscribed on the back in blue crayon 'McCrae 1/5 LF'. The top and the lower sections are missing, but I know it to be a 1:20,000 scale. Unfolded, there are layers of print. The top, in red, is marked, 'Enemy organization 17.7.18'. This provided the most recent intelligence about enemy dispositions. 'Railways-used' and 'disused', 'much used', 'much activity', supply dumps of ammunition, camps and huts are all indicated.

Some of these show information added by William's hand. Looking more closely, I can see red crayon lines sketched in and out of the terrain, with round pencil marks and squares, sometimes numbered. Small squares with tiny triangular flags above them are drawn, as well as positions of the battalion headquarters and lines sketched across a swathe of the country marking the next objective behind the enemy lines. Certainly, officers would have gone forward beyond enemy lines for reconnaissance. This is a snapshot of battalion positions captured at that moment in time, an illustration of what happened before the release of the next updated official map.

At the start of the war, British military commanders thought that they had adequate maps of the area. Yet once both sides had dug in for the stalemate of trench warfare, it became evident that there was a need for far more detailed and accurate mapping. Belgian and French maps were available, but it was going to be difficult to work from these, especially to produce others in a larger scale. This was due to the different systems of measurement used in the different countries. Exact distances were imperative for the artillery to range their targets. Therefore, the dangerous work of resurveying took place from 1914 onwards. Aerial photography was particularly vital for detail of enemy positions, especially for trenches, artillery positions, wire entanglements and observation posts. Capturing this intelligence and transferring it to maps was key to combat.[60] Large-scale maps were at first printed by the Ordnance Survey in Southampton, but production soon moved to France and Belgium. From the middle of 1916, printing in the field was possible. Thousands of sheets could be produced each day.

The second map was complete and headed 'France Sheet 51 SW 1:20,000 Ordnance Survey. March 1918. Edition 2a (local)'. Again, in red overprinted on this was 'Reference of Enemy Organisation: 15.10.18. Forest of Mormal.' Large areas are coloured red, a patchwork effect, indicating where the trees still stood, at that time, in this forest. Other areas were hatched in red, where trees had been felled or thinned. Roads through this forest were labelled fit for mechanical transport (MT) or roads fit for horse transport only (HT). I realized that this map not only showed enemy organization, but also information concerning the condition of the roads, perhaps in preparation for attack. The Battle of the Forest de Mormal was the last major British offensive in the Great War and took place only sixteen days after the map was printed.

On the 7 November the 1/5 Lancashire Battalion was tasked along with the rest of the 42nd Division to take the high ground west of Hautmont and, if possible, capture the town.

Some insight into the role that William's battalion played at this time can be gleaned from a speech that Major General A. Solly-Flood, commanding the 42nd Division, gave to the men on 11 November 1918. He refers to the Armistice bringing operations to a premature conclusion and continues:

> Generally speaking, the recent fighting was not of the violent nature in which you have previously taken part, and so greatly excelled. At the commencement of the operation however, it was sufficiently

severe, and the conditions imposed by the Forest of Mormal and the bridgeless River Sambre were such as to call for the highest soldierly qualities.

After long marches at night in bad weather over boggy forest tracks, although cold and wet, hungry and tired, you attacked and defeated the enemy with your customary indomitableness ... in the face of severe enemy fire.[61]

The Armistice

There exists one final piece of William's writing, on a loose sheet of paper, describing in moving detail the events of the last few hours of the war.

```
It was the afternoon of 10th November '18. All day we had
heard rumours of the impending cessation of hostilities.
The enemy, who had been at close quarters the day before
holding up our advance by heavy machine gun fire, was far
away and definitely on the run.
    He was systematically blowing up dumps, roads and
bridges. His progress in the direction of the Fatherland
being marked by huge columns of dust and debris, which
rose suddenly on the horizon and slowly descended, followed
many seconds later by the dull, reverberating thunder of
the far explosion.
    As it was getting dusk we received orders to leave our
positions in and about the Fort D'Hautmont, which we had
captured the previous day, and return into billets in the
town of that name.
    On the outskirts of the town we were met by the regimental
drum and fife band, who placing themselves at our head,
led us, playing lively marching tunes, into the town.
Flags had been brought out from their hiding places, and
decked the fronts of the houses. The inhabitants came to
their doors and windows. Boys with flaring torches darted
hither and thither, in front and beside us, lighting our
way. There was a general chorus of "Bravos."
    Tired, famished and battle stained we brightened up,
thrust our chests and marched along with more of a swagger.
Had not we actually delivered this same town from out of
the hands of their oppressors.
    That night we were billeted in the school. The next
morning dawned mild and bright. The day of days for
```

which millions had been longing through weary years of bloodshed and horror.

At 10.45 am the battalion formed up in the school yard. The C.O. told us in a few words that Germany had unconditionally surrendered and that an Armistice had been signed. He then read out the official order for the cessation of hostilities at 11am and taking out his watch stood waiting for that hour.

The sun shone down in golden splendour on a peaceful countryside clad in the delicately tinted dress of late autumn. Yellow leaves fluttered down from the trees in a ceaseless procession, or swirled gaily in the fitful breeze. This was a region far removed from the marred battle-scarred area which had seen most of the fighting.

The deep silence was broken every minute by the boom-boom of a gun still firing at a distant enemy, and now and again there was a distant rumble as another mine or dump went into the air.

Suddenly the CO put away his watch and shouted "Battalion Shun." There was a gruff order to the buglers, and the clear notes of the Cease Fire rang out. On each side of us, some near, some distant we could hear buglers of other regiments taking up the call and could visualise the long line of our army, stretching from north to south, some no doubt were in direct contact with the enemy, obeying this liberating call.

The Armistice was established. Peace was with us again. Strangely however that gun still went on firing and did not cease for some hours.

We spent the rest of the day very quietly. It seemed difficult to convince ourselves that the long nightmare was over. We felt like pinching ourselves to see if we were awake. We seemed to be walking on air.

Epilogue

'The Battalion gave three cheers for "The Allies and Victory".'[1]

The 1/5 Lancashire Fusiliers were to remain in Hautmont for some time after the signing of the Armistice (see plate 25). Training, recreational training, route marches and church parades continued. On 1 December, George V visited Hautmont to inspect the 42nd Division.

A week later, on 8 December, William, along with twenty-eight other ranks, proceeded to the Citadel in Namur to take over from the Canadians who were guarding ordnance ceded by the Germans.[2] He was to remain there for the next month, during Christmas and the New Year. Once relieved of this duty, he returned to Charleroi where the rest of the battalion was billeted in Belgian infantry barracks.[3] By the time William returned, an educational scheme had been set up for the men, with instructors being found within the battalion, to teach classes in reading, writing, arithmetic, French, history, typewriting and shorthand. Lectures were also organized, including one entitled 'The Submarine' given by a member of the Royal Navy accompanied with slides. On 16 January, the battalion concert party, known as 'the Pivotal Pierrots' entertained the men.[4]

The 1/5 Lancashire Fusiliers war diary states that on 30 January 1919, eighty days after the Armistice: '2nd/Lt. W. McCrae plus 27 Other Ranks proceeded to UK for demobilisation.'[5]

He passed through the dispersal unit in Dover, where a form was signed and stamped on 1 February 1919, indicating that he would no longer receive any pay from the next day. He was entitled to wear his uniform for just one further week.[6]

On his return his sisters said that he had changed from how he was before the war. Quieter.

Difficult times were ahead for the whole country, with the loss of so many men. Not only did families have to cope with the loss of so many of their loved ones, but they also had to come to terms with the extent of the trauma, both physical and mental, that had been inflicted on those who had returned. In addition, many of those who came back from the front found it difficult to find employment.

William was lucky, as he had his previous job waiting for him, as an insurance clerk at the Royal London Mutual Insurance Company. He was to remain in their employment until he retired at the age of 65, commuting into London every day on the train, and then walking back along the long road from the station, looking forward to seeing his wife and daughter and to tend to his garden.

Dartmoor, forty years later

He had forgotten his walking stick. Reaching the gate at the end of the footpath, I was sent running back to where we had sat, by the water, eating our picnic. A warm day, dry as I remember, one summer, sometime in the 1960s, when I was around 10 years old. I guess he had a rucksack of sorts, definitely his binoculars and a map. A special day, just me and my grandfather, my younger brothers not yet old enough for the long walk across a southern edge of Dartmoor, down to a river and back along the small twisting lanes to the village, where we waited for the bus to take us back home to Plymouth. We sat at the front, on the top deck. Just us.

It was a carefully planned route, just far enough to complete with a youngster in tow, with a stop for lunch, and a walk back, in time to catch the bus. He must have visited before on his own, finding the footpath on the map, as the spot was quite hidden.

According to my grandmother, he would frequently head out alone to walk. She never knew where he was, apart from being somewhere 'on the moors'. I think how he would have looked, wearing a sturdy, cream-coloured gabardine mac' which fitted over his tweed jacket and woollen trousers. Stout leather shoes. Where did he go? What did he think as he strode out across the open, wild landscape? Did he think much about the Great War he had fought in? Did he think about the Second World War when his wife and daughter were evacuated, while he stayed in London to act as a firewatcher? Or did he just feel a sense of peace, and become uplifted and strengthened by the beauty of the open space and sky around him?

Notes

Chapter 1: The Journey to War
1. Barlow, Robin, *Wales and World War One* (Ceredigion: Gomer Press, 2014) p. 44.
2. Griffith, Llewelyn Wyn & Riley, J. (ed.), *Up to Mametz and Beyond* (Barnsley: Pen & Sword, 2010). Introduction by Jonathon Riley, p. xv.
3. Glover, M. & Riley, J., *That Astonishing Infantry: The History of the Royal Welch Fusiliers 1689-2006* (Barnsley: Pen & Sword, 2008).
4. Griffith, Llewelyn Wyn & Riley, J. (ed.), *Up to Mametz and Beyond* (Barnsley: Pen & Sword, 2010). Introduction by Jonathon Riley, p. xv.
5. Ibid.
6. Memorial to the Royal Welch Fusiliers: www.londonremembers.com/memorials/royal-welch-fusiliers [Accessed 30 August 2021].
7. Barlow, Robin, *Wales and World War One* (Ceredigion: Gomer Press, 2014) p. 44.
8. Van Emden, R. & Humphries, S., *All Quiet on the Home Front* (London: Headline Publishing, 2003) p. 7.
9. Hughes, Colin, *Mametz: Lloyd George's 'Welsh Army' at the Battle of the Somme* (first published privately by Orion Press, 1982; Huddersfield: Gliddon Books, 1990) p. 30.
10. Ibid., p. 29.
11. Griffith, Llewelyn Wyn & Riley, J. (ed.), *Up to Mametz and Beyond* (Barnsley: Pen & Sword, 2010). Introduction Jonathon Riley, p. xvi
12. Barlow, Robin, *Wales and World War One* (Ceredigion: Gomer Press, 2014) p. 49.
13. Lock, Col N., Trustee of the RWF Museum – correspondence 8 October 2021.
14. Hughes, Colin, *Mametz: Lloyd George's 'Welsh Army' at the Battle of the Somme* (first published privately by Orion Press, 1982; Huddersfield: Gliddon Books, 1990) p. 36.
15. Barlow, Robin, *Wales and World War One* (Ceredigion: Gomer Press, 2014) p. 51.
16. Hughes, Colin, *Mametz: Lloyd George's 'Welsh Army' at the Battle of the Somme* (first published privately by Orion Press, 1982; Huddersfield: Gliddon Books, 1990) p. 31 re inspection by Lloyd George in Llandudno.
17. Barlow, Robin, *Wales and World War One* (Ceredigion: Gomer Press, 2014) p. 54.

18. The National Archives WO 95/2556/1 War Diary, 15th Royal Welsh Fusiliers.
19. Great War Forum search for Winnall Down note posted by Moonraker. Old Sweats, 30 July 2013: www.greatwarforum.org/topic/197449-training-camps/ [Accessed 27 September 2020].
20. Great War Forum search for Winnall Down note posted by Dave Key. Old Sweats, 30 July 2013: www.greatwarforum.org/topic/197449-training-camps/ [Accessed 27 September 2020].
21. Remarque, Eric Maria, *All Quiet on the Western Front*. (London: Vintage Classics, 1996).
22. Sassoon, Siegfried, *Memoirs of an Infantry Officer* (London: Faber & Faber, 1965) p. 205.

Chapter 2: Rouge Croix and Christmas

1. The National Archives WO 95/2556/1 War Diary, 15th Royal Welsh Fusiliers.
2. The Post Office and the First World War: www.postalmuseum.org/collections/ww1/ [Accessed 4 May 2021].
3. The National Archives WO 95/2556/1 War Diary, 15th Royal Welsh Fusiliers, 19 December 1915.
4. William refers to being attached to the 2nd Battalion of the Grenadier Guards initially and then acknowledges that they had at first been attached to the wrong battalion. See reference 6.
5. Christmas Truce of 1914. History.com editors: www.history.com/topics/world-war-i/christmas-truce-of-1914 [Accessed 7 May 2021].
6. The National Archives WO 95/2556/1 War Diary, 15th Royal Welsh Fusiliers, 19 December 1915. B Company attached to the 3rd Battalion of the Grenadier Guards.
7. Trueman, C. N., Christmas 1915 World War One: www.historylearningsite.co.uk/world-war-one/the-western-front-in-world-war-one/christmas-1915-world-war-one/ 31 March 2015 [Accessed 7 May 2021].
8. Bourne N., 1915 WW1 diary gives account of second Christmas truce: www.bbc.co.uk/news/uk-wales-35120354 26 December 2015 [Accessed 23.11.20].
9. Riley J., The Second Christmas Truce 1915: http://generalship.org/royal-welch-fusiliers-articles/2nd-christmas-truce-1915.html [Accessed 24.11.20].
10. Dilworth, Thomas, *David Jones in the Great War* (London: Entitharmon Press 2012) pp. 71–2.
11. Griffith, Llewelyn Wyn & Riley, J. (ed.), *Up to Mametz and Beyond* (Barnsley: Pen & Sword, 2010) pp. 14–15.
12. In this early period of the war there was very little instruction in trench warfare back in Britain. Later, when subsequent drafts were taken into training at the new very large Kinmel Park Camp, practice trenches were built in the parkland around Bodelwyddan Castle. These can still be seen from the air.

Chapter 3: Trench and Billet

1. Griffith, Llewelyn Wyn & Riley, J. (ed.), *Up to Mametz and Beyond* (Barnsley: Pen & Sword, 2010) p. 19.
2. The National Archives WO 95/2556/1 War Diary, 15th Royal Welsh Fusiliers.
3. Griffith, Llewelyn Wyn & Riley, J. (ed.), *Up to Mametz and Beyond* (Barnsley: Pen & Sword, 2010) pp. 18–19 . This event is also described here by Griffith. He thought it likely that the enemy had probably seen them march into Richebourg St Vaast, resulting in the battalion being heavily shelled for an hour and causing the first casualties, killing two people and injuring five.
4. Richebourg St Vaast: https://film.iwmcollections.org.uk/record/3179. This film, made 'possibly as early as late 1915', shows the ruined church and churchyard as described by William.
5. Ibid., p. 28, Griffith refers to these isolated posts as islands.
6. Ibid., p. 37.
7. Tunnelling Companies of the Royal Engineers (underground warfare): www.longlongtrail.co.uk/army/regiments-and-corps/the-corps-of-royal-engineers-in-the-first-world-war/tunnelling-companies-of-the-royal-engineers-underground-warfare/ [Accessed 10.6.2021].
8. Ibid.
9. Macdonald, Lyn, *They Called It Passchendaele* (London: Papermac, Macmillan Publishers, 1983) p. 17.
10. Ibid., pp. 23–4.
11. Nouix. The nearest match to this I can find with a somewhat similar name is Noeux-les-Mines. However, The National Archives W.O.95/2556/1 War Diary, 15th Royal Welsh Fusiliers states that the battalion was at Locon during this time, from 9–16 February 1916, undergoing training.
12. The National Archives WO 95/2556/1 War Diary, 15th Royal Welsh Fusiliers. Entry for 20 February 1916 confirms a company of the 17th Battalion Lancashire Fusiliers, otherwise known as the Bantams, was attached to the battalion for instruction.
13. Griffith, Llewelyn Wyn & Riley, J. (ed.), *Up to Mametz and Beyond* (Barnsley: Pen & Sword, 2010) p. 38.

Chapter 4: A Sanctuary and Holding a Line

1. Unit History: King's (Liverpool Regiment): www.forces-war-records.co.uk/units/259/kings-liverpool-regiment/ [Accessed 16 March 2021].
2. MacRae-Gilstrap, Ella, *The Clan MacRae with its Rolls of Honour and of Service in the Great War* (Aberdeen: Rosemount Press, 1923) p. 94.
3. The Seaforth Highlanders: www.visitscotland.com/about/history/ww1-centenary/scottish-regiments/the-seaforth-highlanders/ [Accessed 11 March 2021].
4. The National Archives WO 372/12/201497 Record detail for Alan J. McCrae (Seaforth Highlanders).

5. Pals: Britain was the only major power not to begin the First World War with a mass-conscripted army. Thousands of men volunteered when war first broke out. It was thought that they were more likely to join up if they were able to be in the same battalion as their friends and relatives. Thus, the birth of the Pals battalions: www.iwm.org.uk/history/the-pals-battalions-of-the-first-world-war [Accessed 15 March 2021].
6. Blunden, Edmund, *Undertones of War* (London: Penguin Modern Classics, 2000) pp. 27–8.
7. The Derby Scheme was also known as the Group Scheme, named after the then Director General of Recruiting, Edward Stanley, 17th Earl of Derby. Launched in autumn 1915, when it became clear that more recruits would be necessary, canvassers visited eligible men to persuade them to volunteer. Many still did not comply and therefore compulsory conscription was introduced in January 1916 when the Military Service Act became law: www.longlongtrail.co.uk/?s=the+derby+scheme [Accessed 15 March 2021].
8. William McCrae's 20th birthday was on 23 April 1916.

Chapter 5: The Raid
1. The National Archives WO 95/2556/1 War Diary, 15th Royal Welsh Fusiliers, 7 May 1916.
2. Ibid. Narrative of the raid, pp. 38–9.
3. William's account of the raid matches closely with that in the 15th RWF War Diary. The names of those taking part in the raid do not match. I do not know why this is so, although I have found examples of names being replaced with pseudonyms in other accounts of events in the First World War.
4. Griffith, Llewelyn Wyn & Riley, J. (ed.), *Up to Mametz and Beyond* (Barnsley: Pen & Sword, 2010) p. 57.
5. Ibid., pp. 58–60.
6. Dilworth, Thomas, *David Jones in the Great War* (London: Entitharmon Press 2012) p. 95.
7. Hughes, Colin, *Mametz: Lloyd George's 'Welsh Army' at the Battle of the Somme* (first published privately by Orion Press, 1982; Huddersfield: Gliddon Books, 1990) p. 59.
8. Raiding was seen as an important vehicle for demonstrating fighting spirit and aggressive action against the enemy. A number of infantry battalions enjoyed recognition as been the most proficient and active raiding units. In many cases this would be a direct reflection of the commanding officer's direction. Whether this was born out of a desire to engender an offensive spirit in their unit, or to attract the positive attention of the chain of command, should be judged on a case-by-case basis. 2 RWF was well recognized as a highly proficient raiding unit. This was in part due to the fact it did not suffer the same losses as most regular battalions in 1914 and so retained much of its regular and highly trained manpower well into the war.

Chapter 6: Craters and the Colour Blue
1. The National Archives WO 95/2556/1 War Diary, 15th Royal Welsh Fusiliers.
2. 'Pack up your Troubles' was written by a Welshman, Felix Lloyd Powell in 1915. The words were written by his brother George Henry Powell (under the pseudonym George Asaf): www.bbc.com/news/uk-wales-25968407 [Accessed 2 October 2021].
3. Griffith, Llewelyn Wyn & Riley, J. (ed.), *Up to Mametz and Beyond* (Barnsley: Pen & Sword, 2010) p. 141.
4. Pegler, Martin, *Sniping in the Great War* (Barnsley: Pen & Sword, 2017) p. 96.
5. Edmund Blunden and the Red Dragon Crater: www.1914-18.co.uk/blunden/reddragon.htm [Accessed 7 July 2021].
6. Ibid.
7. Blunden, Edmund, *Undertones of War* (London: Penguin Modern Classics, 2000) p. 55.
8. The Tunnellers Memorial, Givenchy: www.tunnellersmemorial.com/red-dragon-survey/ [Accessed 20 June 2021].

Chapter 7: The Somme and Mametz Wood
1. Hicks, Jonathan, *The Welsh at Mametz Wood: The Somme 1916* (Wales: Y Lolfa, 1916) p. 9.
2. Hughes, Colin, *Mametz: Lloyd George's 'Welsh Army' at the Battle of the Somme* (first published privately by Orion Press, 1982; Huddersfield: Gliddon Books, 1990) p. 78.
3. Lewis-Stempel, J., *Where Poppies Blow: The British Soldier, Nature, the Great War* (London: Weidenfeld & Nicolson, 2017) p. 24.
4. The figure on the dome of Albert Church fell in April 1918, caused by British fire during an effort to drive out the occupying Germans. It is now completely restored with a shining golden Virgin Mary holding up the Christ child with her outstretched arms, as it was in the past: www.bottesfordhistory.org.uk/content/catalogue_item/bottesford-local-history-archive/photographs-donated-glenys-claricoats/damage-to-the-town-of-albert-in-ww1 [Accessed: 1 October 2020].
5. Robinson, Peter, *A Welsh Response to the Great War: The 38th (Welsh) Division on the Western Front 1914–1919* (Cardiff University: MPhil thesis, 2017): https://orca.cardiff.ac.uk/111318 [Accessed 25 July 2019], cites Pryce-Davies papers, p. 79.
6. Hicks, Jonathan, *The Welsh at Mametz Wood: The Somme 1916* (Wales: Y Lolfa, 1916) p. 63.
7. The National Archives WO 95/2556/1 War Diary, 15th Royal Welsh Fusiliers indicates the following distances and destinations during the battalion's march to the Somme: Puchevillers 12md 31 June 1916 travelled 9.7km to Lealvillers 2 July, then 16km to Ribemont on 4 July; on 5 July Ribemont to Mametz Wood area 18km where occupied advanced trenches

of the 7th Division, relieved 1st Warwick in Queen's Nullah, Bottom Wood etc at 8 pm.
8. Robinson, Peter, *A Welsh Response to the Great War: The 38th (Welsh) Division on the Western Front 1914–1919* (Cardiff University: MPhil thesis, 2017): https://orca.cardiff.ac.uk/111318 [Accessed 25 July 2019] pp. 73 & 82.
9. Griffith, Llewelyn Wyn & Riley, J. (ed.), *Up to Mametz and Beyond* (Barnsley: Pen & Sword, 2010). Wyn Griffith's original book was entitled *Up to Mametz*. Jonathon Riley discovered additional material with the Griffith family which continued the story past the Battle of Mametz, hence the added 'and beyond' part of the title to the updated and expanded version.
10. Robinson, Peter, *A Welsh Response to the Great War: The 38th (Welsh) Division on the Western Front 1914–1919* (Cardiff University: MPhil thesis, 2017): https://orca.cardiff.ac.uk/111318 [Accessed 25 July 2019] p. 87.
11. The National Archives WO 95/2556/1 War Diary, 15th Royal Welsh Fusiliers.
12. Griffith, Llewelyn Wyn & Riley, J. (ed.), *Up to Mametz and Beyond* (Barnsley: Pen & Sword, 2010) p. 112.
13. Ibid., p. 114.
14. Hicks, Jonathan, *The Welsh at Mametz Wood: The Somme 1916* (Wales: Y Lolfa, 1916) p. 83.
15. The National Archives WO 95/2556/1 War Diary, 15th Royal Welsh Fusiliers. The War Diary indicates they reached Ribemont by 6.30 pm on 11 July 1916.
16. Ibid. The War Diary indicates the battalion was entrained at Mericourt bound for Longprie, then marched from Longprie to Ergnies, on 12 July 1916. William refers to travelling by lorry rather than train.
17. Griffith, Llewelyn Wyn & Riley, J. (ed.), *Up to Mametz and Beyond* (Barnsley: Pen & Sword, 2010) pp. 122–3.
18. Glover, M. & Riley, J., *That Astonishing Infantry. The History of the Royal Welch Fusiliers 1689–2006* (Barnsley: Pen & Sword, 2008) p. 131.
19. Hughes, Colin, *Mametz: Lloyd George's 'Welsh Army' at the Battle of the Somme* (first published privately by Orion Press, 1982; Huddersfield: Gliddon Books, 1990) p. 135.
20. Hicks, Jonathan, *The Welsh at Mametz Wood: The Somme 1916* (Wales: Y Lolfa 1916) p. 198.
21. Hughes, Colin, *Mametz: Lloyd George's 'Welsh Army' at the Battle of the Somme* (first published privately by Orion Press, 1982; Huddersfield: Gliddon Books, 1990) p. 136.
22. Hicks, Jonathan, *The Welsh at Mametz Wood: The Somme 1916* (Wales: Y Lolfa, 1916) p. 355.
23. Robinson, Peter, *A Welsh Response to the Great War: The 38th (Welsh) Division on the Western Front 191 –1919* (Cardiff University: MPhil thesis, 2017): https://orca.cardiff.ac.uk/111318 [Accessed 25 July 2019] p. 126.

24. Jones, David, *In Parenthesis* (London: Faber & Faber, 2014).
25. Graves, Robert, *Goodbye to All That* (London: Penguin, 1960) p. 175.
26. Graves, Robert, *A Dead Boche*: https://allpoetry.com/A-Dead-Boche [Accessed 2 September 2021].
27. Accounts of the Battle of Mametz Wood collected by A. Colin Hughes: https://archiveshub.jisc.ac.uk/data/gb1239-461 [Accessed 1 September 2021].
28. Sheers, Owen, *Mametz: A Play* (London: Samuel French Publishers, 2016).
29. War's Hell Exhibition (2016) National Museum, Cardiff. https://museum.wales/cardiff/whatson/8949/Wars-Hell-The-Battle-of-Mametz-Wood-in-Art/footer/ [Accessed 5 January 2020].

Chapter 8: A Respite of Sorts

1. Van Emden, R. & Humphries, S., *All Quiet on the Home Front* (London: Headline Publishing, 2003) p. 83.
2. Ibid.
3. IWM 1: www.iwm.org.uk/history/key-facts-about-the-battle-of-the-somme [Accessed 15 August 2021].
4. Pals battalions: www.iwm.org.uk/history/the-pals-battalions-of-the-first-world-war [Accessed 15 March 2021].
5. Van Emden, R. & Humphries, S., *All Quiet on the Home Front* (London: Headline Publishing, 2003) p. 90.
6. IWM: www.iwm.org.uk/history/geoffrey-mails-and-the-battle-of-the-somme-film [Accessed 15 August 2021].
7. IWM: www.iwm/history/how-the-battle-of-the-somme-was-filmed [Accessed 15 August 2021].
8. The National Archives WO 95/2556/1 War Diary, 15th Royal Welsh Fusiliers, 18 July 1916 bivouacked near Coigneux.
9. The National Archives WO 374/43769 personal file of 2nd Lieutenant William McCrae, The Duke of Wellington's (West Riding Regiment).
10. Hallett, Christine E., *Nurses of Passchendaele* (Barnsley: Pen & Sword, 2017) p. 28.
11. Ibid.
12. Ibid., p. 29.
13. Shanks, G. D., 'How World War 1 Changed Global Attitudes to War and Infectious Diseases', *Lancet*, 8 November 2014, 384:1699–1707.
14. Sassoon, Siegfried, *Memoirs of an Infantry Officer* (London: Faber & Faber, 1965) pp. 120 & 123.
15. German measles vaccine: www.gov.uk/government/publications/vaccination-timeline [Accessed 15.8.21]. First vaccine for German measles was licensed in 1969 and became available for immunization in 1970.
16. Shanks, G. D., 'How World War 1 Changed Global Attitudes to War and Infectious Diseases', *Lancet*, 8 November 2014, 384:1699–1707.

Chapter 9: The Yser Canal

1. Robinson, Peter, *A Welsh Response to the Great War: The 38th (Welsh) Division on the Western Front 1914–1919* (Cardiff University: MPhil thesis, 2017): https://orca.cardiff.ac.uk/111318 [Accessed 25 July 2019] p. 133.
2. Griffith, Llewelyn Wyn & Riley, J. (ed.), *Up to Mametz and Beyond* (Barnsley: Pen & Sword, 2010) p. 131.
3. Château des Trois Tours is now called Kasteel drie Torens. It is located to the west of Brielen, which is north-west of Ypres on the road to Elverdinge (N8): www.greatwarforum.org/topic/93365-chateau-des-trois-tours/ Post 1, March 2008 [Accessed: 25 February 2021].
4. There is a fingernail sketch of the mask in the original account.
5. Warner, Philip, *World War One: A Chronological Narrative* (Barnsley: Pen & Sword, 2008) p. 57.
6. Clayton, Albert, *Long Before Daybreak* (independently published by M. J. Duckworth, 2020). contains a good description of carrying heavy loads along the trenches. Albert was an officers' mess runner in the Royal Fusiliers.
7. The idea here of taking part in a wiring party in no man's land at night being 'peaceful' perhaps goes against expectations. 'Peaceful' in the context of men who are constantly immersed in such a dangerous environment this may be seen as comparative, and it also excused men form further work that night. David Jones preferred to take part on patrols in no man's land for that reason. Reference: Dilworth, Thomas, *David Jones in the Great War* (London: Entitharmon Press 2012) p.85.
8. The Derby Scheme was also known as the Group Scheme, named after the then Director General of Recruiting, Edward Stanley, 17th Earl of Derby. Launched in autumn 1915, when it became clear that more recruits would be necessary, canvassers visited eligible men to persuade them to volunteer. Many still did not comply and therefore compulsory conscription was introduced in January 1916 when the Military Service Act became law: www.longlongtrail.co.uk/?s=the+derby+scheme [Accessed 15 March 2021].
9. Hesketh-Prichard, H. V., *Sniping in France* (Barnsley: Pen & Sword, 2014) p. 1.
10. Pegler, Martin, *Sniping in the Great War* (Barnsley: Pen & Sword, 2017) pp. 17–18.
11. Ibid., p. 25.
12. Ibid., p. 21.
13. www.greatwarforum.org/topic/291901-38th-division-sniping-company-1916-1918/?tab=comments#comments-3030013 [Accessed 14 July 2021].
14. Lewis, Harold, *Crow on a Barbed Wire Fence* (Australia: Angus & Robertson Publishers, 1973) p. 211.
15. Lewis, Harold, *Bluey* (Australia: Angus & Robertson Publishers, 1985) p. 78.

16. Ibid., pp. 80–2.
17. Ibid., p. 88.
18. www.longlongtrail.co.uk/army/regiments-and-corps/the-british-infantry-regiments-of-1914-1918/welsh-regiment/. The 19th (Service) Battalion (Glamorgan Pioneers) provided the pioneer battalion for the 38th (Welsh) Division at this point of the war. The pioneer battalions were often recruited from mining areas as they included a high number of men experienced in manual labour. They performed non-specialist field engineering tasks such as trench defences and support tasks such as road-making in the divisional rear area. When the division was conducting offensive or active defensive operations, the pioneer battalions were expected to fight as infantry.
19. Lewis, Harold, *Bluey* (Australia: Angus & Robertson Publishers, 1985) p. 91.

Chapter 10: Sniping School and Observation
1. Hesketh-Prichard, H. V., *Sniping in France* (Barnsley: Pen & Sword, 2014) p. 85.
2. Pegler, Martin, *Sniping in the Great War* (Barnsley: Pen & Sword, 2017) p. 172.
3. Ibid., p. 21.
4. Ibid., p. 179.
5. Hesketh-Prichard, H. V., *Sniping in France* (Barnsley: Pen & Sword, 2014) p. 1.
6. Pegler, Martin, *Sniping in the Great War* (Barnsley: Pen & Sword, 2017) p. 18.
7. Crum, F. M., *Memoirs of a Rifleman Scout*. (Barnsley: Frontline Books, 2014) p. 212.
8. Hesketh-Prichard, H. V., *Sniping in France* (Barnsley: Pen & Sword, 2014) p. 14.
9. Ibid., p. 40.
10. Ibid., p. 14.
11. Ibid., p. 19.
12. Ibid., p. 4.
13. Pegler, Martin, *Sniping in the Great War* (Barnsley: Pen & Sword, 2017) p. 56.
14. Hesketh-Prichard, H. V., *Sniping in France* (Barnsley: Pen & Sword, 2014) p. 20.
15. Ibid., p. 11.
16. Ibid., p. 114.
17. Ibid., p. 7.
18. Lewis, Harold, *Bluey* (Australia: Angus & Robertson Publishers, 1985) p. 89.
19. Pegler, Martin, *Sniping in the Great War* (Barnsley: Pen & Sword, 2017) p. 141.

20. Ibid., pp. 140–1.
21. Hesketh-Prichard, H. V., *Sniping in France* (Barnsley: Pen & Sword, 2014) p. 28.
22. Ibid., p. 105.
23. The YMCA during World War One: www.westernfrontassociation.com/the-latest-wwi-podcast/ep-146-the-ymca-during-ww1-kathryn-white/ [Accessed 28 June 2021].
24. Talbot House: www.greatwar.co.uk/ypressalient/museum-talbot-house-history.htm. [Accessed 28 June 2021].
25. Pegler, Martin, *Sniping in the Great War* (Barnsley: Pen & Sword, 2017) p. 132.
26. Crum, F. M., *Memoirs of a Rifleman Scout* (Barnsley: Frontline Books, 2014) p. 269.
27. Hesketh-Prichard, H. V., *Sniping in France* (Barnsley: Pen & Sword, 2014) p. 54.
28. Ibid., p. 127.
29. Ibid.
30. Ibid., p. 82.
31. Pegler, Martin, *Sniping in the Great War* (Barnsley: Pen & Sword, 2017) p. 99.
32. Ibid., chapter 7.
33. Hesketh-Prichard, H. V., *Sniping in France* (Barnsley: Pen & Sword, 2014) pp. 122–4.
34. Ibid., p. 80.
35. The National Archives: WO-372-23-124036. Edwin Hurley –awarded Military Medal.
36. Robinson, Peter, *A Welsh Response to the Great War: The 38th (Welsh) Division on the Western Front 1914–1919* (Cardiff University: MPhil thesis, 2017): https://orca.cardiff.ac.uk/111318 [Accessed 25 July 2019] p. 150.

Chapter 11: 1917–1918

1. Macdonald, Lyn, *They Called It Passchendaele* (London: Papermac, Macmillan Publishers, 1983) p. 4.
2. Griffith, Llewelyn Wyn & Riley, J. (ed.), *Up to Mametz and Beyond* (Barnsley: Pen & Sword, 2010) p. 139.
3. Macdonald, Lyn, *They Called It Passchendaele* (London: Papermac, Macmillan Publishers, 1983) p. 5.
4. Robinson, Peter, *A Welsh Response to the Great War: The 38th (Welsh) Division on the Western Front 1914–1919* (Cardiff University: MPhil thesis, 2017): https://orca.cardiff.ac.uk/111318 [Accessed 25 July 2019] p. 155.
5. The National Archives WO 95/2556/1 War Diary, 15th Royal Welsh Fusiliers, 1 February 1917.
6. Robinson, Peter, *A Welsh Response to the Great War: The 38th (Welsh) Division on the Western Front 1914–1919* (Cardiff University: MPhil thesis, 2017): https://orca.cardiff.ac.uk/111318 [Accessed 25 July 2019] p. 135.

7. The National Archives WO 95/2556/1 War Diary, 15th Royal Welsh Fusiliers, 5 February 1917.
8. Ibid., February & March.
9. The National Archives WO 95/2556/2 War Diary, 15th Royal Welsh Fusiliers, 17 April 1917.
10. The National Archives WO 374/43769 personal file of 2nd Lieutenant William McCrae, The Duke of Wellington's (West Riding Regiment).
11. The National Archives WO 95-2540-1 38th Division War Diary, 5 April 1917.
12. Hesketh-Prichard, H. V., *Sniping in France* (Barnsley: Pen & Sword, 2014) p. 107.
13. Ibid., p. 98.
14. Ibid.
15. Ibid., p. 198.
16. Pegler, Martin, *Sniping in the Great War* (Barnsley: Pen & Sword, 2017) p. 179.
17. Position of William McCrae calculated using the Ordnance Survey Trench Map corrected to 1 April 1917, scale: 1:20,000 Sheet of Grid reference: 28NW.B.6.c.6.1 (National Library of Scotland: https://maps.nls.uk/ww1/trenches [Accessed 31 August 2021]).
18. Robinson, Peter, *A Welsh Response to the Great War: The 38th (Welsh) Division on the Western Front 1914–1919* (Cardiff University: MPhil thesis, 2017): https://orca.cardiff.ac.uk/111318 [Accessed 25 July 2019] p. 143.
19. The National Archives WO 374/43769 personal file of 2nd Lieutenant William McCrae, The Duke of Wellington's (West Riding Regiment).
20. Robinson, Peter, *A Welsh Response to the Great War: The 38th (Welsh) Division on the Western Front 1914–1919* (Cardiff University: MPhil thesis, 2017): https://orca.cardiff.ac.uk/111318 [Accessed 25 July 2019] p. 48.
21. The National Archives WO 95/2556/2 War Diary, 15th Royal Welsh Fusiliers, June 1917.
22. Ellis, Humphrey Evans: www.rwfmuseum.org.uk/nb_heddwyn.html [Accessed 27 July 2021].
23. Robinson, Peter, *A Welsh Response to the Great War: The 38th (Welsh) Division on the Western Front 1914–1919* (Cardiff University: MPhil thesis, 2017): https://orca.cardiff.ac.uk/111318 [Accessed 25 July 2019] p. 149.
24. Ibid., p. 149.
25. Ibid., p. 150.
26. Ellis, Humphrey Evans 'Hedd Wyn': http://www.rwfmuseum.org.uk/nb_heddwyn.html [Accessed 27 July 2021].
27. The National Archives WO 374/43769 personal file of Second Lieutenant William McCrae, The Duke of Wellington's (West Riding Regiment).
28. The National Archives WO 95/2556/2 War Diary, 15th Royal Welsh Fusiliers, 31. July 1917.

29. Robinson, Peter, *A Welsh Response to the Great War: The 38th (Welsh) Division on the Western Front 1914–1919* (Cardiff University: MPhil thesis, 2017): https://orca.cardiff.ac.uk/111318 [Accessed 25 July 2019] pp. 122 &126.
30. Lewis, Harold, *Bluey* (Australia: Angus & Robertson Publishers, 1985) p. 93.
31. Ibid., pp. 91–4.
32. The National Archives WO 95/2556/2 War Diary, 15th Royal Welsh Fusiliers, p. 47.
33. The National Archives WO 374/43769 personal file of 2nd Lieutenant William McCrae, The Duke of Wellington's (West Riding Regiment).
34. MacRae-Gilstrap, Ella, *The Clan MacRae with its Rolls of Honour and of Service in the Great War* (Aberdeen: Rosemount Press, 1923) p. 41. This reference indicated that Alan was missing, presumed killed in action. More recent records show that he is buried at Brown's Copse Commonwealth War Graves Commission Cemetery, Roeux, Headstone 907 (CWGC Certificate A. J. McCrae. S/17591).
35. The Death of the 2nd Seaforths, 11 April 1917: https://newbattleatwar.com/murderonthehill.htm [Accessed 20 April 2021].
36. Arras offensive, 1917 (Battle of Arras): www.longlongtrial.co.uk/battles/battles-of-the-western-front-in-france-and-flanders/the-arras-offensive-1917-battle-of-arras/ [Accessed 26 August 2021].
37. Von Ranke, F. M., Zanetti G., Hochhegger B. & Marchiori E., 'Infectious Diseases Causing Diffuse Alveolar Hemorrhage in Immunocompetent Patients: A State-of-the-art Review', *Lung* 191 (2013): 9–18.
38. Personal papers of Andrew McCrae, application for disability pension. Paper copy.
39. Eltham Hill School: www.elthamhill.com/90/history-of-e;tham-hill-tbc [Accessed 26 August 2021].
40. Ibid.
41. Ibid.
42. Gillies, Sir Harold: www.gilliesarchives.org.uk [Accessed 3 August 2021].
43. Prior Park College history: www.priorparkcollege.com/welcome/our-history [Accessed 14 July 2021].
44. Hentel, Magdalena J., 'Temporary Gentlemen: The Masculinity of Lower-Middle-Class Temporary British Officers in the First World War', PhD thesis (The University of Western Ontario, 2017): https://ir.lib.uwo.ca/cgi/viewcontent.cgi?article=6411&context=etd [Accessed 1 August 2019].
45. Ibid.
46. *No. 18 Officer Cadet Battalion 26 November 1916 to 20 February 1919* (Bath: *Bath Chronicle* booklet. With kind permission from Prior Park School Archives).
47. Ibid.
48. Hentel, Magdalena J., 'Temporary Gentlemen: The Masculinity of Lower-Middle-Class Temporary British Officers in the First World War', PhD

thesis (The University of Western Ontario, 2017): https://ir.lib.uwo.ca/cgi/viewcontent.cgi?article=6411&context=etd [Accessed 1 August 2019].
49. Ibid.
50. Sassoon, Siegfried, *Memoirs of an Infantry Officer* (London: Faber & Faber, 1965) p. 127.
51. Hentel, Magdalena J., 'Temporary Gentlemen: The Masculinity of Lower-Middle-Class Temporary British Officers in the First World War', PhD thesis (The University of Western Ontario, 2017): https://ir.lib.uwo.ca/cgi/viewcontent.cgi?article=6411&context=etd [Accessed 1 August 2019].
52. Mather, Philip, Research Officer, The Fusilier Museum, Bury, Moss Street, Lancashire. Correspondence 23 July 2021.
53. Flaving, Scott, Honorary Secretary to Duke of Wellington's Regiment Museum Trustees and Regimental Archivist, Halifax. Correspondence 16 April 2021.
54. Mather, Philip, Research Officer, The Fusilier Museum, Bury, Moss Street, Lancashire. Correspondence 23 July 2021.
55. Flaving, Scott, Honorary Secretary to Duke of Wellington's Regiment Museum Trustees and Regimental Archivist, Halifax. Correspondence 16 April 2021.
56. Ibid. He remained a 'duke' and his medals entitlement was made out to Duke of Wellington's (West Riding) Regiment.
57. Mather, Philip, Research Officer, The Fusilier Museum, Bury, Moss Street, Lancashire. Correspondence 23 July 2021.
58. The National Archive. WO 95-2654-2_2 War Diary 1/5 Lancashire Fusiliers, 9 April 1917.
59. Mather, Philip, Research Officer, The Fusilier Museum, Bury, Moss Street, Lancashire. Correspondence 23 July 2021.
60. Chasseaud, Peter, *Mapping the First World War* (Glasgow: Imperial War Museum/Harper Collins, 2013).
61: The National Archive. WO 95-2654-2_2 War Diary 1/5 Lancashire Fusiliers, 9 April 1917, p. 66.

Epilogue
1. The National Archives WO 95-2654-2_2 War Diary 1/5 Lancashire Fusiliers, p. 55.
2. Ibid., p. 69.
3. Ibid., p. 82.
4. Ibid., p. 85.
5. Ibid., p. 86.
6. The National Archives WO 374/43769 personal file of 2nd Lieutenant William McCrae, The Duke of Wellington's (West Riding Regiment).

Abbreviations

ASC	Army Service Corps
ATMB	Artillery Trench Mortar Battalion
BHQ	Battalion Headquarters
BQMS	Battalion Quarter Master Stores
BC	Battalion Cook
CO	Commanding Officer
CT	Communication Trench
CQMS	Company Quarter Master Sergeant
FOO	Forward Observation Officer
MS	Mess Sergeant
Mk III	Short Magazine Lee–Enfield Mark III
NCO	Non-Commissioned Officer
OC	Officer Commanding
OR	Operations Room
QMS	Quarter Master Sergeant
RWF	Royal Welsh Fusiliers
SB	Stretcher Bearer
SM	Sergeant Major
SWB	South Wales Borderers

Glossary

bacho: Welsh term of endearment.

Blighty: soldiers would talk of 'getting a Blighty' meaning that they had an injury that would qualify them to return home to Great Britain.

chaffed: Made fun of, ridiculed.

clay-kickers: the men who worked excavating the clay when they were digging the tunnels for the London Underground system. Using a sharp-pointed spade the miners would dig at an angle and kick the clay out as they went. It was a far more efficient method than using the usual broad-bladed pick.

clinching: grappling with boxing opponent.

colloquy: conversation.

enfilade: a volley of gunfire along a line from end to end

ennui: feeling of listlessness and dissatisfaction arising from lack of occupation or excitement.

epithet: word expressing a quality or attribute regarded as characteristic of the person or thing mentioned.

essaying: to try and do something.

fatigue duty: labour assigned to military men that does not require the use of armament.

Flying Pig: the nickname for a large-calibre mortar which became the standard British heavy mortar from the autumn of 1916. It weighed 298lb, was about five foot long and shaped like a pig. It carried a light in the tail which went out as soon as the shell began to descend.

ghillie: a man who assisted in deer hunting, deer stalking or fly-fishing expeditions in the Scottish Highlands.

ghillie suit: a type of camouflage clothing designed to resemble the background environment. A net or cloth garment covered in loose strips of cloth, or twine, sometimes made to look like leaves and twigs. Pieces of foliage from the area can be woven in to provide more camouflage.

glassmen: a pre-war term used for observers in the context of hunting animals. Someone with a skill in using 'glasses' such as binoculars or a telescope.

jackeroo: an Australian term referring to a young man working on a sheep or cattle station.

Jack Johnson shell: a shell that emits black smoke when it explodes. It was named after Jack Johnson, the first black American world heavyweight boxing champion.

ju-jitsu: a Japanese discipline of unarmed combat and physical training which has been used in the military since the early 1900s.

lance jack: lance corporal

limber: a two-wheeled horse-drawn vehicle used to pull a field gun.

Machonochie: a tinned stew made of vegetables, haricot beans and beef, used as a food ration for British soldiers in First World War trenches.

Mesopotamia: the name of the 'land between the rivers', the Tigris and Euphrates, which is now part of Iraq and Syria.

MM (Military Medal): given to those below commissioned rank for acts of bravery.

nose-cap: the tip of a shell, commonly made of brass.

Pals battalions: specially constituted battalions of the British Army comprising of men who had enlisted together in local recruiting drives.

parados: a bank at the back of a trench or other fortification, away from the enemy line, giving protection from being fired on from the rear.

qui vive: on the alert or on the lookout.

redcaps: military police.

told off: instructed to undertake a task.

Tickler's Jam: Tickler's based in Grimsby was at the time one of the biggest producers of jam in the England and was chosen to supply the army with plum and apple jam during the First World War. Empty jam tins were often used by troops to make homemade grenades.

trench mortar: a short stumpy tube designed to fire a projectile at a steep angle so that it falls straight down on the enemy.

Verey/Very light: the most common type of flare gun, named after Edward Wilson Very (1847–1910), an American naval officer who developed and popularized this single-shot breech-loading snub-nosed pistol that fired flares.

vituperative: bitter and abusive.

Bibliography

Books and Papers

Adams, Bernard, *Nothing of Importance* (first published 1917 London: Methuen; London: Naval & Military Press, 2009).
Arthur, Max, *Forgotten Voices of the Great War* (London: Ebury Press, 2002).
Barlow, Robin, *Wales and World War One* (Ceredigion: Gomer Press, 2014).
Blunden, Edmund, *Undertones of War* (London: Penguin Modern Classics, 2000).
Borden, Mary, *The Forbidden Zone* (London: Modern Voices, 2008).
Chasseaud, Peter, *Mapping the First World War* (Glasgow: Collins, 2013).
Clayton, Albert, *Long Before Daybreak* (independently published by M. J. Duckworth, 2020).
Crum, F. M., *Memoirs of a Rifleman Scout* (Barnsley: Frontline Books, 2014).
Dilworth, Thomas, *David Jones in the Great War* (London: Entitharmon Press, 2012).
Fussell, P., *The Great War and Modern Memory* (Oxford: Oxford University Press, 1977).
Gillies, Midge, *Army Wives* (London: Aurum Press, 2016).
Glover, M. & Riley, J., *That Astonishing Infantry: The History of the Royal Welch Fusiliers 1689–2006* (Barnsley: Pen & Sword, 2008).
Graves, Robert, *Goodbye to All That* (London: Penguin, 1960).
Graves, Robert, *A Dead Boche* https://allpoetry.com/A-Dead-Boche [Accessed 2 September 2021].
Griffith, Llewelyn Wyn & Riley, Jonathon (ed.), *Up to Mametz and Beyond* (Barnsley: Pen & Sword, 2010).
Hallett, Christine E., *Nurses of Passchendaele* (Barnsley: Pen & Sword, 2017).
Hentel, Magdalena J., 'Temporary Gentlemen: The Masculinity of Lower-Middle-Class Temporary British Officers in the First World War', PhD thesis (The University of Western Ontario, 2017) https://ir.lib.uwo.ca/cgi/viewcontent.cgi?article=6411&context=etd [Accessed 1.8.2019].
Hesketh-Prichard, H. V., *Sniping in France* (Barnsley: Pen & Sword, 2014).
Hope, Anna, *Wake* (Great Britain: Black Swan, 2015).
Hughes, Colin, *Mametz: Lloyd George's 'Welsh Army' at the Battle of the Somme* (first published privately by Orion Press, 1982; Huddersfield: Gliddon Books, 1990).
Hughes, Colin A., 'Collected Accounts of the Battle of Mametz Wood' https://archiveshub.jisc.ac.uk/data/gb1239-461 [Accessed 1 September 2021].
Hicks, Jonathan, *The Welsh at Mametz Wood: The Somme 1916* (Wales: Y Lolfa, 1916).
Jones, David, *In Parenthesis* (London: Faber & Faber, 2014).

Korte, B. & Einhaus. A. M. (eds.), *The Penguin Book of First World War Stories* (London: Penguin, 2007).
La Motte, Ellen N., *The Backwash of War* (London: Conway, 2014).
Lewis, Harold, *Crow on a Barbed Wire Fence* (Australia: Angus & Robertson Publishers, 1973).
Lewis, Harold, *Bluey* (Australia: Angus & Robertson Publishers, 1985).
Lewis-Stempel, J., *Where Poppies Blow: The British Soldier, Nature, the Great War* (London: Weidenfeld & Nicolson, 2017).
Macdonald, Lyn, *They Called It Passchendaele* (London: Papermac, Macmillan Publishers, 1983).
MacRae-Gilstrap, Ella, *The Clan MacRae with its Rolls of Honour and of Service in the Great War* (Aberdeen: Rosemount Press, 1923).
No. 18 Officer Cadet Battalion November 26th 1916 to February 20th 1919 (Bath: *Bath Chronicle* booklet. With kind permission from Prior Park School Archives).
Pegler, Martin, *Sniping in the Great War* (Barnsley: Pen & Sword, 2017).
Raby-Dunne, Susan, *John McCrae: Beyond Flanders Fields* (Canada: Heritage, 2016).
Remarque, Eric Maria, *All Quiet on the Western Front* (London: Vintage Classics, 1996).
Robinson, Peter, *A Welsh Response to the Great War: The 38th (Welsh) Division on the Western Front 1914–1919* (Cardiff University: MPhil thesis, 2017) https://orca.cardiff.ac.uk/111318 [Accessed 25 July 2019].
Sassoon, Siegfried, *Memoirs of an Infantry Officer* (London: Faber & Faber, 1965).
Shanks, G. D., 'How World War 1 Changed Global Attitudes to War and Infectious Diseases', *Lancet*, 8 November 2014, 384:1699–1707.
Sheers, Owen, *Mametz – A Play* (London: Samuel French Publishers, 2016).
Speller, Elizabeth, *At the Break of Day* (London: Virago Press, 2013).
Teodorescu, Bianca & Călin Răzvan, A., 'The Base Articulations of the Liminality Concept', *Review of European Studies* Vol. 7, (2015) No. 12 https://ir.lib.uwo.ca/cgi/viewcontent.cgi?article=6411&context=etd [Accessed: 20.1.2020].
Van Emden, R. & Humphries, S., *All Quiet on the Home Front*. (London: Headline Publishing, 2003).
Von Ranke, F. M., Zanetti G., Hochhegger B. & Marchiori E., 'Infectious Diseases Causing Diffuse Alveolar Hemorrhage in Immunocompetent Patients: A State-of-the-art Review', *Lung* 191 (2013)
Warner, Philip, *World War One: A Chronological Narrative* (Barnsley: Pen & Sword, 2008).

Correspondence
Flaving, Scott, Honorary Secretary to Duke of Wellington's Regiment Museum Trustees and Regimental Archivist, Halifax. Correspondence 16 April 2021.
Mather, Philip, Research Officer, The Fusilier Museum, Bury, Moss Street, Lancashire. Correspondence 23 July 2021.

The National Archives
The National Archives WO 95-2540-1 38th Division War Diary.
The National Archives. WO 95-2540-2 War Diary 38th Division. 3 August 1917.

The National Archives WO 95-2654-2-2 War Diary 1/5 Lancashire Fusiliers.
The National Archives WO 95/2556/1 War Diary, 15th Royal Welsh Fusiliers.
The National Archives WO 95/2556/2 War Diary, 15th Royal Welsh Fusiliers.
The National Archives: WO-372-23-124036. Edwin Hurley – awarded Military Medal
The National Archives WO 374/43769 personal file of 2nd Lieutenant William McCrae, The Duke of Wellington's (West Riding Regiment).
The National Archives WO 372/12/201497 Record detail for Alan J. McCrae (Seaforth Highlanders).

Other Sources
Arras offensive, 1917 (Battle of Arras): www.longlongtrial.co.uk/battles/battles-of-the-western-front-in-france-and-flanders/the-arras-offensive-1917-battle-of-arras/ [Accessed 26 August 2021].
Battle of the Somme, Imperial War Museum: www.iwm.org.uk/history/key-facts-about-the-battle-of-the-somme [Accessed 15 August 2021].
Bourne N., 1915 WW1 diary gives account of second Christmas truce: www.bbc.co.uk/news/uk-wales-35120354 26 December 2015 [Accessed 23 November 2020].
Christmas Truce of 1914 History.com editors: www.history.com/topics/world-war-i/christmas-truce-of-1914 [Accessed 7 May 2021].
Riley J., The Second Christmas Truce 1915: http://generalship.org/royal-welch-fusiliers-articles/2nd-christmas-truce-1915.html [Accessed 24 November 2020].
Trueman, C. N., Christmas 1915 World War One: www.historylearningsite.co.uk/world-war-one/the-western-front-in-world-war-one/christmas-1915-world-war-one/ 31 March 2015. [Accessed 7 May 2021].
The Derby Scheme: www.longlongtrail.co.uk/?s=the+derby+scheme [Accessed 15 March 2021].
Edmund Blunden and the Red Dragon Crater: www.1914-18.co.uk/blunden/reddragon.htm [Accessed 7 July 2021].
Ellis Humphrey Evans: www.rwfmuseum.org.uk/nb_heddwyn.html [Accessed 27 July 2021].
Eltham Hill School: www.elthamhill.com/90/history-of-e;tham-hill-tbc [Accessed 26 August 2021].
Film of the Battle of the Somme. Imperial War Museum: www.iwm.org.uk/history/geoffrey-mails-and-the-battle-of-the-somme-film [Accessed 15 August 2021].
Film of the Battle of the Somme: How it Was Made. Imperial War Museum: www.iwm/history/how-the-battle-of-the-somme-was-filmed [Accessed 15 August 2021].
German measles vaccine: www.gov.uk/government/publications/vaccination-timeline.
Gillies, Sir Harold: www.gilliesarchives.org.uk [Accessed 3 August 2021].
Great War Forum search for 38th Divisional Sniping Company: www.greatwarforum.org/topic/291901-38th-division-sniping-company-1916-1918/?tab=comments#comments-3030013 [Accessed14 July 2021].

Great War Forum search for Winnall Down note posted by Dave Key. Old Sweats, 30 July 2013: www.greatwarforum.org/topic/197449-training-camps/ [Accessed 27 September 2020].

Great War Forum search for Winnall Down note posted by Moonraker. Old Sweats, 30 July 2013: www.greatwarforum.org/topic/197449-training-camps/ [Accessed 27 September 2020].

Memorial to the Royal Welch Fusiliers: www.londonremebers.com/memorials/royal-welch-fusiliers [Accessed 30. August 2021].

'Pack up your Troubles' was written by a Welshman, Felix Lloyd Powell, in 1915. The words were written by his brother George Henry Powell (under the pseudonym George Asaf) www.bbc.com/news/uk-wales-25968407 [Accessed 2 October 2021].

PALS battalions: www.iwm.org.uk/history/the-pals-battalions-of-the-first-world-war [Accessed 15 March 2021].

The Post Office and the First World War: www.postalmuseum.org/collections/ww1/ [Accessed 4 May 2021].

Prior Park College history: www.priorparkcollege.com/welcome/our-history [Accessed 14 July 2021].

The Seaforth Highlanders: www.visitscotland.com/about/history/ww1-centenary/scottish-regiments/the-seaforth-highlanders/ [Accessed 11 March 2021].

The Death of the 2nd Seaforths, 11 April 1917: https://newbattleatwar.com/murderonthehill.htm [Accessed 20 April 2021].

Talbot House: www.greatwar.co.uk/ypressalient/museum-talbot-house-history.htm [Accessed 28 June 2021].

The Tunnellers Memorial, Givenchy: www.tunnellersmemorial.com/red-dragon-survey/ [Accessed 20 June 2021].

Tunnelling Companies of the Royal Engineers (underground warfare): www.longlongtrail.co.uk/army/regiments-and-corps/the-corps-of-royal-engineers-in-the-first-world-war/tunnelling-companies-of-the-royal-engineers-underground-warfare/ [Accessed 10 June 2021].

Unit History: King's (Liverpool Regiment): www.forces-war-records.co.uk/units/259/kings-liverpool-regiment/ [Accessed 16 March 2021].

War's Hell. Exhibition (2016) National Museum, Cardiff: https://museum.wales/cardiff/whatson/8949/Wars-Hell-The-Battle-of-Mametz-Wood-in-Art/footer/ [Accessed 5 January 2020].

The YMCA during World War One: www.westernfrontassociation.com/the-latest-wwi-podcast/ep-146-the-ymca-during-ww1-kathryn-white/ [Accessed 28 June 2021].

Acknowledgements

I would like to thank all of those who have encouraged and supported me in writing this book.

Thanks go to Midge Gillies and Elizabeth Speller and fellow students on the Creative Non-Fiction Writing course at Madingley Hall, University of Cambridge in 2017/18. Thank you, Midge, for your encouragement despite me missing the opportunity to publish during the centenary of the First World War. Thank you, Elizabeth, for your enthusiasm, direction, and your deep knowledge of the First World War.

I must give special thanks to Colonel Nick Lock in his role as a trustee of the Royal Welch Fusiliers Museum, Caernarfon, who encouraged me from the outset to publish this book. He first provided me with key information that enabled me to become familiar with the rich history of the 15 RWF, and later thoroughly checked through the final draft. Thank you too to Keith Jones for his interest and introducing me to the trustees. Thank you Tim Jones for your enthusiasm and encouragement and giving me invaluable information about First World War military life and the ubiquitous acronyms. Also, to Peter Robinson whose detailed account of the 38th (Welsh) Division on the Western Front, provided me with a great deal of background information, and who also helped me find the link to William McCrae's personal file in The National Archives.

Thank you to Christopher Southwell for putting me in touch with Scott Flaving, the Duke of Wellington Regimental Archivist, who unlocked the key to William's life as a second lieutenant in that regiment. I would otherwise never have found him, especially as, although he continued to be a 'Duke', he actually served in the 1/5 Lancashire Fusiliers. Thank you too to Philip Mather, Research Officer at the Fusilier Museum in Bury, Lancashire, who provided me with much information of that time.

Grateful thanks also goes to Carole Laverick at Prior Park School Archive for her help with sourcing information about the 18th Officer Cadet Battalion that was based there during the First World War.

Acknowledgements

I would like to acknowledge how invaluable a resource both websites, The Long, Long Trail and The Great War Forum, have been in my research.

Thank you to Claire Hopkins of Pen & Sword Books for her guidance and belief in the value of this book. Also many thanks to Chris Cocks for his invaluable scrupulous copy-editing.

Lastly, thank you to my family who have cheered me on over the last two years, despite the separation that Covid-19 lockdown caused. Special thanks to Nick Boase whose constructive comments and thoughts on the final draft were invaluable, and of course to Clive who has been at my side constantly, endlessly discussing events in the First World War, and keeping me fed.

Index

1/5 Lancashire Fusiliers xi, 177–80, 183
1st Royal Irish Fusiliers 171
2nd Army 125, 156–7
2nd Black Watch (Royal Highlanders) 56, 171
4th King's Liverpool Regiment 55–6, 171
11th Hussars 119
13th (1st London) Royal Welsh Fusiliers (13 RWF) 8
14th (1st London) Royal Welsh Fusiliers (14 RWF) 8
14th Welsh Regiment (Swansea Pals) xiii, 93
15th (1st London) Royal Welsh Fusiliers (15 RWF) x, 2, 4–5, 7–9, 23, 29–30, 32, 50, 70, 72, 85–86, 92, 99–100, 112, 115, 122, 125, 139, 141, 166–170, 178
16th (1st London) Royal Welsh Fusiliers (16 RWF) 8, 129
18th Officer Cadet Battalion *see also* Prior Park, Bath xi, 174, 177, 207
34th Infantry Base Depot 177
38th (Welsh) Division viii, xii, 7–8, 11, 95, 111–12, 125, 136, 161–2, 164, 166, 169
38th Divisional Sniping Company 10, 135, 161, 166, 168
113th Infantry Brigade (North Wales Brigade) 8
42nd Division 178, 180, 183
254 Tunnelling Company 92–3

Aire-sur-la-Lys 16, 18
Albert 96
Battle of 179
Allison, Capt 38
Amiens 121–2, 154
Armentières 127
Armistice xi, 5, 163, 180–3
Army Service Corps 23
Arras, Battle of 171
Auchonvillers 115–16
Australian troops 157–8
Authie St Leger 115–16

Bantams 24, 44–5, 89, 92
Bapaume, Second Battle of 179
Barber, Pte 58, 129–32
Barrett, Thomas 143
Bayencourt 116
Béthune 52, 62
Blendecques 18
Blunden, Edmund 5, 57, 93
Boer War 8, 154, 158
Boesinghe 126, 128, 163, 167
Bond, Pte 58
Bowen, Col Ivor 9
Bowers, WOII 74, 83
British Expeditionary Force (BEF) 20, 135, 166
Brown, Cpl 81

Camerlynck, Coevoet 156
Canadian troops 157–8, 183
Canal du Nord, Battle of the 179
Christmas 27–32, 68, 183
Church, 'Windy' 93–4
cinematography 114–15, 172
Clayton, Rev Philip 'Tubby' 156
Collins, Thomas 93
communications trenches (CTs) 39–40, 45, 65–6, 92, 116, 127–31, 151, 159–60
Contalmaison 98, 102, 104–7
Couin Wood 117
Couin Wood Field Hospital 117
Courcelles 116
Crum, Maj F. M. 144, 154, 156
Cuinchy 32, 48, 52, 59, 62

Davies, Pte 66–7, 103, 131–2, 141–2
Davies, batman 137
Davies, WOII *also* Davis 58, 70
Davison, Capt 74, 81, 85
Davis, Pte 121
Day, Pte 120
Dean, Pte 1
Delville Wood, Battle of 112
disease 123–4
Duck's Bill Crater 43, 89, 92
Duke of Wellington's Regiment (West Riding Division) viii–ix, xi, 177

English Channel 3, 12, 17, 25, 114, 165, 171, 173
Estaires 70, 72, 89
Etaples 177
Evans, Ellis Humphry (Hedd Wyn) viii, 169
Evans, Gen 100
Evans, Sir Vincent 6

Felstead, Bertie 30
Festubert 45, 57, 60
Field Dressing Stations 140
Fléchin, 169
Forest de Mormal, Battle of the 180
Fort D'Hautmont 181
Fox-Pitt, Col W. A. L. 8
Fraser, Pte 66
Fricourt Valley 97–8, 106

Gallipoli campaign 73, 120, 158
gas 10, 41, 123, 125, 132–3, 167, 169–70
George V, King 175, 183
Gillies, Harold 173–4
Givenchy-lès-la-Bassée 32
Goulding, Brud 62
Graves, Robert viii, 4, 112
Grenadier Guards 8, 23–7, 29–31, 44, 63

Hackett, William 93
Hautmont 180, 183
Hebuterne 116, 178
Hesketh-Prichard, Capt Vernon 143–4, 146–8, 154, 156–8, 161
High Wood, Battle of 112
Hindenburg Line 179
Humphries, Cpl 117
Hunter-Weston, Gen Sir 125
Hurley, Edwin 161
hygiene 31, 162, 165–6

Inn of the Red Hart 45, 48

Jones, David viii, 4–5, 30, 85, 112–13
Jones, Pte 1, 20–2, 29, 34, 53,
Jones, WOI 170

Keating, Robert 30
Kemp, Pte 83
King's Royal Rifle Corps 144
Kitchener, Lord Herbert 6–7, 9, 57, 114

La Bassée 63, 65, 68
La Bassée Canal 44
La Gorgue 23, 32, 70, 86, 95
La Rouge Croix x, 18–31

Langemark *also* Langemarque 160, 162, 168
Lavantie 23
Le Havre 12–13
Lee–Enfield rifle 10, 147
Lewis, 2Lt Harold 134–9, 141, 148, 150, 154, 156, 170
Llandudno, training in viii, 8–9, 56, 62, 86
Lloyd George, David 6–9, 113
Lochnagar Crater 43
Lovat Scouts 154, 158

Malins, Geoffrey 114
Mametz Wood, Battle of 168, 170
Matthews, Pte J. 84
McCrae, Agnes 2, 69, 172–3
McCrae, Alan 56, 171
McCrae, Andrew 2, 56, 171
McCrae, Nettie 2, 68–9, 172
McCrae, Robert 2, 56
McCrae, Robert and Isabella 2
McCrae, William 'Mac' viii–xi, 2–10, 12–13, 16, 18, 27, 29, 31, 43, 51–2, 56, 68, 70, 75, 85, 88, 90, 92, 96–7, 99–100, 102–3, 107, 110–14, 123–5, 129–30, 137, 142, 146–8, 154–6, 161–8, 170, 173–81, 183–4
McCrae, William snr viii, x, xiii, 2
McDowell, John 114
Meadows, Cpl 34
Menin Road 127
Merville 32, 70, 83–4
Merville Field Hospital 83
Mesopotamia campaign 56, 171
Messines Ridge, Battle of 156
Miles Pte W. 173

Namur 183
Neuve Chapelle x, 23–5, 35, 63, 86, 89
New Army 6
New Zealand troops 72, 158, 173, 179
No. 25 Stationary Hospital 124
Norman, Sgt 159
Nouix 43

O'Hara, Pte 47
Ordnance Survey 180
Owen, batman 136–8, 141–2
Owen, Wilfred 4

Passchendaele, Battle of 162, 169
Pelling, Sgt 67–8, 89, 130
Penny, Sgt 57
Philipps, Gen Ivor 7

Pilckem Ridge, Battle of 129, 160–2, 164, 168–70
Pioneer battalions 106, 141
Piper, Lt 65, 67, 100–1
Pope, 2Lt 74, 79
Poperinghe 122, 126, 144, 154–6, 171
Post Office Rifles 21
Preble, Pte 99
Prince of Wales' Light Horse 8
Prior Park, Bath see also 18th Officer Cadet Battalion xi, 174–5

Queen's Hospital 173
Queen's Nullah xii, 102–3

RAMC see Royal Army Medical Corps
rations 21, 23, 26, 31, 37, 46, 48, 59, 62, 91, 96–7, 99, 131, 175
RE see Royal Engineers
Red Dragon Crater 43, 92–3
religion 7, 30–1, 65–6, 73, 155–6, 168, 175, 183
Richebourg l'Avoué 33, 39, 44
Richebourg St Vaast 32, 38, 58
River Lys 70, 86
Roberts, Pete 71–3, 76, 82–3
Rowlands, L/Cpl 86
Royal Army Medical Corps (RAMC) 52–3, 106, 168, 172
Royal Engineers (RE) 39, 60, 63, 82, 92, 116, 154, 166
Royal London Mutual Insurance Society x, 7
Royal Sussex Regiment 57
Royal Welch Fusilier Regiment vii, ix
Rue du Bois 35
rum ration 29, 31, 81–2

Sassoon, Siegfried viii, 4–5, 12, 124, 176
Sayers, Pte 20, 22, 29, 34, 52
School of Scouting, Observation and Sniping see Sniping School
Scots Guards 27
Seaforth Highlanders 56, 171
Selle, Battle of the 179
Shields, Sammy 139, 141
sniping ix, 34, 36–7, 50, 89–91, 128, 134–6, 139–40, 142–8, 150–2, 154, 156–9, 161, 166–8, 177–8

Sniping School (Mont des Cats) 156
Sniping School (Fort Mahon) 178
Solly-Flood, Gen A. 180
Somme, Battle of the x, 21, 43, 86, 95–99, 101, 114–15, 179
South Staffordshire Regiment 143
South Wales Borderers (SWB) 159
Southampton 2–3, 5–6, 11, 17, 21, 180
St Pol 97
Swansea Pals see 14th Welsh Regiment

telescopic sights 141, 144, 147–8, 152–3, 157
Tracey, 2Lt 74
Training Reserve Brigade 171, 174
trench raids x, 35, 41, 50, 58, 70–4, 78, 81–7, 91–2, 121–2, 130, 149, 167
tunnelling and mining 40, 42–3, 93, 136, 177
Turnbull, Pte 60–1

Vauchelles-lès-Authie 178

Walker, 'Johnny' 151, 153, 155–6, 159, 163
War Office 114
war poetry viii, 4, 12, 112, 169
Ward, Douglas 11, 19, 30, 34, 46, 49, 53–5, 57, 60, 62, 70–1, 75, 80, 87–8, 91–2, 100, 115–16, 132
Welsh Army Corps 6
Western Front viii, x–xi, 2, 10–12, 14, 16, 20–1, 56, 70, 95, 123, 139, 143–4, 151, 155, 172, 174, 177
Wilkins, sniper 144, 147–50
'Windy Corner' 45, 48, 60
Winnall Down Camp, Winchester 1, 10
Wyn Griffith, Watcyn 102
Wyn Griffith, Llewelyn viii, 4, 39, 99–100, 110, 113, 165

YMCA 10, 155
Ypres Second Battle of 133
Ypres Third Battle of see Passchendaele, Battle of
Yser Canal x, 125–6, 167, 169–71, 174, 178